The Demand for Children: The Economics of Fertility in the United States

The Demand for Children: The Economics of Fertility in the United States

Boone A. Turchi
University of North Carolina
Chapel Hill

Ballinger Publishing Company ● Cambridge, Mass.
A Subsidiary of J.B. Lippincott Company

This book is printed on recycled paper.

International Standard Book Number: 0–88410–353–6

Library of Congress Catalog Card Number: 75–22111

Printed in the United States of America

Library of Congress Cataloging in Publication Data

Turchi, Boone A
    The demand for children.

    Bibliography: p.
    1. United States—Population. 2. Family Size.
I. Title. [DNLM: 1. Fertility. 2. Socioeconomic factors. HB903.F4 T932d]
HB915.T87   301.32′1′0973   75–22111
ISBN 0–88410–353–6

To My Parents

Contents

List of Figures

List of Tables

Acknowledgments

Many persons and institutions have made the writing of this book a less arduous task than it might have been. I have been fortunate to be associated with two institutions whose value to a population scholar cannot be underestimated: The Population Studies Center at the University of Michigan, and the Carolina Population Center at the University of North Carolina. In particular I wish to acknowledge the programming assistance I received from J. Michael Coble and Albert F. Anderson of the Population Studies Center, and the editorial and financial assistance received from Henry C. Cole of the Carolina Population Center. While at Michigan I was partially supported by the Population Council of New York during 1969–70 when I was a Population Council Fellow. My thanks also extend to Mrs. Betsy Pierce of the Economics Department, University of North Carolina for her careful and cheerful typing of the final draft.

The most important gift a scholar can receive from his colleagues is a careful and critical reading of his work. George B. Simmons, Lester D. Taylor, Ronald Freedman, and Frank P. Stafford, all of whom served as members of my dissertation committee, provided generously of their time to criticize an early version of this study. In addition, Beverly Duncan provided some valuable suggestions during the initial phase of the empirical analysis. Joseph J. Spengler, Peter Lindert, Krishnan Namboodiri, Solomon Polachek, and an anonymous reviewer all provided exceedingly useful comments which materially improved this study.

Finally, I wish to thank my wife, Janet, and children, Francesca and Alexander, for their forbearance in giving up many hours that were rightfully theirs. Their sacrifices cannot be fully compensated but they remain enormously appreciated all the same.

Chapter One

Introduction:
A Framework
for Fertility Analysis

THE ECONOMIC APPROACH TO
FERTILITY ANALYSIS

During the past few years economists have begun to apply the microeconomic theory of consumer behavior to the analysis of human fertility in the United States.[a] Their interest has been spurred in part by the relative lack of success that sociologists and demographers have had in explaining the determinants of family size. As the American population has become more homogeneous over time, attempts to explain fertility differentials and trends on the basis of differential social correlates have become considerably less promising. However, the recent economic contributions to the literature on human fertility have not met with a particularly enthusiastic reception outside the economics profession; thus a major objective of this study is to improve that reception by developing a microeconomic theory of fertility that is firmly placed in the social and psychological context within which family size decisions are made.

It is my contention that the analysis of fertility requires a model appropriate to the study of resource allocation decisions made under constraint. At the same time, analysis of these decisions cannot be divorced from the social and cultural context within which they are made. Unfortunately, many of the current writings on the economics of fertility continue this separation while at the same time failing to convince noneconomists that it is warranted.

This study has three major goals: (1) to analyze in some detail the role of the microeconomic theory of the consumer in the analysis of fertility;

---

[a]Throughout this study "fertility" will refer to the actual birth performance of parents while "fecundity" will be reserved to indicate the physiological capacity to reproduce.

(2) to present in rigorous fashion an integrated socioeconomic theory of fertility that allows noneconomic determinants to interact in a plausible way with economic determinants; and (3) to estimate this model statistically using currently available national sample survey data. In addition, the analytical development of the socioeconomic model of fertility will produce some secondary goals of independent interest. The most important of these goals is the construction of estimates of the cumulative cost of children. These estimates, which are necessary to allow the statistical estimation of the fertility model, will represent new and independent measures of both the money cost and time cost of an American child, and can be compared with other recent estimates such as those prepared for the United States Commission on Population Growth and the American Future (see Chapter Four for such a comparison).

A new study of the determinants of family size is timely for a number of reasons. Discretionary control over fertility has, with the arrival of legalized abortion in the United States, become more widespread and more complete than at any time in the nation's history. Since aggregate fertility is the only major component of population change not subject to effective policy control, it is the main source of uncontrolled population growth, or decline and of instability in aggregate rates of population growth. Population has received increasing attention in recent years as a major contributor to environmental decay and cyclical economic fluctuations, and there is therefore a good chance that fertility will become the target of explicit government policy in the not too distant future.

Currently, fertility researchers understand relatively little about the underlying determinants of fertility decisions, and what is known appears to be ill suited to the task of providing policy tools by which to influence fertility. Family size cannot simply be legislated; parenthood is a social and cultural role of profound dimensions and efforts to coerce couples directly are bound to be met with strong resistance. One of the fruits of a better understanding of the determinants of fertility may well be the discovery of alternative channels by which fertility rates can be influenced without the social and political side effects of some of the more extreme policy measures that have recently been suggested.[1]

Some Limitations

Perhaps the major omission of this study is that nonwhites are excluded from the analysis because of a data base insufficient to support the full statistical treatment required to test the theory. Nonwhites —and blacks in particular—have experienced life in the United States from a vantage point quite distinct from that of the majority of whites, and adequate treatment of white-nonwhite differentials in the context of decision theory would require data that are currently unavailable. Collection of the new data described in Chapter Seven would eliminate this problem and would allow ready access to the analysis of racial differentials.

The second major limitation is the restriction of the study to the analysis of marital fertility. The model of fertility proposed in the following chapters requires that the decision makers involved in the production of a child make their decisions in a reasonably stable environment that allows them to make at least minimal plans about the future. Extramarital fertility would not appear to occur in a stable enough environment to warrant the application of the described decision model.

The third limitation is that biological and health factors that may affect fertility are, in general, not included in the analysis. For example, although demonstrably subfecund or sterile couples are omitted from the statistical analyses, no attempt is made to assess the impact of differing degrees of fecundity or of differing frequencies of sexual intercourse upon completed family size. Likewise, the impact of infant and fetal mortality on fertility decisions is assumed to be homogeneous among the white couples analyzed.

Finally, this study does not attempt to explain the variations in aggregate fertility rates that have occurred in the United States over the past few decades. However, the decision framework presented here may ultimately prove to be a useful tool in explaining variations in completed family size over time.

OUTLINE OF THE STUDY

This chapter is the first of two dealing with a general theory of marital fertility. In it a framework for fertility analysis, based on the economic theory of the consumer, is presented and discussed in some detail. A rationale for the adoption of an allocative decision making framework is presented and defended, and special attention is paid to the manner in which economic and noneconomic determinants of fertility may interact. The sociodemographic literature on fertility is briefly reviewed with the intention of illustrating how it fits in the decision framework adopted for the study. Moreover, the decision process itself is discussed and the conditions are enumerated under which "rational" behavior by parents can plausibly be assumed.

Chapter Two presents the microeconomic theory of the family size decision. Again, the theoretical discussion makes explicit the manner in which noneconomic factors influence fertility within the consumer theory framework. After a theory of individual fertility decisions is presented and analyzed, the theory is expanded to encompass an explanation of fertility differentials among sociodemographic groups. Next, the policy implications of the theory are reviewed. It is argued that the integrated socioeconomic theory advanced in this study offers an excellent vehicle by which to compare the various policy alternatives available to affect aggregate fertility. Finally, the theory's relationship to other economic analyses of fertility is discussed in some detail.

Chapters Three and Four are empirical chapters within which measures of the total cost of a child for different income groups are developed. These chapters are necessary because the theoretical model of Chapter Two requires variables that have never been directly measured; however, they afford the added benefit of providing new estimates of the cost of children that can be compared with other recent estimates.

Chapter Five is another empirical chapter within which estimates of a couple's long range income potential are developed. Again, the additional estimations are required to produce proxy variables for theoretical variables required by the analysis. Chapter Six presents attempts to estimate statistically the demand for children. It is based on the theoretical development of Chapters One and Two and utilizes the empirical proxies generated in Chapters Three, Four, and Five. Chapter Seven concludes the study and suggests directions for future research. In particular, directions are suggested for new attempts to gather data appropriate to the economic analysis of the family size decision.

1. THE CONTEXT OF THE FERTILITY DECISION

The basic principle underlying this study is that the fertility of most American couples is the result of a conscious decision to limit family size. Moreover, this decision involves the allocation of scarce parental resources among a number of activities—child rearing being one—that provide psychic rewards to the couple. Given that these resources (time and money) are scarce, the couple must decide how best to allocate them among child rearing and other competing activities.

This view of the family size decision has led in recent years to attempts, mainly by economists, to analyze the fertility of American couples in the context of the economic theory of the consumer. Consumer theory pictures the consumer as attempting to satisfy a number of competing wants subject to the limitations of restricted wealth. Couples also must choose among child rearing and other activities that consume scarce resources and provide pleasure in varying degrees; therefore, the problem they face is formally equivalent to the standard consumer allocation problems traditionally analyzed by economists.

Although the fertility decision may be formally equivalent to other consumption decisions, it represents both in magnitude and substance a problem of considerably greater impact on the couple than any other consumption activity they are likely to undertake. Aside from the size of the resource expenditures entailed, child rearing is associated with social and cultural ramifications totally absent from most of the other consumption activities undertaken by the couple. The importance of these sociocultural factors dictates that fertility cannot successfully be studied as an allocation problem unrelated to the institutional context within which it exists.[a]

A highly simplified picture of this context is presented in Figure 1–1.[b] In the diagram a couple is pictured as making decisions about family size on the basis of experience (various social and background variables), personal preferences (resulting both from social influences and from additional independent aspects of personality), expectations regarding the resources potentially available to the couple, and predictions about the resource costs of child rearing. This is the type of decision with which consumer theory has previously dealt, but economists have typically utilized an extremely simplified version of this framework, concentrating almost entirely on the decision (i.e., the "Fertility Decision" box, Fig. 1–1) and on the quantity demanded. Moreover, they traditionally have assumed away the possibility of systematic differences in preference structures. For ordinary consumption problems the assumption may well have been valid; however, fertility is not an ordinary consumption decision, but one which represents a profound alteration of a couple's life and a truly significant expenditure of its lifetime supply of scarce resources. Therefore, although this study utilizes the analytical framework of consumer theory to study the determinants of family size, it seeks to incorporate systematically a theory of the ways in which noneconomic factors might modify the outcome of the decision process.

Two avenues of influence are thought to be especially important. First, there is ample reason to believe that couples' preferences for children versus other consumption activities vary systematically with membership in specific sociodemographic groups, and the empirical analysis of Chapter Six will pay particular attention to some of the factors that have been emphasized in the sociological literature: religion, age at first marriage, farm background, and cohort. Second, it will be

---

[a]A reviewer has argued that a "professional division of labor" is appropriate to the study of fertility; economists might treat the resource allocation problem while sociologists and psychologists would study the other aspects of the process. As will presently become quite clear, this study. proceeds under the view that such a division of labor will inhibit the attainment of a true understanding of the fertility process.

[b]In particular, the diagram has been simplified by the omission of all attempts to illustrate how fertility regulating behavior is influenced by social, psychological, and economic factors. As will be elaborated below, this behavior is not a primary subject of the present study. In Chapter Two it will be shown how data problems will force an even more drastic simplification of the analytical structure.

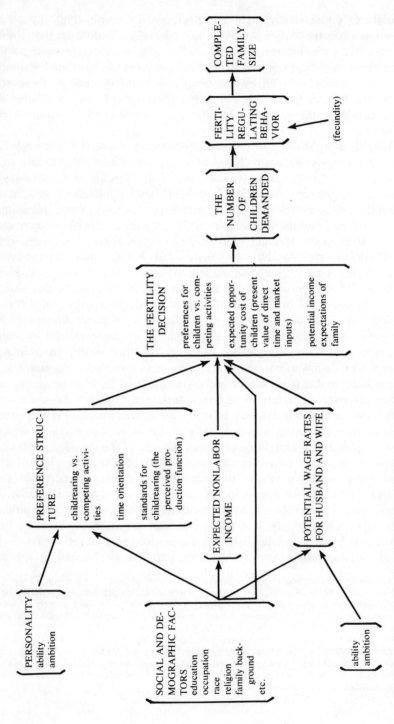

Figure 1-1.   A Framework for Fertility Analysis

argued in Chapter Two that there are strongly differentiated norms governing resource expenditures on children from differing socioeconomic strata. Indeed, we will argue in the following chapter that many previous studies regarding the impact of family income on completed fertility have presented unimpressive empirical findings precisely because of the failure to consider the effect of status related differentials in the cost of children.

Figure 1–1 illustrates that a parental decision regarding optimal family size must be translated into actual fertility through the adoption of fertility regulating behavior designed to achieve the goal. It is not enough to desire a family of a given size if the couple is unable or unwilling to undertake the behavior necessary to achieve it. As a result some economists,[1a] argue that the fertility decision cannot be successfully divorced from the decisions to engage in fertility regulating behavior. This argument has merit and is discussed more extensively later in this chapter (The Decision Process).

The model of fertility presented in Figure 1–1 is static; that is, it pictures a couple at a point in time and assumes that the decision made then is the long run equilibrium family size decision. Theoretically there is nothing wrong with this point of view—empirical evidence relating to the fertility behavior of American couples indicates that the vast majority do reach their ultimate completed family size long before the onset of subfecundity.[2] It is not unreasonable, therefore, to argue that there is a point during the wife's fecund period when final decisions are made regarding long run equilibrium family size.

Furthermore, static analysis of an essentially dynamic process is permissible and appropriate if it can be demonstrated (1) that a static long run equilibrium does in fact exist, (2) that it is stable, and (3) that there is reasonably rapid convergence toward it. All these stipulations would appear to hold for the couples included in this study.[3] However, we must further assume that the factors influencing fertility decisions (see the figure) also stabilize by the decision point, or at least that they cease to have a significant impact on the couple's choice of an ultimate family size. Many students of fertility may not be willing to make such an assumption. Moreover, there are certain aspects of the study of fertility that manifestly cannot be undertaken in a static framework, the most obvious of these being studies of spacing and timing of births as well as analyses of various aspects of fertility regulating behavior. Research of this type will have to rely on the type of dynamic analyses suggested by Namboodiri and others.[4]

Even if it is thought to be analytically permissible to undertake a static analysis of completed fertility, serious empirical problems remain. Couples may well reach a final decision about family size before the onset of subfecundity, but the location of this "decision point" is likely to vary widely among couples. Furthermore, it may not even be identified for some time after couples have actually made their final decision—indeed, as long as the wife retains her fecundity, "final" decisions may be reversed. To avoid such problems, some researchers limit their analyses to couples past the fecund period and analyze only completed fertility.[5] However, this approach may lead to new sources of bias and to the loss of much useful information available for younger couples.

Despite its limitations, the static approach will be utilized in this study. It enables a marked simplification in the analytical discussion and it is far better suited to the available cross-section data with which the model will be tested. Lamentably, this concession may introduce bias into our statistical findings and, in the absence of well controlled experiments, the nature and direction of this bias will be difficult to interpret. However, let this discussion serve as a warning to the reader to remember the problem of dynamics versus statics in fertility analysis.

It is a paradox of the economics of demand analysis that the preference function of the consumer plays a central role in consumer demand theory but virtually no role at all in the empirical estimation of demand curves.[6] Indeed, most empirical demand studies do not even test demand functions which have been constrained to be consistent with underlying preference orderings satisfying the basic postulates of consumer theory.[7] Moreover, empirical demand analyses rarely have allowed for the possibility of systematic variations in preference structures among consumers, relying instead on the assumption that if these differences do exist they are statistically independent of the explicitly specified determinants of demand. Such an assumption seems to be unwarranted with regard to the demand for children, and specific attempts are made in Chapter Six to account explicitly for differentials in the relative taste for children among couples. Unfortunately, direct measures of relative preferences are virtually nonexistent and heavy reliance will be placed on empirical proxies. The measurement of preferences regarding child rearing and other activities is an underdeveloped field that promises to be very important for subsequent analyses of fertility that utilize the decision framework outlined in this section.[8] Consequently, although the Preference Structure block in Figure 1-1 is conceived to be of major importance in the analysis of the demand for children, our empirical measures of the dimensions of this structure remain in an unsatisfactory state, which can be improved only by some extensive efforts to gather new data of this type in the context of a decision model of fertility.

The model of fertility presented and analyzed in this book is organized around the principle that the couple's family size decision is basically a decision to maximize the couple's happiness subject to the limitations of time and wealth available. In this sense, the fertility decision of Figure 1–1 is formally equivalent to the utility maximizing consumption choice of traditional consumer theory. The couple is pictured as attempting to maximize its utility given its relative preferences for children and other consumption activities, its perceptions of the cost of children, and its expectations about future resources.

All these factors may be influenced in nontrivial ways by the social structure within which the decisions are made, and a major task of the following chapter is to present a theory of the avenues by which sociodemographic variables influence the demand for children. Once the theory of fertility presented in Chapter Two is fully explained, the remainder of the study is devoted to an empirical formulation and test of the theory. Chapters Three and Four present empirical estimates of the expected costs of child rearing for couples of differing socioeconomic strata. Chapter Five develops empirical estimates of expected future resources, and Chapter Six brings the full model together in order to confront it with data.

The remainder of this chapter is concerned with the task of integrating the insights of a number of scholars (primarily from the discipline of sociology) into the decision framework presented in this section. In addition, further discussion of selected parts of the framework are presented and some additional limitations on the goals of the study are advanced.

2. SOCIOLOGICAL APPROACHES TO DIFFERENTIAL FERTILITY

The Normative Explanation of Fertility Differentials

Nineteen fifty-five marked the beginning of a period of intensive and accelerated collection of information regarding the family size desires, contraceptive practices, and fecundity of American women. Besides providing volumes of descriptive information on these topics, these data gathering efforts allowed sociologists to explore a number of hypotheses regarding the social correlates of differential fertility.

The sample survey was the primary method of data collection for the two different types of fertility research begun in that period. The first type was the national sample survey of married women of childbearing age, beginning with the Growth of American Families studies (GAF) of 1955 and 1960, continuing with the National Fertility Studies (NFS) of 1965 and 1970, and culminating with the assumption in recent years by the federal government of the responsibility for continuing these studies.[9] These surveys have provided a tremendous amount of information, and even if one believes, as I do, that this series in its present form has entered a period of diminishing returns, one still must acknowledge that most of what we know about the determinants of American fertility stems from it.

The second line of survey research begun in the 1950s was the metropolitan area survey as exemplified by the Princeton Study, the Detroit Area Surveys, and, later, the Rhode Island Surveys.[10] The Princeton Study was a longitudinal survey of white couples living in seven of the largest metropolitan areas in the United States. It was designed as a direct descendant of the Indianapolis Study of 1941, which was the first survey designed to acquire data useful for the analysis of factors affecting fertility. Both the Detroit Area Surveys and the Rhode Island Surveys have also incorporated the longitudinal design essential both in analyzing fertility behavior over time and in the verification of responses obtained in the initial interviews.

These surveys have reached some fundamental conclusions about American fertility and family planning that are of major importance for this study:

1. Fecundity impairments are very widespread in the American population but they are not quantitatively important in determining the course of aggregate population trends. However, the existence of subfecundity poses empirical problems in the assessment of the demand for children. These complications are treated in more detail in Chapter Six.
2. Family limitation is almost universally practiced and approved. The 1955 GAF study reported that 79 percent of the women interviewed (white couples only) had used or expected to use contraception at the time of the survey. By 1965 the proportion had risen to 90 percent; furthermore, 97 percent of white wives classified as fecund in 1965 had used or expected to use contraception.[11] Moreover, this high use rate combined with the wider diffusion of the oral contraceptive and the intrauterine device has led in recent years to an impressive decline in the rate of unwanted fertility among all groups in the population.[12] We can view this evidence as providing support for the assertion that family size is, indeed, a subject of conscious decision for most American couples. Later, the empirical problem of identifying couples by their ability to regulate family size will be treated in some detail; however, the accumulated evidence would appear to support our choice of a decision model as a framework for fertility analysis.

3. American couples from all classes have come to share a preference for families of moderate size. Virtually all couples cite a family size in the two- to four-child range as being desirable (see Table 1-1), and actual expectations also tend to cluster in this narrow range. Even given the narrow range of family size desires, however, aggregate fertility in the United States has varied significantly in the twentieth century (Figure 1-2). The total fertility rate, which reached 3.77 in 1957, plummeted in the intervening sixteen years to a low of 1.9 in 1973.[13] This decline is explained in part by the shifts in family size within the two- to four-child range. For example, in 1960 the proportion of wives expecting two children was 25 percent and the proportion expecting three or four children was 47 percent. By 1974 expectations had shifted to 43.2 percent of all wives expecting two children and only 34 percent expecting three or four children.[14] These changes in expectations and the concomitant decline in period fertility rates during the 1960s attests to the control that American couples exercise over their childbearing. Given the aggregate instability now characteristic of fertility in the United States and other developed nations, an understanding of the basic determinants of these shifts would appear to be even more important for public policy purposes than ever before.

In the face of the obvious control over reproduction being exercised by couples in the United States, sociologists began an intensive study of the social factors influencing differences in fertility rates. In contrast to economists' emphasis on individual behavior, sociologists have until recently tended to concentrate upon the normative influences affecting fertility behavior. Many of our earliest insights regarding the determinants of differential fertility can be traced to the sociological assertion that individual behavior may often be the result of group pressure.

Although the definition of the term "norm" is not completely precise, its usage in the sociological literature generally conforms to at least one of the following three definitions:

(1) a collective equation of behavior in terms of what it *ought* to be; (2) a collective expectation as to what behavior *will be;* and/or (3) particular *reactions* to behavior, including attempts to apply sanctions or otherwise induce a particular kind of conduct.[15]

Thus the normative explanation of fertility centers upon procreation and child rearing as social process shaped and influenced by the attitudes, beliefs, and actions of the social, racial, or economic class within which the parents reside. In effect, the normative explanations of differential

Table 1-1. Percent Distribution by Number of Children Considered Ideal: 1941, 1945, 1955, 1960, 1965, 1974

Number of Children Considered Ideal	American Institute of Public Opinion[a]		Growth of American Families[b]			NFS 1965	Current Population Survey[c] 1974
			1955	1960			
	1941	1945	White Wives	White Wives	All Wives	All Wives	All Wives
All replies	100	100	100	100	100	100	100
None	—	—	—	—	—	.1	5
1	1	1	—	—	—	.4	9.9
2	40	25	19	20	20	24.4	43.2
3	32	33	32	31	30	33.0	23.5
4	21	31	41	41	41	34.5	10.5
5	3	7	4	4	4	3.9	7.9[d]
6 or more	3	3	4	4	5	3.7	—
Average number	3.0	3.3	3.4	3.5	3.5	3.29	2.55

[a]Data are for all single and married women, 21–34 years of age.

[b]Data are mean distributions of the minimum and maximum replies of wives, 18–34 years of age.

[c]Data are for number of children expected by wives aged 18–39.

[d]Percentage of wives expecting five or more children.

Source: First five columns from Pascal K. Whelpton, Arthur A. Campbell, John E. Patterson, Fertility and Family Planning in the United States (copyright © 1966 by Princeton University Press), Table 12, p. 34. Reprinted by permission of Princeton University Press. Ryder and Westoff, op. cit., p. 28 (column six). U.S. Bureau of the Census. Current Population Reports, Series P-20, No. 269, "Prospects for American Fertility: June 1974," Washington, D.C.: U.S. Government Printing Office, September 1974 (column seven).

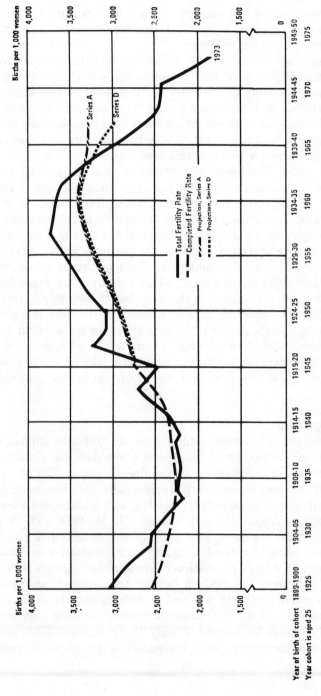

Figure 1–2. Completed Fertility Rates for Birth Cohorts of Women with Birth Years 1899–1900 to 1941–42, and Total Fertility Rates for Calendar Years 1925–1973: United States

Source: U.S. Bureau of the Census, *The Methods and Materials of Demography*, Henry S. Shryock, Jacob S. Siegel and Associates, Washington, D.C.: U.S. Government Printing Office, 1971, p. 490.

fertility that are reviewed below attempt to relate the "Social and Demographic Factors" of Figure 1–1 directly to the fertility decision, without benefit of the intervening variables.

In the contemporary United States, reliance solely upon normative arguments in the explanation of fertility differentials is clearly insufficient. Explanations of fertility differentials on the basis of membership in varying social, ethnic, and economic groups have been unimpressive statistically, and, over time, those differentials which have been discovered have begun to disappear, at least with respect to the analyses of *direct* relationships between social norms and fertility.

The decision model developed and tested in this study does not disregard normative influences on fertility; rather, these influences are pictured as operating either directly on preferences for children or indirectly through other variables not usually considered in the normative context. For example, the education of a husband and wife may operate directly on the relative preferences of the couple for children versus other activities, or indirectly by influencing the quantity of resources available to the family and the manner in which resources are expended in child rearing. Indeed, it is argued in the following chapter that normative influences play an important role in influencing the cost of child rearing, and thereby have a powerful indirect effect on the demand for children. In the remainder of this section a brief review of some of the major normative influences on fertility is undertaken, with a view toward the integration of these insights into the decision model outlined above.[16]

Family Background

In the literature on differential fertility prior to 1959 little attention was paid to the geographic origin of couples on whom data was gathered for the assessment of differentials by socioeconomic status. Data from the 1910 and 1940 censuses as well as the Indianapolis Survey seemed to indicate that fertility was negatively correlated with such status measures as education, occupation, and income.[17] In 1959 and 1960 Goldberg advanced the argument that most of the observed negative correlation between completed family size and socioeconomic status was due to the presence of a large proportion of rural-urban migrants in the cities.[18] Using data from the 1952–58 Detroit Area Studies, and considering only those older cohorts that had completed their families, he demonstrated that most of the differences in fertility between high and low status families were eliminated if only those families with two generations of urban experience were considered. As a result he concluded:

1. Socioeconomic differences in completed family size among two generation urbanites were small and inconsistent. There was no distinct inverse or direct pattern.
2. Farm migrants exhibited a sharp inverse fertility pattern.
3. Farm migrants, on the average, had a larger number of children than two-generation urbanites.
4. Farm migrants were disproportionately selected into the lower socioeconomic groups after their arrival in the urban area.
5. Findings 2, 3, and 4 produced the usual inverse fertility pattern for the total sample of metropolitan Detroit.[19]

Goldberg's reanalysis of the Indianapolis data produced similar results, leading immediately to the conclusion that the traditionally accepted negative correlations between fertility and status in urban areas were the product of the high incidence of farm migrants in the lower socioeconomic groups. Duncan, in a 1965 paper, confirmed Goldberg's results and concluded:

In the [the older] cohorts, a sufficient condition for controlled fertility was indicated by either of two characteristics—two generations of nonfarm residence in the history of both spouses or attainment of high levels of schooling. It is as though a commitment to the "modern" fertility pattern could be made with either nonfarm rearing or by prolonged contact with the educational system.[20]

Other evidence, however, has proved contradictory. The 1955 GAF study provided evidence in confirmation of Goldberg's findings but the 1960 GAF data produced disagreement:

. . . the earlier farm experience of neither the husband or wife appears to have much effect upon the expected fertility of couples that had not lived on farms after marriage. In fact, the expected number of births is somewhat lower for such couples than for couples with no farm background at all.[21]

A recent analysis of data from the 1967 Survey of Economic Opportunity finds, however, that fertility (as measured by the number of children ever born per woman standardized by age) and size of place of origin are negatively correlated. Rural-urban migrants have higher fertility than urban-urban migrants or urban nonmigrants; however, when current residents of urban areas were classified by size of place, the effect of rural origin was irregular.[22] These last results, while suggestive, provide no insight into the mechanism by which rural origin is translated into higher fertility. If rural origin merely signifies the effects of lower education and income, consideration of the latter two variables will obviate the need to include origin as a variable for analysis. If, however, a rural origin affects tastes and attitudes independently, then its inclusion in the analysis of a demand equation for children may be justified.

A rural origin may indeed represent by proxy a taste for children. Duncan et al. have argued that there is a small positive correlation between the size of families of orientation of a husband and wife and their own fertility decisions.[23] They hypothesize that ". . . children learn in their families of orientation a set of solutions for the problems they face later in forming their own families as adults . . . they tend to attempt to recreate this setting in their own families as adults . . . in order to mobilize familiar resources, relationships, and roles."[24] If persons from large families have come in the main from rural areas, part of the higher fertility of persons of rural origin may stem from a taste for larger families.

In any case, rural origin and large families of orientation are fast losing quantitative importance in the determination of fertility. The cohorts now entering the childbearing years will exhibit an increasing incidence of nonrural origin and small families of orientation as the nation's recent history of urbanization and moderate family size manifests itself. However, rural origin may prove to be a valuable proxy for the preference structure measures desired but unavailable for the empirical analysis of Chapter Six.

Religion

The national fertility studies have added authoritative confirmation to the general belief that Catholics desire and produce more children than non-Catholics.[c] The investigators for the 1955 GAF study found that among the major religious groups Catholics were the least likely to be users of contraception, the least likely to have completely planned fertility, and the most likely to experience accidental pregnancies.[25] Controls on variables such as educational attainment, income, farm background, and place of residence did not result in elimination of the religious differential.

[c]Ryder and Westoff, analyzing data from the 1970 National Fertility Study, have found a marked narrowing in wanted fertility between white Catholic and non-Catholic couples in the youngest (1946–50) cohort. If the Catholic–non-Catholic differential is indeed disappearing, normative explanations of fertility differentials will have been dealt another blow. See Norman B. Ryder and Charles F. Westoff, "Wanted and Unwanted Fertility in the United States: 1965 and 1970," in U.S. Commission on Population Growth and the American Future, *Demographic and Social Aspects of Population Growth,* Charles F. Westoff and Robert Parke, Jr., Eds., Vol. I of Commission research reports (Washington, D.C.: U.S. Government Printing Office, 1972, pp. 475–476.)

Differences in family planning practices were accompanied by corresponding differences in desired and expected family size. Whelpton, Campbell, and Patterson report, "Within every major social and economic group, we find Catholic wives expecting a substantially larger number of births than Protestant and Jewish wives."[26] Furthermore, the Catholic–non-Catholic differential is accentuated when degree of religious commitment is considered. Data from the NFS (1965) and the Princeton Study show that both completed family size and fertility expectations are positively correlated with degree of religiousness among Catholics; however, among Protestants and Jews this relationship does not hold.[27]

Important for the present study are recent findings concerning contraceptive practices of Catholics who have reached intended family size. Bumpass and Westoff find that even for Catholic women the proportion using contraception increases markedly so that by the time of the third interview of the Princeton Study (mean age of wives was 35.6 years), 87 percent of these women were using contraception or were sterile.[28] Furthermore, even though Catholics have been shown to be prone to contraceptive failure, the overall proportion experiencing number failure is quite similar to the proportion of non-Catholics experiencing number failure. This is due to three interrelated factors: (1) white Catholics desire, on the whole, more children than do white non-Catholics;[d] (2) this implies that they experience a shorter exposure to the risk of an unwanted birth; (3) this exposure to risk occurs at a higher average age for Catholics than for non-Catholics and therefore, presumably, the fecundity of Catholic women is lower.[29]

The fact that Catholic women practice contraception after family size desires are fulfilled provides some reassurance that use of a model positing rational planning behavior will not be inappropriate. Catholic women have larger families than do non-Catholics but their completed families remain considerably smaller than would be predicted if they took no measures of control. If Catholics merely exhibited a taste for larger families than non-Catholics, the statistical treatment of Catholics in our analysis would be relatively simple. In the final demand equation for children a variable denoting religion might be included to account for these taste differences. The matter is, however, not so simple: denominational differences appear to interact with different measures of socioeconomic status to produce contrasting effects of status on fertility. For example, the 1960 GAF study found that for non-Catholics both the wife's and husband's education was negatively related to total number of

[d]Fecund white Catholic wives wanted between 17 and 30 percent larger families than comparable non-Catholics in 1970.

births expected, while for Catholics the relationship appeared to be U-shaped with expectations being higher for the low and high ends of the status distribution.

Results from the 1965 NFS demonstrate even more clearly the existence of an interaction effect between religion and socioeconomic status. For Protestant wives number of children expected declines from 3.9 for those women with a grade school education to 2.7 for those women with four or more years of college. For Catholic women, however, expected family size falls from 4.7 (grade school) to 3.5 (college, 1–3 years) and then rises to 4.5 for women with a college degree. The interaction remains, although not as strongly, when husband's occupational status and income are compared with expected fertility.[30]

Finally, as will be more fully discussed in Chapter Three, it is possible that Catholics and non-Catholics differ significantly in their child rearing practices, resulting in higher opportunity costs for child rearing in Catholic families. Thus a substantial amount of evidence suggests that religious differences are the source of important interaction effects that, if neglected, might seriously confuse the analysis of the effects of status differentials on fertility.

To complicate matters still further, Bumpass has suggested that much of the Catholic–non-Catholic differential may in fact be due to differences in age at marriage.[31] Bumpass demonstrates that, for Catholics and non-Catholics alike, the strong negative relationship between fertility and status declines with advancing age at marriage. To the degree that Catholics tend to marry later than non-Catholics, observed differentials between them may be due more to the age at marriage interaction than to religious differences.

Bumpass proposes two plausible explanations for the existence of the age at marriage interaction. From a sociologist's perspective he argues that age at marriage has little effect on high status women, but that early marriage reduces alternative role possibilities for lower status women. As a result these women might tend to favor larger families than they would if they had been able to work, attend college, or gain other extrafamilial experience before marriage. That is, early marriage has prevented them from acquiring a "taste" for nonfamilial roles that compete with motherhood.

Second, he argues that an early age at marriage is selective of women with high fecundity, resulting in larger families for low status women who marry early. Bumpass suggests:

> Insofar as premarital pregnancies play a role in young ages of marriage and are related to low education, women who marry at later ages may be a less fecund residual of the population of low-education women. On the other

hand, few women who marry young go on to college after becoming pregnant, and consequently women who marry young and still attend college may be relatively subfecund.[32]

Bumpass presents data on childlessness to support this claim but, while they are suggestive, they are insufficient to bear the whole weight of his argument.

If age at marriage does account for much of the Catholic–non-Catholic fertility differential it should be included as an explanatory variable in the analysis of the demand for children. In Chapter Six age at marriage will be utilized both as a predetermined variable in the demand equation and as a criterion variable in the analysis of possible interaction effects; and, to anticipate, its inclusion as an explanatory variable seems amply justified, while its role as an interaction variable remains doubtful.[e]

Income

One of the dependable relationships in fertility research has been the negative correlation between income and fertility. This relation, which has been noted both in time series and cross-sectional analyses, lies at the heart of a number of the theories of the demographic transition from high to low fertility; however, it is important not to confuse the relation between income and family size over time with the cross-sectional relation at one point in time. The well established negative correlation noted in most time series analyses is not inconsistent with a positive relation cross-sectionally, nor is the longitudinal relationship between fertility and income always negative as the example of the United States during the period 1945–1957 demonstrates.

Although our concern in this study is primarily with the cross-sectional relation between income and fertility, time series studies are not without interest. Studies relating aggregate birth rates to short run changes in business conditions,[33] and the work of Richard Easterlin and others [34] on longer term cyclical variations, pose an interesting question: Why does income, which appears to influence fertility over time, not bear a stronger relationship to fertility in the cross-section?

Judith Blake has marshalled data from eleven Gallup and Roper polls (see Table 1–2) conducted between 1936 and 1966 to demonstrate that ideal family size generally varies little with income and that when it does

[e]In the life cycle models of human capital accumulation and fertility favored by adherents of the "Chicago School" of fertility analysis (see Chapter Two for a discussion of this literature), inclusion of age at marriage would be inappropriate, since by assumption the marriage decision, the fertility decision, and the life cycle human capital accumulation and work-leisure decisions are made simultaneously. I prefer to think of the decision to marry as essentially independent of the decision regarding completed family size—although marriage and the desire to have at least some children are in general closely linked.

Table 1-2. Number of Children Considered Ideal by White Females According to Economic Status or Income, United States, Selected Years, 1936–1966

Date	Age Range	Economic Status or Income	0	1	2	3	4	5	6+	Total	(N)	$\bar{X}$
1936	21+	Average+	—	3	32	35	24	3	3	100	(177)	3.1
		Average	—	2	37	29	28	3	1	100	(202)	3.0
		Poor+	—	2	28	31	26	8	5	100	(155)	3.3
		Poor	—	2	23	41	19	8	7	100	(53)	3.4
		Total	—	2	32	32	26	5	3	100	(527)	3.1
1952	21+	Average+ & Wealthy	—	1	23	35	33	5	3	100	(77)	3.3
		Average	—	1	22	33	35	5	4	100	(277)	3.4
		Poor	1	2	29	24	32	5	7	100	(539)	3.3
		Total	—	2	26	28	33	5	6	100	(893)	3.3
1966	21+	10,000+	—	1	13	40	38	4	4	100	(129)	3.4
		7,000–9,999	—	2	23	33	34	4	4	100	(109)	3.3
		5,000–6,999	—	2	21	27	43	4	3	100	(154)	3.4
		3,000–4,999	—	2	12	38	34	7	7	100	(89)	3.6
		Under 3,000	—	1	12	29	48	4	6	100	(69)	3.6
		Total	—	2	17	33	39	5	4	100	(550)	3.4

Source: Judith Blake, "Income and Reproductive Motivation," *Population Studies* XXI (3) (November 1967): 190–191. The data for the table above come from Gallup polls and are extracted from Blake's Table 1.

the relation is usually inverse. The 1960 GAF study and the 1965 NFS both found that the relation of income to fertility depended upon the religion of the respondent. For Protestants the relation between the husband's current income and expected family size was weakly inverse. For Catholics, the relation was U-shaped with couples at both ends of the income distribution expecting more children than those in the middle.[35]

Students of fertility, and especially Blake, have assessed the zero order correlations between income and fertility and have argued that the level of current income reported by a family has little to do with the family size chosen by a couple. Furthermore, Blake has expanded her argument to insist that the economic theory of consumption offers little in the way of explanation of differential fertility.[36]

At least two objections would appear to make such an extreme conclusion premature. First, since child rearing is a long term process, long term income may be the relevant measure of income, not current income. This distinction would appear to be especially important in the analysis of fertility predictions of younger couples whose current income may be considerably below their expected future income. Both Stafford and Freedman have called attention to the effect of higher than average income expectations on current and future fertility, and reliance solely on current income would appear to be ill advised.[37] Second, the effect of income on fertility cannot be assessed independently of the cost of rearing children.

This point is obscured by Gary Becker in his pathbreaking article on fertility because he incorrectly argues that all parents face the same prices for child rearing and that any resulting differences in expenditure on children are the result of preferences for "higher quality" children. If these preferences were uniform throughout the income distribution, neglect of the expenditures parents make on their children might not affect our assessment of the effect of income on fertility. As is amply demonstrated in Chapters Three and Four, however, expenditures on child rearing are positively correlated with the long range income of parents, and there is a strong theoretical case for postulating status related differentials in child rearing standards.

The result, then, of considering only the simple correlation between income and family size is that the potentially powerful negative effect of price on the demand for children is overlooked. The weak correlation between income and fertility may be nothing more than the net effect of two strongly offsetting income and price effects, as is argued in detail in the next chapter.

Education and Occupation

The couple's education and the husband's occupation are closely allied to the family's income and status. Protestant women exhibited a strongly negative correlation between their education and expected family size in all three of the national fertility surveys. For Catholic wives, however, evidence of the U-shaped distribution persists.[38] Due to the predominance of non-Catholics in the population the overall relationship is negative. Fertility expectations by husband's occupational class are again negative for Protestant couples and U-shaped for Catholic couples.[39]

None of the national studies tabulates the wife's fertility expectations by the husband's education, presumably because husband's education and occupational class are highly correlated; but as is demonstrated in the subsequent chapters, the husband's education and occupation as well as the wife's education each have an independent importance in the study of fertility. Simple tabulation of each of these variables separately is not sufficient to measure their joint impact on fertility. Education and occupation can enter the demand equation for children directly as taste variables and indirectly as determinants of the couple's resources and expenditures on children. Analysis of each of the factors independently fails to produce understanding of either of the direct effect of the variable or possible indirect and joint effects.

Current Place of Residence

Differences in fertility among residents of cities, suburbs, towns, rural areas, and farms have long been cited as one of the major aspects of differential fertility. The 1955 GAF study documented these differentials by size of place, using data on birth expectations; and Cho, Grabill, and Bogue have added confirmation, using data on children ever born from the 1960 Census.[40] The 1960 GAF and the 1965 NFS provide somewhat less conclusive evidence: with the exception of rural farm residents, expected fertility by place of residence shows no clear pattern.[41]

Why might the Census provide different evidence from the sample surveys? The probable reason is that the Census data concern only that fertility which has already occurred, while the fertility studies report expected fertility. If couples move out of central cities as family size increases, we might expect that the Census data will show a preponderance of couples with small families in central cities, many of whom will move as their family size grows. The sample surveys, on the other hand, are reporting on the *prospective* fertility of couples who may well be planning to move before the completion of their fertility.

Thus it is not surprising to find little variation in expected family size by current place of residence since place or residence may well be a function of current family size. Current residence is expected to be an especially poor predictor of fertility for younger couples who have not yet moved in response to a growing family. For older couples, however, size of place of current residence might be relevant for the prediction of fertility, since location in a central city may represent a stronger than average taste for activities that compete directly with child rearing and that induce the couple to pay more for child rearing in order to enjoy them. Thus the use of current place of residence in conjunction with expected fertility may provide little in the way of meaningful information regarding the causal interaction of the two variables.[42]

Other Activities

Child rearing, as is demonstrated in Chapter Three, takes an inordinate amount of time. It competes for the husband's and wife's time with a wide range of other consumption activities and market work. The model developed in Chapter Two illustrates in a formal way the influence that the time requirements of child rearing might be expected to have on the demand for children.

Our purpose in this section is to review very briefly some of the voluminous literature relating fertility to nonparental activities. The issues here are enormously complex and assignments of causality are dubious, to say the least. For example, the work history of the wife since marriage has been shown to be strongly related to her fertility expectations. Data from all three of the national studies of fertility have repeatedly shown (1) that wives who work after marriage exhibit lower current and expected fertility, (2) that there is an inverse relation between length of the wife's work after marriage and her expected fertility, and (3) that wives who work because they "like to" have fewer children and expect fewer than wives who work because they "need the income."[43] Furthermore, the relation holds when fecundity of the wife is controlled, eliminating those wives who are in the labor market as a result of sterility or subfecundity.

What are we to make of the causal implications of this? The general conclusion drawn by many students of fertility is that women decide to work in lieu of additional children, but as Sweet points out, "An equally compelling case can be made, however, for the reverse causal sequence: that women who have smaller families, for whatever reason, have more time to work and fewer constraints on work."[44]

This view is implicitly shared by the numerous labor economists who have studied labor force participation of married women and who treat family composition as a predetermined variable. Data demonstrating that the presence of children under six is a major determinant of a wife's labor force participation have been gathered from the 1955 GAF study, from the 1964 Productive Americans survey, from the 1967 Survey of Economic Opportunity, and from the 0.1 percent 1960 Census sample.[45]

Market work is not the only activity claiming the time not devoted to child rearing. The husband and wife may participate in a wide range of nonparental consumption activities as diverse as reading, bowling, moviegoing, gardening, etc. These activities and others also lay claim to the couple's time, and sociologists have speculated that the wider the set of alternatives open to a couple the smaller the family they choose. Data supporting these speculations are hard to come by. Pratt and Whelpton, analyzing data from the Indianapolis Study, found that both a wife's work and her involvement in outside activities (clubs, lodges, meeetings, dances, parties, etc.) tended to reduce the family's actual and desired fertility.[46] More recent work, utilizing a sample of wives of college teachers, provides some support for the notion that housewives engaged in "creative" activities have fewer children than those who do not, but contradicts Pratt and Whelpton's findings regarding the effect of participation in clubs and organizations.[47]

The role of nonparental activities in a theory of fertility is extremely complex. Theoretically, wives may work because they prefer it to additional child rearing or because they have larger families as a result of choice or contraceptive error. Also, work at different times in the life cycle may well imply different things about completed fertility. However, the state of our current knowledge about the dynamics of time allocation to parental and nonparental activities is very poor. The dynamic aspect of the time allocation choices made regarding nonparental activities would appear to be extremely important, but we do not as yet have the data necessary to test our theories effectively.[f] The systematic inclusion of nonparental activity into a model of fertility will have to await the acquisition of data suitable to test it.

Generational Aspects of Differential Fertility

In the study of differential fertility our primary goal is to isolate groups in the population that display distinctive fertility patterns and to explain the reasons for these differentials. In this chapter we have been concerned with those differentials related to various social, economic, and demographic variables, but we have not as yet explored the significance of time as a variable in differential fertility research. Each married couple exists as a discrete and finite entity in the continuum of the life of the population. The fertility decision made by the couple and the relation of this decision to other decisions made by other couples cannot be divorced from the explicit historical situation in which the couple completes its life cycle. It is, therefore, very risky to provide explanations of fertility differentials by social, economic, or demographic classes without regard to the effect of the passage of time.

The 1955 and 1960 GAF studies provide ample evidence that fertility differentials by social and economic variables depend in part upon the age of the couples being studied. The two GAF studies contain frequent instances in which the negative relation between expected fertility and socioeconomic status is reduced or even reversed when the youngest cohorts are analyzed separately.[48] For some commentators these reversals signal the arrival of a truly "modern" fertility pattern in the

---

[f]Many of the microeconomic models of fertility reviewed in the following chapter suggest that fertility, labor force activity, and nonmarket allocations of time to children and other activities are jointly determined. I take the position that the family size decision implies a commitment of time to child rearing but that it does not necessarily imply a lifetime allocation of the remaining time between market work and other nonmarket activities. The fertility decision must be made based on estimates about the future time requirements of children, but this does not mean that *other* time allocation decisions must also be made so early in the couple's life cycle.

United States in which the changes wrought by the industrialization and urbanization of the nation have been largely absorbed, regional differences dissolved, and social and class differences reduced to a degree that makes them irrelevant for the study of fertility differentials. Indeed, a close study of the sociological literature on differential fertility tends to foster the suspicion that many of the traditional variables associated with differential fertility research will in the none too distant future cease to possess much, if any, explanatory power.

Different cohorts exhibit wide variations in fertility, as reference to Figure 1-2 will confirm. In this figure the completed fertility of cohorts of women spanning the period 1899–1900 to 1941–42 is displayed. The completed fertility rate is the average number of children born per thousand women of a given cohort, registered when women of the cohort have reached age 25 (the approximate center of the peak childbearing period). For example, completed fertility of women born in 1909–10 is approximately 2,300 and this quantity is graphed at the year 1935 when these women were 25 years of age. As is evident from a comparison of both the completed fertility rate and the total fertility rate, much of the aggregate change in period measures of fertility can be traced to intercohort differentials.

Given that intercohort variations are important in the analysis of the course of aggregate fertility,[49] what role do they play in the analysis of differentials by economic and social status? Given the model presented in Chapter Two, two situations may occur, the first being decidedly less serious than the second.

1. Tastes and preferences regarding desired family size do change, but norms regarding child rearing behavior do not. In this situation the experience of a cohort may lead to tastes for more or less children than for other cohorts but child rearing practices and the responsiveness of couples to changes in the costs of child rearing do not change—or if they do change, the changes are uniform. The statistical remedy for complications of this sort is a standard analysis of first order interaction effects.

2. The second situation is more serious in that norms regarding child rearing practices also change from cohort to cohort but the changes are not uniform among social and economic groups. For example, assume that a college educated, high status occupation couple of the 1940–41 cohort intends to spend less on child rearing (relative to other couples of the same cohort but different status levels) than did a couple of similar status in the 1930–31 cohort. Unless this difference in child rearing behavior can actually be quantified the interaction

effect cannot be analyzed. As will become apparent in Chapters Two through Four, the data presently available do not allow analysis of this sort of interaction.[g]

In any case, because tastes, preferences, and norms may change over time, an analysis of intercohort differentials is necessary to insure that an important interaction effect is not obscuring underlying behavioral relationships. Interactions of the first type will be analyzed in Chapter Six, but those of the second type cannot be treated with the data currently available.

3. THE DECISION PROCESS

Joint Maximization versus Conflict Resolution

It is ironic that, in a discipline so concerned with the antecedents to and the outcomes of optimizing decisions, economists have spent so little effort in the analysis of the decision process itself.[50] In the vast majority of economic research, the process by which decisions are reached is treated somewhat as a funnel through which prior decision criteria are passed and out of which the decision outcomes are produced. This omission is often justified by the somewhat circular argument that if the observed outcomes of decision processes are consistent with the theoretical hypotheses underlying the analysis, specific attention to the decision process is unnecessary. This may be the case in some instances, but the research pertaining to decision processes in large organizations just cited and the rather special nature of the fertility decision suggest otherwise.

The social and psychological literature on fertility suggests the presence of a considerable level of conflict between husband and wife over the couple's target family size, and it is clear that the outcomes of exercises in conflict resolution often do not resemble those of a joint utility maximization. Nevertheless, we will reluctantly follow in the tradition and assume that the husband and wife act jointly so as to maximize their joint utility with regard to the fertility decision.[51] Moreover, it will be assumed that the decision process itself is neutral in influencing the outcome of couples' fertility decisions—although evidence will be presented in Chapter Six that suggests that the assumption of neutrality may be misplaced.

One of the most important items on the agenda for further fertility research should be an assessment of the impact of the decision process

---

[g]Another problem centers around the fact that, in cross-section surveys conducted at one point, age and cohort are identical, prohibiting the separation of age effects from cohort effects.

upon levels of and differentials in fertility. The data available in the national fertility surveys of the 1960s and early 70s will not, however, support such an analysis, which will have to wait for new data collected especially for that purpose.

"Rationality" and the Family Size Decision

Given the assumption of joint utility maximization, our adaptation of consumer theory requires that husband and wife work together "rationally" to achieve an optimal family size. Rationality has many different meanings in behavioral research,[h] but its meaning in the consumer theory context is reasonably well defined, as illustrated by the following quotation:

> Given the set A, rational (consistent) choice is defined as follows: As between any two actions a_1 and a_2 in A, the actor either prefers one to the other [or] is indifferent between them. Further, preference and indifference are transitive; if a_1 is preferred to a_2 and a_2 is preferred to a_3, then a_1 is preferred to a_3. Each action is indifferent to itself. Given an actual opportunity to choose an action from a subset B of A, the actor will choose an action to which no action in B is preferred, provided that there is such an action. That is, the actor will choose one of the "most preferred" actions in B.[52]

Or, to acknowledge the utilitarian origins of this concept of rationality, the decision maker acts so as to maximize his utility. In the remainder of the book, rational-consistent behavior on the part of the couple is assumed.

This assumption requires at least an attempt at justification, since skepticism regarding this assumption extends to numerous students of fertility.[53] The problem is to consider conditions under which assumption of the rational-consistent model is plausible. Winter suggests that two conditions must hold if the assumption of consistent choice is to be tenable: (1) the costs of making a decision about fertility should be low relative to the potential costs or gains resulting from the decision; and (2) the conditions in which the decision makers find themselves are relatively stable.[54]

With regard to the first condition, the fertility decision would appear

[h]Sidney Winter identifies six common and mutually independent connotations of rationality as used in behavioral research: (1) rationality as consistent choice, (2) rationality as conformity in goals and belief, (3) rationality as creative problem solving, (4) rationality as sound decision procedure, (5) rationality as viability, and (6) rationality as learning ability. See his "Concepts of Rationality in Behavioral Theory," Institute of Public Policy Studies Discussion Paper No. 7 (University of Michigan (August 1969), p. 4).

to fit: the consequences of a wrong decision have an enormous impact on the couple. At the same time, the information on which a decision about family size might be based is either very inexpensively obtained—e.g., observation of peers, relatives, etc.—or is infinitely expensive (exact knowledge of future income, child rearing expenses, personality patterns of future children, etc.). Thus it would appear that the information upon which parents actually base their family size decisions is inexpensive relative to the consequences of those decisions.

The second condition is more problematic. Schumpeter, in his advocacy of the rational-consistent model for certain uses, argues:

> The assumption that conduct is prompt and rational is in all cases a fiction. But it proves to be sufficiently near to reality, if things have time to hammer logic into men. Where this has happened, and within the limits in which it has happened, one may rest content with this fiction and build theories upon it.[55]

The central issue as Schumpeter sees it is whether the social structure is stable enough over time to permit couples to make decisions with reasonable confidence that the expectations under which they are made will be reasonably close to subsequent events. For the couple attempting to choose a family size the required stability conditions might relate to the future of the family as a social institution, to employment prospects in the near and long term, and to the political and social stability of the country.

The last few years in America do not present particularly compelling evidence of long term stability, and the political, social, and economic events of the decade may be in part responsible for the sharp decline in marital fertility reported earlier. The growth of the women's liberation movement and the resulting unfavorable publicity accorded the family as an institution may be responsible for the sharp fall in the proportion of women married during the ages 20 to 24.[i] However, the proportions married at older ages do not seem to have declined nearly so severely and the Hoffmans' dictum that "nothing . . . has occurred to diminish the importance of the family as the major primary group," appears to remain valid today.[56]

This is not to deny that instability of the institutional structure can cause vast changes; rather it is to suggest that the sort of instability

---

[i]This proportion fell from 71.6 percent in 1960 to 60.4 percent in 1974. U.S. Bureau of the Census, *Current Population Reports,* Series P-20, No. 271, "Marital Status and Living Arrangements: March 1974" (Washington, D.C.: U.S. Government Printing Office, 1974, p. 3).

witnessed during the last decade has not fundamentally altered the prospects and expectations of most white Americans to the point that the underlying decision process surrounding fertility choice has been fundamentally altered or upset. If this is indeed the case, the assumption of rational-consistent choice is at least plausible in the context of the fertility decision.

"Rational" Behavior and Contraceptive Efficacy

Figure 1–1 emphasized that overt behavior must occur in order to translate the demand for children into actual fertility. This is a problem with which economists dealing with standard commodity demand problems do not have to deal. In orthodox consumption studies it is assumed (although not demonstrated) that consumers can purchase the exact amount of each commodity demanded.[j] Systematic errors in the attainment of intended quantities are thus implicitly ruled out of the analysis.

Although it might be agreed that this assumption is relatively innocuous with respect to consumer demand studies, it is entirely unsuitable for the analysis of fertility. Since the demand for sexual relations exists quite independently of the demand for children, pregnancy is often the unintended outcome of coition. Investigators have, over time, become quite successful in identifying those couples who are not effectively controlling completed family size, but the problem of how to incorporate them into the decision framework presented above remains.

Formally, if noneconomic factors are disregarded, the problem is not particularly difficult: couples demand the ability to regulate fertility and this ability entails both psychic and economic costs. The degree of contraceptive effectiveness chosen by the couple can then be considered to be a function of the costs of the particular method and of the consequences of a pregnancy.[k] Thus, fertility regulating behavior can be viewed as another aspect of utility maximization under constraint, with couples choosing a degree of contraceptive effectiveness that maximizes their utility.[57]

Viewed in this way, contraceptive failures cannot be characterized as the outcomes of irrational behavior; rather, they should ideally be considered as part of the total fertility decision process and be analyzed as such.[58] An unwanted birth occurs, it might be argued, because the

---

[j]A subtler student of consumer demand might disagree, arguing instead that what is assumed is that errors in consumption are distributed randomly and independently of the determinants of demand.

[k]It is assumed here for the sake of argument that the cost of a method and its effectiveness are positively related. Obviously, this need not be the case.

marginal costs of employing a more effective means of contraception exceed the marginal benefit to be gained from the reduction in the probability of an unwanted conception. There is ample support for this view of fertility regulating behavior.

Fertility studies have long shown that the efficacy of contraceptive behavior increases drastically as desired family size is approached among all types of couples, indicating that as the costs of an unwanted birth rise, more effective measures are chosen. However, contraceptive failure is closely associated with socioeconomic status, and a disproportionate share of the unwanted births occur to couples with the least education and income.[59] Since the model to be developed in the following chapter assumes that couples are able to achieve their intended family size, it is necessary either to develop a model to explain contraceptive failure or to exclude failure prone couples from the analysis.

In the absence of data sufficient to test a behavioral model of fertility regulation, the latter course is chosen for this study. Consequently, many couples from the lowest status levels will be excluded from the analysis and the result may reduce the scope of the results more than would be desirable. However, given the data limitations, it seems best to eliminate this potential source of bias at the beginning of the analysis. When data sets designed for the analysis of decision models of fertility are collected it will be possible to test a unified model of the fertility decision and fertility regulating behavior.

The decision model presented in Chapter Two will not explicitly deal with contraceptive behavior for those couples retained for analysis. Aside from the fact that the requisite cost data are not available, it is my suspicion that the analysis of fertility regulating behavior is not a necessary concomitant of the analysis of completed fertility. As an example, consider the following behavioral model of contraceptive behavior. Assume that a married couple with full information about available contraceptive methods attempts to minimize the sum of the (economic and psychic) cost of avoiding pregnancy (C_e) and the expected cost of a contraceptive failure (EC_f) in a given period of risk. That is, the couple minimizes:

$$C = C_e + EC_f,$$

where $C_e = \gamma(P_f)$ and $EC_f = P_f \cdot C_{k,f}$, given that P_f is the probability of contraceptive failure in the period, $C_{k,f}$ is the (economic and psychic) cost of a sure contraceptive failure to parents at parity k, and that the cost effectiveness curve C_e is a strictly decreasing function of P_f and is convex.

The cost minimizing level of risk is found by differentiating the expression above with respect to P_f and setting the derivative equal to zero:

$$\frac{dC}{dP_f} = \gamma' + C_{k,f} = 0.$$

For a couple at any given parity, the cost minimizing level of risk (P^*) is shown in Figure 1-3 as the minimum distance between the cost effectiveness curve and the failure curve for the given parity. If the expected cost of an unwanted pregnancy in any period rises with parity, then as parents approach their intended family size (say two children) they choose the most effective methods available. Since our concern is with couples who have a demonstrated ability to control fertility, their contraceptive behavior becomes relatively unimportant for analytical purposes when completed fertility is being analyzed.

Another possibility is that effectiveness and cost are not strictly related. In Figure 1-4, two methods (say the oral contraceptive (A) and the IUD (B)) provide considerably better protection than other methods at a cost lower than at least some of them. In this example, method B (IUD) is adopted by a couple at parities zero and one—not because it is the cheapest, but because it minimizes the sum $C_e + EC_f$. However, at parity two the couple switches to method A (oral contraceptive) even though it is more expensive because of the greatly increased negative consequences of an unwanted birth. In both these cases the couple switches to effective methods as intended family size is reached, thus insuring a high degree of success in the prevention of pregnancy.

Once the couple has attained its desired family size an accidental pregnancy represents a sizable additional cost, and, given the availability of truly effective methods of birth control such as the IUD and the oral contraceptive (not to mention legal abortion), we might expect the incidence of unwanted pregnancy to decline drastically among married couples. Comparative data from the 1965 and 1970 National Fertility Surveys bear out this expectation strikingly.[60]

Thus, for effective contraceptors the achievement of optimal family size probably coincides with the adoption of effective measures, the costs of which are insignificant relative to the cost of an unwanted birth.[1] In the chapters that follow, we assume just that—that the costs of fertility

---

[1]In this analytical framework we might characterize those ineffective contraceptors who are being omitted from this study as possessing cost effectiveness curves that approach infinity for high degrees of effectiveness (low P_f) perhaps because of a lack of information, or because of an aversion to the more effective methods. In the first instance a lack of information might be remedied by public health information campaigns; in the second, tastes would have to be changed, perhaps through government "information" efforts.

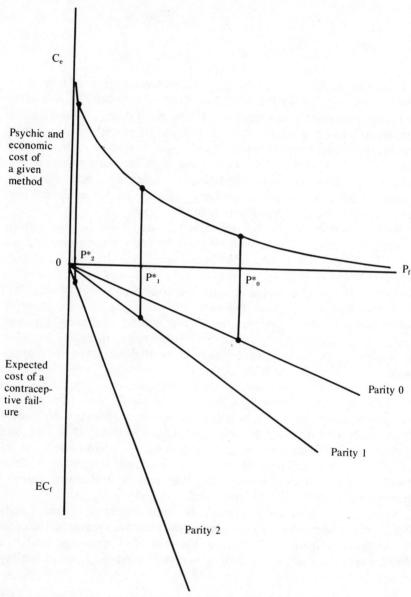

Figure 1–3.   Choice of the Optimal Fertility Control Strategy (i)

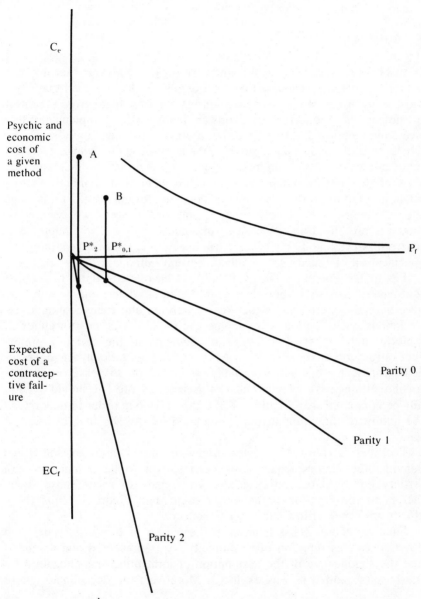

Figure 1–4. Choice of the Optimal Fertility Control Strategy (ii)

control are negligible relative to the costs of contraceptive failure, once intended family size has been achieved.[m]

4. SUMMARY

In this chapter the theoretical framework for the analysis of fertility has been advanced and discussed in some detail. We have argued that since most white American wives cease bearing children long before the onset of subfecundity, conscious decisions are being made to implement effective contraception and therefore, by inference, to limit family size. The existence of these decisions provides the justification for viewing fertility in the context of a decision model. Figure 1–1 represents a diagrammatic view of the way in which social, psychological, and economic factors might interact to produce the couple's demand for children. At this stage the framework is extremely general; only in Chapter Two, where the model is presented and elaborated in some detail, and in Chapter Six, where it is estimated empirically, will specific hypotheses regarding the specification of the model be advanced and defended.

Figure 1–1 presumes the availability of all relevant data. It suggests that background social and demographic factors determine to some degree both the preference structures of parents and their economic expectations regarding long run income and the expected cost of children. Unfortunately, most of the relevant elements of the couple's preference structure have not yet been measured empirically, and sociodemographic factors will eventually be called on to serve as proxies for the missing psychological factors. Indeed, Figure 1–1 should eventually be compared with Figure 2–1 of Chapter Two in order to understand the nature of the simplifications mandated by the shortage of relevant data.

The next section (2) reviewed briefly the more important social and demographic factors which have been shown to be associated with fertility differentials. Initial efforts were made to relate these social factors to the decision framework presented in Figure 1–1 and these efforts are renewed in Chapters Two and Six.

Finally, section 3 has dealt with the nature of the fertility decision process. Our assumption of "rationality" was presented and defended and the significance of the assumption of joint utility maximization by the husband and wife was explored. Moreover, the decision to ignore

---

[m]It is my guess that the real value of analysis of the fertility control decision lies in its applicability to the study of spacing and timing patterns rather than to the analysis of completed fertility.

analysis of fertility regulating behavior was defended on the grounds that, once effective contraceptors are selected for analysis, the cost of effective control becomes minor relative to the cost of exceeding desired family size.

CHAPTER ONE

1. See Daniel Callahan, ed., *The American Population Debate,* Garden City, N.Y.: Doubleday and Co., 1971, selections 16–23.

1a. Notably, Richard A. Easterlin, "Towards a Socioeconomic Theory of Fertility," in S.J. Behrman, L. Corsa, and R. Freedman, eds., *Fertility and Family Planning: A World View,* Ann Arbor, Mich.: University of Michigan Press, 1969; and Richard A. Easterlin, "The Economics and Sociology of Fertility: A Synthesis" (unpublished), University of Pennsylvania, July 1973).

2. Larry Bumpass and Charles F. Westoff, *The Later Years of Childbearing,* Princeton: Princeton University Press, 1970, Chapter III; U.S. Bureau of the Census, *Current Population Reports,* Series P-20, No. 263, "Fertility Histories and Birth Expectations of American Women: June 1971, Washington, D.C.: U.S. Government Printing Office, 1974, Table 12.

3. John R. Hicks, *Capital and Growth,* New York: Oxford University Press, 1965, pp. 16 ff.

4. N. Krishnan Namboodiri, "Some Observations on the Economic Framework for Fertility Analysis," *Population Studies* XXVI (2) (July 1972): 185–206.

5. See, for example, Robert J. Willis, "A New Approach to the Economic Theory of Fertility Behavior," *Journal of Political Economy* 81 (2) Part II (March/April 1973): S14–S64. (This issue of the *Journal of Political Economy* is hereafter referred to as *JPE Supplement, 1973.*) Dennis N. De Tray, "Child Quality and the Demand for Children," *JPE Supplement, 1973:* S70–S95. See also Glen G. Cain and Adriana Weininger, "Economic Determinants of Fertility: Results from Cross-Sectional Aggregate Data," *Demography* 10 (2) (May 1973): 205–224.

6. For a recent exception in the field of the "new home economics" see James J. Heckman, "Effects of Child-Care Programs on Women's Work Effort," *Journal of Political Economy* 82 (2) Part II (March/April 1974): S136–S163. This issue of the *Journal of Political Economy* will hereafter be referred to as *JPE Supplement, 1974.*

7. However, see H.S. Houthakker and L.D. Taylor, *Consumer Demand in the United States* (2d. ed.), Cambridge, Mass.: Harvard University Press, 1970, Chapter 5.

8. A start in the right direction is contained in Kenneth W. Terhune and Sol Kaufman, "The Family Size Utility Function," *Demography* 10 (4) (November 1973): 599–618; see also Lolagene C. Coombs, "The Measurement of Family Size Preferences and Subsequent Fertility," *Demography* 11 (4) (November 1974): 587–612.

9. The basic reports of the studies are: Ronald Freedman, Pascal K. Whelpton, and Arthur A. Campbell, *Family Planning, Sterility, and Population Growth,* New York: McGraw-Hill, 1959 (1955 GAF study); P.K. Whelpton, Arthur A. Campbell, and John E. Patterson, *Fertility and Family Planning in the United States,* Princeton: Princeton University Press, 1965 (1960 GAF study); and Norman B. Ryder and Charles F. Westoff, *Reproduction in the United States: 1965,* Princeton: Princeton University Press, 1971 (1965 NFS).

10. The Princeton Study has produced three principal reports: Charles F. Westoff, Robert G. Potter, Jr., Philip C. Sagi, and Elliot G. Mishler, *Family Growth in Metropolitan America,* Princeton: Princeton University Press, 1961; Charles F. Westoff, Robert G. Potter, Jr., and Philip C. Sagi, *The Third Child,* Princeton: Princeton University Press, 1963; and Larry Bumpass and Charles F. Westoff, *The Later Years of Childbearing,* Princeton: Princeton University Press, 1970. The findings of the Detroit Area and Rhode Island surveys have appeared in numerous journal articles and dissertations emanating from the University of Michigan and Brown University.

11. Ryder and Westoff, *op. cit.,* p. 107.

12. Norman Ryder and Charles F. Westoff, "Wanted and Unwanted Fertility in the United States: 1965 and 1970," in U.S. Commission on Population Growth and the American Future, *Demographic and Social Aspects of Population Growth,* Charles F. Westoff and Robert Parke, Jr., eds., Vol. I of Commission Research Reports, Washington, D.C.: U.S. Government Printing Office, 1972, pp. 482–483.

13. U.S. Bureau of the Census, *Current Population Reports,* Series P-25, No. 521, "Estimates of the Population of the United States and Components of Change: 1973 (with Annual Data from 1930)," Washington, D.C.: U.S. Government Printing Office, 1974, p. 3.

14. Whelpton, Campbell, and Patterson, *op. cit.,* p. 47, and U.S. Bureau of the Census, *Current Population Reports,* Series P-20, No. 269, "Prospects for American Fertility: June 1974," Washington, D.C.: U.S. Government Printing Office, 1974, p. 5.

15. J.P. Gibbs, "Norms: The Problem of Definition and Classification," *The American Journal of Sociology* 70 (5) (March 1965): 589.

16. This literature review is quite selective and the interested reader should consult the following references for a comprehensive survey of the literature: Geoffrey Hawthorn, *The Sociology of Fertility,* London: Collier-Macmillan, 1970; and Ronald Freedman, *The Sociology of Human Fertility: An Annotated Bibliography,* New York: Appleton-Century Crofts, 1974.

17. This relationship was not invariant, however. Among successful number and timing planners in the Indianapolis Survey a direct relationship was found between fertility and status variables. See Clyde V. Kiser and P.K. Whelpton, "Resume of the Indianapolis Study of Social and Psychological Factors Affecting Fertility," *Population Studies* VII (2) (November 1953): 97.

18. David Goldberg, "The Fertility of Two-Generation Urbanites," *Population Studies* XII (3) (March 1959): 214–222; and David Goldberg, "Another Look at the Indianapolis Fertility Data," *The Milbank Memorial Fund Quarterly* XXXVIII (1) (January 1960): 23–36.

19. Goldberg (1960), *op. cit.*, pp. 24–25.

20. Otis Dudley Duncan, "Farm Background and Differential Fertility," *Demography* II (1965): 240–249.

21. Whelpton, Campbell, and Patterson, *op. cit.*, p. 121.

22. P. Neal Ritchey and C. Shannon Stokes, "Residence, Background, Migration and Fertility," *Demography* 9 (2) (May 1972): 217–230.

23. Otis Dudley Duncan, Ronald Freedman, J. Michael Coble, and Doris Slesinger, "Marital Fertility and Size of Family Orientation," *Demography* II (1965): 508–515. Bumpass and Westoff, *op. cit.*, pp. 89–93, find similar results for the women in the Princeton Study; however, they note that the positive relation holds for only Protestants and for those wives who reported that they experienced a happy childhood.

24. *Ibid.*, p. 514.

25. Freedman, Whelpton, and Campbell, *op. cit.*, pp. 104, 107.

26. Whelpton, Campbell, and Patterson, *op. cit.*, p. 72.

27. Ryder and Westoff, *op. cit.*, pp. 70–72; Bumpass and Westoff, *op. cit.*, pp. 79–85.

28. Bumpass and Westoff, *op. cit.*, p. 58.

29. Ryder and Westoff, *op. cit.* (1972), p. 481.

30. Whelpton, Campbell, and Patterson, *op. cit.*, pp. 96–106; Ryder and Westoff, *op. cit.*, pp. 74–79.

31. Larry L. Bumpass, "Age at Marriage as a Variable in Socioeconomic Differentials in Fertility," *Demography* VI (1) (February 1969): 45–54.

32. *Ibid.*, p. 52.

33. Morris Silver, "Births, Marriages and Business Cycles in the United States," *Journal of Political Economy* 73 (3) (June 1965): 237–255; Dudley Kirk, "The Influence of Business Cycles on Marriage and Birth Rates," in Universities—National Bureau of Economic Research, *Demographic and Economic Change in Developed Countries,* Princeton: Princeton University Press, 1960, pp. 241–257; V.L. Galbraith and D.S. Thomas, "Birth Rates and the Interwar Business Cycles," *Journal of the American Statistical Association* 36 (1941): 465–476.

34. Richard A. Easterlin, *Population, Labor Force, and Long Swings in Economic Growth: The American Experience,* New York: Columbia University Press, 1968; Richard A. Easterlin, "Relative Economic Status and the American Fertility Swing" (unpublished), University of Pennsylvania, 1972; and Peter H. Lindert, "Remodelling the Household for Fertility Analysis," Madison, Wis., Center for Demography and Ecology Working Paper 73–14, May 1973.

35. Whelpton, Campbell, and Patterson, *op. cit.*, pp. 103–106; Ryder and Westoff, *op. cit.*, pp. 77–79.

36. Judith Blake, "Income and Reproductive Motivation," *Population Studies* XXI (3) (November 1967): 185–206; Judith Blake, "Are Babies Consumer Durables?" *Population Studies* XXII (1) (March 1968): 5–25.

37. Frank P. Stafford, "Student Family Size in Relation to Current and Expected Income," *Journal of Political Economy* 77 (4) (July/August 1969): 471–77; Deborah Freedman, "The Relation of Economic Status to Fertility," *American Economic Review* LIII (3) (June 1963): 414–426.

38. Ryder and Westoff, *op. cit.,* p. 85.

39. *Ibid.,* p. 78; Whelpton, Campbell, and Patterson, *op. cit.,* p. 113.

40. Freedman, Whelpton, and Campbell, *op. cit.,* p. 312; Lee-Jay Cho, Wilson H. Grabill, and Donald J. Bogue, *Differential Current Fertility in the United States,* Chicago: University of Chicago Community and Family Study Center, 1970, p. 55.

41. Ryder and Westoff, *op. cit.,* p. 90.

42. A recent econometric analysis of rural-urban birth rates seems to miss these points. See Llad Phillips, Harold Votey, and Darold E. Maxwell, "A Synthesis of the Economic and Demographic Models of Fertility, An Econometric Test," *Review of Economics and Statistics* LI (3) (August 1969): 298–308.

43. Whelpton, Campbell, and Patterson, *op. cit.,* pp. 107–109; Ryder and Westoff, *op. cit.,* pp. 80–81.

44. James A. Sweet, "Family Composition and the Labor Force Activity of American Wives," *Demography* 7 (2) (May 1970): 208.

45. See Marion G. Sobol, "Correlates of Present and Expected Future Work Status of Married Women" (unpublished PhD dissertation), University of Michigan, 1960, pp. 36, 58–59; U.S. Department of Labor, Bureau of Labor Statistics Staff Paper No. 4, *A Micro Model of Labor Supply,* M.S. Cohen, S. Rea, R.I. Lerman, 1970, pp. 87–95; James A. Sweet, *loc. cit.*

46. Lois Pratt and P.K. Whelpton, "Extra-Familial Participation of Wives in Relation to Interest and Liking for Children, Fertility, Planning, and Actual and Desired Family Size," in Vol. 5 of C. Kizer and P.K. Whelpton, *Social and Psychological Factors Affecting Fertility,* New York: Milbank Memorial Fund, 1958, pp. 1245–1279.

47. Judith A. Fortney, "Achievement as an Alternative Source of Emotional Gratification to Childbearing" (unpublished), read at the Annual Meetings of the Population Association of America, April 1972.

48. See, for example, Freedman, Whelpton, and Campbell, *op. cit.,* pp. 291–294, 298, 307, 315–317, and Whelpton, Campbell, and Patterson, *op. cit.,* p. 114.

49. See the works of Richard A. Easterlin cited above for an extensive analysis of cohort fertility differentials.

50. The notable exception, of course, is the work of those economists studying "behavioral" theories of the business firm. See, for example, Herbert A. Simon, "Theories of Decision-Making in Economics and Behavioral Science," *American Economic Review* 49 (3) (June 1959): 253–283; Richard M. Cyert and James G. March, *A Behavioral Theory of the Firm,* Englewood Cliffs, N.J.: Prentice-Hall, 1963.

51. Robert Willis, *op. cit.,* presents an ingenious (but, I think, inappropriate) appeal to some theorems in modern welfare economics in order to make a similar assumption.

52. Winter, *op. cit.,* p. 4.

53. Judith Blake, "Are Babies Consumer Durables?" *Population Studies* XXII (1) (March 1968): 5–25; Phillip M. Hauser, "Comments," *Milbank Memorial Fund Quarterly* XLVIII (2) Part 2: (April 1970); 236.

54. *Ibid.,* p. 32 ff.

55. Joseph A. Schumpeter, *The Theory of Economic Development,* Cambridge, Mass.: Harvard University Press, 1949, p. 80.

56. Lois W. Hoffman and Martin L. Hoffman, "The Value of Children to Parents," in *Psychological Perspectives on Population,* James T. Fawcett, ed., New York: Basic Books, 1973, p. 52.

57. Richard A. Easterlin, "Towards a Socioeconomic Theory of Fertility," in *Fertility and Family Planning: A World View,* S.J. Behrman, Leslie Corsa, Jr., and Ronald Freedman, eds., Ann Arbor: University of Michigan Press, 1969, pp. 127–156.

58. An interesting example of this sort of approach can be found in Robert T. Michael and Robert J. Willis, "Contraception and Fertility: Household Production Under Uncertainty," New York: National Bureau of Economic Research, Working Paper No. 21, December, 1973; and Robert T. Michael, "Education and the Derived Demand for Children." *JPE Supplement*, 1973, pp. S128–S164.

59. Whelpton, Campbell, and Patterson, *op. cit.,* p. 256.

60. Ryder and Westoff, *op. cit.* (1972).

An Economic Analysis of the Fertility Decision

1. INTRODUCTION

Given an understanding of the context within which family size decisions take place, we can turn to the fertility decision itself. In this chapter a microeconomic model of fertility is presented and analyzed with special attention being paid to the ways in which noneconomic factors might affect the attainment of a couple's optimal family size. The model to be developed below possesses two features that set it apart from other microeconomic models current in the literature.

First, it characterizes the fertility decision as the first stage of the couple's lifetime allocation of its wealth among alternative consumption activities. Because of biological constraints upon fecundity, couples must, relatively early in the life cycle, commit a large amount of time and money resources to the rearing of their children. This commitment is, to all intents and purposes, irreversible; it binds the couple to a series of resource outlays that will continue until the last child has left home. Consequently, young couples must make the decision early to earmark a significant portion of their lifetime total wealth for the rearing of their children; this decision will in turn determine the quantity of resources left to the husband and wife for allocation to other consumption activities. This requirement for an early and irreversible commitment of resources to child rearing gives rise to some analytical problems, which will be discussed in detail in Section 2.

The second distinguishing feature of the model is the explicit attempt, detailed in the following two sections, to include consideration of the noneconomic factors that influence the cost of rearing a child. In the majority of economic models currently typifying the fertility literature,[a]

[a]See Section 5 of this chapter for a discussion of this literature.

expenditures on children are characterized as being the result of conscious "quality" decisions by parents. The theory articulated in this chapter provides an alternative view in which normative considerations may be decisive in determining the cost of a child. In this way sociological and institutional factors (among others) may exert an important influence upon the fertility behavior of American couples.

2. A COUPLE'S DEMAND FOR CHILDREN

Assumptions

1. The couple behaves rationally in choosing a completed family size that is perceived to maximize its long run welfare. Rationality in this context is as defined in Chapter One—that is, the couple behaves consistently so as to maximize an index representing the couple's joint welfare:

$$U(K, N), \tag{1}$$

where K is the number of children, N is the present value of all resources remaining to the couple after provision has been made for the resource expenditures required in child rearing, and U is the index of welfare or "utility." Both children and other (unspecified) activities provide psychic rewards to the parents and their problem is to determine, at the first stage, the optimal split between children (K) and other activities as represented by the value of uncommitted resources (N). The necessity for choice comes about, of course, because couples are faced with limited economic resources, the scarcity of which forces them to make decisions about the quantity of resources to be allocated among a number of attractive and competing comsumption activities. The nature and importance of the fundamental resource constraint faced by couples will be explored in detail later in this section.[b]

2. Children[c] are considered to be "consumption activities" which are "produced" by the household. That is, the argument K in the utility function is a consumption activity that the parents undertake to produce through the application of scarce resources, market goods and services, and their own time. This notion of a consumption activity is, at least for heuristic purposes, one of the most important advances in consumer

[b]Note that this formulation of the couple's utility maximization problem also assumes that the couple is able to achieve its optimal family size. For the reasons discussed in Chapter One we will assume for the remainder of the theoretical development that couples are indeed able to achieve optimal family size and that this ability to regulate fertility is both perfect and costless.

[c]Or more specifically "child rearing," which is defined to be synomymous with the number of children.

theory in recent years. It is associated with Gary Becker and Kelvin Lancaster,[1] and allows for the treatment of nonmarket allocative activities such as child rearing in a plausible manner within the framework of consumer theory.

The household production approach has been extensively utilized in recent research on the economics of fertility, and, although its analytical usefulness has recently been called into question,[2] it has had the merit of making the consumer theory approach more palatable to noneconomists, who have objected to the identification of children as "consumer durables." The fact that the consumption activity child rearing requires scarce resources that must be allocated by the husband and wife is the primary justification for the adoption of a modified consumer theory approach.

The decision to bear and rear children implies a sizable long range commitment of parental resources that is, in essence, irreversible. It is in the size of this commitment that child rearing and the purchase of consumer durables can be compared; however, parenthood is a complex social process, and it exhibits many features that make any facile comparison between it and other consumer durable purchases very dangerous. Indeed, the primary thrust of this chapter is that consumer theory must be modified explicitly to take account of the social and institutional constraints on parents if it is to provide an accurate understanding of the fertility decision.

3. Parents choose their completed family size based on prior notions of the opportunity cost of child rearing. That is, we assume that parents take the cost of each child as a datum when they make their fertility decisions. This assumption stands in direct opposition to the assumption—current in the economics literature on fertility[d]—that the fertility decision involves a decision as to both the quantity of children and the "quality" of children to be chosen. Rather than making some conscious quality versus quantity choice as a part of the family size decision, couples are here pictured as entering into the fertility decision process with a preconceived notion of the cost of a child. Since it runs counter to the dominant assumptions of much of the current literature, this assumption will be elaborated and defended later in this chapter.[e]

4. The reference period for the fertility decision extends far past the

[d]See the literature review in Section 5 of this chapter.

[e]Whether or not couples actually make conscious quality-quantity tradeoffs is, of course, an empirical question. In a pretest for a national sample survey now being prepared by J. Richard Udry, Karl E. Bauman, and me, husbands and wives were asked whether they would consider spending less on all their children so that they might be able to afford another child. About 71 per cent of husbands and wives replied that they would probably not or definitely not consider the tradeoff. Between 18 and 23 percent replied that they would probably or definitely consider the tradeoff.

decision period per se. The decision to have a child is one of the few resource allocation decisions that the couple makes that implies an essentially irrevocable commitment to a stream of expenditures over a long period of time. This is an essential difference between children and consumer durables, since, once the child arrives, there is no recourse to a resale market nor to a local humane society. This commitment, combined with the biological necessity to reproduce early in the life cycle, forces parents to set aside future resources for child rearing long before other consumption requirements that will occur contemporaneously are recognized or budgeted. Thus, when they make their family size decision, couples are essentially dividing their expected future resources into two parts: expenditures on children and expenditures on everything else. Since no decisions have to be made regarding the latter, it is reasonable to suspect that parents really judge the economic impact of children in terms of the proportion of their expected total wealth that will be required in child rearing.[3]

The model presented below does not, therefore, require that all resource allocations over the life cycle be made concurrently with the fertility decision. What is required at the time of the fertility decision is a division of expected resources between child rearing and other activities, with no requirement that the share allocated to the latter be committed to any specific collection of consumption activities. Note that this does not imply that couples do not plan ahead with respect to other consumption or labor force participation. What is implied is that children represent an irreversible commitment while other activities such as taking a job, obtaining further education, buying a house, etc. do not. It is the early decline in female fecundity and the irreversibility of the commitment to children that forces the early budget division reflected in the model.[f]

The Production Function for
and the Cost of Children

When parents make their final decisions about family size, they do so on the basis of their initial child rearing experiences and on the basis of

[f]Fertility decisions are based on expectations of future expenditures and income flows, and it is generally assumed by economists that current decisions are affected more by current expenditures and income flows than by their future counterparts. This view is formalized by the common practice of working with discounted present values of future expenditures and income in the analysis of consumer decision problems. We will follow this practice by assuming that our consumers discount all expenditures and income streams at some constant rate and that all couples exhibit the same subjective rate of time preference. See Chapter Five, Section 5 for a discussion of the empirical problems associated with the implementation of this assumption.

their expectations about the future resource requirements of a child. These expectations and perceptions about the resource requirements of child rearing may be represented formally by the couple's "production function" for children, shown here in implicit form:

$$\phi^{\bar{s}}(K, x, t) = 0,\tag{2}$$

where K is the number of children, x is a u-element vector of market goods and services utilized in child rearing, t is a v-element[g] vector of total time inputs of the husband and the wife during the children's presence in the family, and $\bar{s}$ is an index representing a set of biological, psychological, and normative factors that determine the parameters of each couple's production function. The bar over the s indicates that this set is fixed for any particular couple. This production function, which for convenience will be assumed to possess the convexity and homogeneity properties normally ascribed to such functions in economic theory,[4] represents the couple's perceptions of the minimum combinations of parental time and market goods and services necessary to raise a given number of children.

Parental perceptions regarding the possibilities for rearing children are represented by one production function because we suspect that, in general, parents have a standard that applies to all their children equally,[h] and that they do not perceive a wide range of possible modes of child rearing available to them as they make their fertility decisions. This latter view runs counter to that fostered by Gary Becker in which parents perceive a wide latitude for choice regarding expenditures per child and consciously trade off expenditures per child versus numbers of children in the course of the fertility decision. In my opinion, that view gives far too little weight to the normative constraints placed on child rearing both by society in general and by a couple's peer group in particular. Consequently, the model presented in this chapter is offered as an alternative to Becker's formulation, an alternative that places

[g]The time inputs into child rearing must be represented by a vector not only because two persons (or more, including relatives, friends, etc.) are providing child rearing inputs but also because the child rearing process may require different types of time. For example, an hour of a mother's time in the morning may not be completely substitutable for an hour of her time in, say, the late afternoon. Indeed, this hypothesized lack of substitutability of different types of a mother's time inputs may be a major contributing factor to the low labor force participation rates of mothers with young children.

[h]Remember, it is the perceived production function for children at the time of the fertility decision that is at issue here. There is no evidence available that suggests that parents *initially* plan to discriminate among their children with respect to time and money inputs; however, as the children develop, the parents may indeed begin to tailor their inputs to match the differences in character and ability exhibited by their children.

specific emphasis upon the social and psychological constraints faced by couples as they project the cost of their children.[i]

In form the production function for children is very general. It allows for the substitution of inputs and does not rule out increasing or decreasing returns to scale.[j] However, for analytical simplification, the comparative static analysis developed below proceeds on the assumption that parents perceive child rearing as a constant returns to scale activity.[k]

Given their perceptions of the production function for children, their expectations regarding the prices of market inputs into child rearing, and the valuation they make of their own time inputs, couples can develop present value estimates of the cost of child rearing. Assuming that parents choose the least cost manner of producing children consistent with their personal standards as embodied in the production function, we can characterize the development of their cost function for children as the minimization of:

$$C = p \cdot x + w \cdot t \tag{3}$$

subject to the production function:

$$\phi^{\bar{s}}(\bar{K}, x, t) = 0. \tag{4}$$

C is the opportunity cost[l] of child rearing, p and w are u and v-dimensional vectors of discounted prices of market goods and parental time, and the bar over K indicates that opportunity cost is minimized for

[i]A compromise between these two approaches might be to characterize the couple as considering a small set of possible alternative production functions; however, my experience with a national sample survey currently in the field suggests that couples' projections are simply not that precise and that to suggest that they clearly differentiate even a small number of alternative production functions is to ascribe a precision that is not present.

[j]Again, note that parents might perceive constant returns to scale when they make fertility decisions, while the actual child rearing process, objectively measured, may exhibit increasing or decreasing returns to scale.

[k]This assumption may not be too inaccurate. In a pretest of a national sample survey conducted in Greensboro, North Carolina, husbands and wives were asked (in simpler language!) whether they thought child rearing was an increasing, decreasing, or constant returns to scale activity. Wives, on the average, thought that it was a constant returns to scale activity, with the distribution of responses leaning marginally toward diminishing returns to scale. Husbands, on the other hand, were more disposed toward viewing child rearing as a mildly increasing returns to scale activity. The differences may reflect the divergent roles that husband and wife assume in child rearing.

[l]I define the opportunity cost of child rearing as the total value of resources committed to that activity. Thus the opportunity cost of child rearing is the sum of the money cost of children (the inner product $p \cdot x$) and the time cost of children (the inner product $w \cdot t$). The vector p represents market prices of goods and services, but the source of the values for w is more difficult to ascertain and is discussed at length in the following subsection.

any given family size. The result of this minimization is the total cost function, which depends upon family size, prices and wages:

$$C = C^{\bar{s}}(K, p, w). \tag{5}$$

This cost function expresses the parents' expectations of the total opportunity cost of child rearing. It quantifies their expectations that child rearing will exhibit increasing or decreasing returns to scale and it also reflects their perceptions about the substitutability of inputs in the child rearing process.

The average cost of a child may be represented as:

$$\frac{C}{K} = \frac{C^{\bar{s}}(K, p, w)}{K}, \tag{6}$$

while the marginal cost of a child is given by:

$$\frac{\partial C}{\partial K} = C_K^{\bar{s}}(K, p, w),^{m} \tag{7}$$

or, since constant returns to scale is assumed, marginal cost equals average cost equals the price of a child, P:

$$P = \frac{C}{K} = \frac{\partial C}{\partial K} = C^{\bar{s}}(l, p, w) \tag{8}$$

and the price of a child is independent of family size. The perceived price of a child may vary from couple to couple either because of differences in the level of inputs per child due to differences in the perceived production function, ϕ^s, or because the prices that parents face for the inputs into child rearing vary.

Surely there is every reason to suppose that husbands and wives of differing occupation, education, ability, or tastes value the time spent in child rearing differently. For example, men and women who are able to command high market wages sacrifice more in the way of market goods and services when they spend time in child rearing, and it is to be expected that differences in market wage potentials are intimately connected to the valuation that couples place on their time spent in child rearing.

Moreover, couples may not face the same prices for market goods

---

[m]Strictly speaking, children arrive in discrete quantities, and characterization of the marginal cost as a partial derivative is inappropriate. However, for purposes of analysis we will resort to Alfred Marshall's time honored artifice of the "representative couple" that stands for the actions of a large group of couples identical with respect to social and psychological characteristics and differing only with respect to potential wage rates and wealth. Then it is possible to discuss truly marginal changes in family size and total cost of child rearing.

and services. For instance, certain very low income families are eligible for food stamps, which reduce the prices they must pay for selected staples. At the same time, children from low and middle income families may be eligible for scholarships based on need, which are not available to upper income families. Likewise, public housing and various forms of rent subsidies such as those found in major cities that impose rent control result in varying prices for constant quality housing space.

Of course it is not enough that these price differentials actually exist; they must be perceived to exist by parents making fertility decisions if they are to be relevant to those decisions. Moreover, the degree to which differential price and wage expectations might affect the expected cost of a child will depend upon the nature of the price differences and the degree of substitutability among inputs perceived to exist by parents.[n]

The Time Frame of the Fertility Decision

Assumption 4 characterizes the fertility decision as being the first stage of a two-stage lifetime resource allocation problem. Because of the legally and culturally mandated responsibilities of parenthood, the fertility decision is characterized by an irreversibility not associated with other allocative decisions such as the purchase of major consumer durables, the decision to seek more education or training, or the decision to enter or leave the labor force. Moreover, the early decline in the wife's fecundity requires that fertility decisions be made relatively early in the life cycle, before other allocation decisions are necessary or even contemplated.

Of course, couples may well be making plans about other activities at the same time that they are choosing a family size. Indeed, the argument N in the utility function (1) is a representation in value terms of the other consumption possibilities considered by the couple as they make the fertility decision. As a polar case, the husband and wife may make *all* future consumption, labor force participation, and human capital accumulation decisions concurrently with the family size decision. In fact, this is the assumption employed by Robert Willis in what is the fullest exploration of a Gary Becker type of fertility model to date.[5] In this model the husband and wife are assumed to adopt, at the outset of marriage, a utility maximizing lifetime plan for childbearing, human capital accumulation, and labor force participation by the wife. Willis's

---

[n]In the empirical work that follows, the absence of suitable data will force us back to Gary Becker's original position that all parents face the same prices for market inputs of constant quality. However, the price of parental time utilized in the child rearing process does vary from couple to couple, depending upon such factors as education, occupation, and ability.

approach has the advantage that all lifetime allocation decisions are thereby determined and can be analyzed simultaneously with the fertility decision. Unfortunately this is a very strong assumption, one that would appear to be manifestly incongruent with reality.

The alternative formulation employed here characterizes the couple as making only the fertility decision in the first stage. Subsequent consumption and labor force behavior decisions are assumed to control those activities—indeed, the children resulting from the fertility decision become constraining factors upon the parents' time and money allocation decisions in the second stage. Strictly speaking, this assumption is also a distortion. Some couples do make other plans, or they at least have a rough idea of other activities that they intend to pursue. In fact, for some couples it is the wife's career or education plans that determine the perceived time and money resources remaining for child rearing at the time of the fertility decision.

Nevertheless, the tentative commitments that couples make to other activities simply are not accompanied by the collection of legal and normative constraints that characterize child rearing. Practically speaking, therefore, it is parenthood that involves the irreversible resource commitments, not the other allocative activities open to parents.[6] Ideally it would be possible to observe couples in order to determine the strength of their consideration of alternative activities as they make fertility decisions; perhaps then it would be fruitful to develop a model that specifies the degree of commitment to particular types of alternative activities. However, in the absence of the data necessary to implement such an approach, it would appear preferable to characterize the fertility decision as is done here: as an attempt to decide, in the face of uncertainty about future consumption and work activities, the optimum split between child rearing and an alternative collection of potential consumption activities, many of which are only dimly perceived or are not yet perceived at all.

The Overall Budget Constraint

In the following subsection couples will be formally characterized as attempting to maximize a long range utility function subject to an overall resource constraint. This constraint will represent their intentions not to consume more time and dollar resources than are expected to be available to them. Of course, it is the couple's perceptions about these future resources that are relevant to the fertility decision; therefore, we need measures of the predicted values of p, the vector of discounted market prices for inputs into child rearing, V the present value of expected income from nonlabor sources,[o] T the v-element vector representing the

[o] V is a scalar, not a vector.

total amount of each type of time available to the couple in each period over the life cycle, and w the v-element vector of discounted market wage rates associated with each element of T.[p]

It is market wages that are relevant to the fertility decision because, from a resource allocation standpoint, the essence of the family size decision is the problem of allocating scarce life cycle resources between child rearing and other activities, including market work. Consequently, we are concerned with the value of time as a predetermined parameter of the couple's intertemporal budget constraint, as a measure of consumption foregone by having a certain number of children.[q] Therefore, the expected value of the husband's and wife's market wage for each type of time and for each period into the future is the value that is necessary in order to evaluate foregone consumption alternatives in future periods.[r]

The overall resource constraint may be derived by first noting the various constraints that must be satisfied. First is the time constraint faced by the couple:

$$t_k K + t_{OA} + t_{LF} = T \tag{9}$$

where t_k is a vector of time inputs per child for a particular set of market prices, p, and wages, w, t_{OA} is the time devoted to other nonmarket activities, t_{LF} is a vector of time inputs into market work, and T is the vector of total time available. Each of these vectors contains v elements each of which is greater than or equal to zero. The couple also faces a market budget constraint:

$$(p \cdot x)K + M = V + w \cdot t_{LF}, \tag{10}$$

where $(p \cdot x)$ is a scalar representing the present value of market inputs

[p]Average wages for each type of time in each period are assumed constant for convenience; consequently, average and marginal wage rates are equal.

[q]Note that this is exactly the opposite approach to that taken by Reuben Gronau,[7] who treats the number of children as exogenous in order to explain the impact of children on the shadow value of a housewife's time.

[r]Mincer and Polachek [8] have presented evidence that the periodic absence from the labor force of married women adversely affects their accumulation of human capital and hence their market wage. Since the presence of children is often associated with nonparticipation or reduced participation in the labor force, a causal relation between fertility and the wage rate of the wife is implied. Whether or not wives actually perceive a wage rate effect associated with child rearing, and whether they act upon their perceptions in choosing a family size, is an empirical question the answer to which has not yet been ascertained. It is not sufficient to demonstrate the existence of a job interruption effect upon wages; what must be demonstrated is that husbands and wives perceive wage effects associated with fertility. Consequently, we proceed under the assumption that couples do not perceive wage effects associated with fertility; however, the model could be modified in order to incorporate simultaneity between K and w.

into child rearing per child (given market price expectations), M is the present value of other consumption, V is the present value of nonlabor income, and $w \cdot t_{LF}$ is the present value of labor income.[s] By rearranging equation (9) and substituting for t_{LF} in (10) and collecting terms in the new expression, we arrive at the overall budget constraint:

$$(p \cdot x + w \cdot t_k)K + M + w \cdot t_{OA} = V + w \cdot T. \tag{11}$$

Then, since long range work-leisure decisions have not been imposed on the couple, and since constant returns to scale in child rearing have been assumed, the overall budget constraint can be rewritten as:

$$PK + N = V + w \cdot T, \tag{12}$$

where P $(= p \cdot x + w \cdot t_k)$ is the opportunity cost, or price, of a child; $V + w \cdot T$ is the potential income [9] available to the couple; and N $(= M + w \cdot t_{OA})$ is the present value of resources remaining for the couple's use after provision is made for the resource expenditures required in child rearing.

The potential income constraint is a representation in present value terms of the couple's estimates of the total quantity of resources to be available to them over the life cycle. For most couples the major component of potential income will be their own time, which can be utilized in nonmarket activities such as child rearing or in market work in order to obtain funds to purchase other scarce commodities on the open market.[t]

The Optimum Number of Children

Now that the couple's perceived potential income constraint has been derived and its expected cost function for children described, the fertility decision may be presented. The couple is viewed as attempting to choose that split of potential income between child rearing and all other activities that maximizes its utility. The problem is:

Maximize: $U = U(K, N)$ (13)

Subject to: $PK + N = I,$ (14)

---

[s]It is assumed that the couple's net borrowing equals zero in the long run; however, it is possible to allow for bequests simply by adding another constraint to the system.

[t]I assume that couples do not expect any monetary income from their children because there is little or no evidence that expected income from children's labor is a factor in fertility decisions in the United States. This assumption might not be justified were a microeconomic model of fertility to be applied to natality in developing countries.

where $I\ (= V + w \cdot T)$ is potential income and where maximization of the associated Lagrangian function:

$$L = U(K, N) - \lambda(PK + N - I) \tag{15}$$

leads to the first order conditions:

$$\begin{aligned}
U_K - \lambda P &= 0 \\
U_N - \lambda \ &= 0 \\
PK + N - I &= 0.
\end{aligned} \tag{16}$$

In theory, the system of first order conditions (16) can be solved for K, N, and λ in terms of the predetermined variables P and I—or in terms of the actual market price and wage vectors p and w and the nonlabor income term V—to produce a derived demand equation for children:

$$K = K(P, I) = D(p, w, V). \tag{17}$$

That is, the demand for children depends upon the couple's perceived price of children and on potential income, or, more fundamentally, on the prices of the various inputs into child rearing, w and p, and the present value of nonlabor income. Chapter Six of this study will be devoted to attempts to estimate statistically variants of this demand equation. If the general form of the utility function were known, the functional form of the demand equation could also be specified a priori; however, in the absence of this information the empirical specification of the demand equation will depend upon other factors, which will be reviewed in Chapter Six.

For the representative couple the influence of noneconomic factors on the demand for children is manifested in two ways: directly, through the functional operator K, and indirectly through the perceived price of a child, P. If all couples were homogeneous with respect to their tastes for children relative to other activities, and if they all perceived the same production function ϕ as operative in child rearing, it would be possible to estimate equation (17) directly. However, it is a fundamental proposition of this study that couples are not homogeneous and that there are social forces that act systematically upon the tastes and perceptions of couples to produce differentials in fertility in addition to those predicted by differentials in potential income. In Section 3 of this chapter the microeconomic model of fertility is expanded to encompass those determinants of fertility not specifically economic in nature.

First, however, it is useful to explore some of the behavioral implications of the narrower theory presented thus far. Of particular interest to economists are the comparative static effects on optimum family size of changes in the predetermined variables, P and I, or in the input prices p and w. To determine the effects of price and income changes on optimal family size the system of first order conditions (16) can be differentiated totally and, when terms are collected, we have the system:

$$\begin{bmatrix} U_{KK} U_{KN} & -P \\ U_{KN} U_{NN} & -1 \\ -P & -1 & 0 \end{bmatrix} \begin{bmatrix} dK \\ dN \\ d\lambda \end{bmatrix} = \begin{bmatrix} \lambda dP \\ 0 \\ K^* dP - dV - d(w \cdot T) \end{bmatrix} \quad (18)$$

where $V + w \cdot T$ has been substituted for I.[u] Solving the system for the vector of differentials we have:

$$\begin{bmatrix} dK \\ dN \\ d\lambda \end{bmatrix} = \frac{1}{A} \begin{bmatrix} A_{11} & A_{12} & A_{13} \\ A_{21} & A_{22} & A_{23} \\ A_{31} & A_{32} & A_{33} \end{bmatrix} \begin{bmatrix} \lambda & 0 & 0 \\ 0 & 0 & 0 \\ K^* & -1 & -1 \end{bmatrix} \begin{bmatrix} dP \\ dV \\ d(w \cdot T) \end{bmatrix} \quad (19)$$

where A is the determinant of the bordered Hessian matrix in (18) above and the A_{ij} are elements of the matrix which is the adjoint of the same bordered Hessian. Finally, the total impact on family size of changes in any of the determining variables can be expressed as:

$$dK = \frac{1}{A} \left[(\lambda A_{11} + K^* A_{13}) dP - A_{13} dV - A_{13} d(w \cdot T) \right]. \quad (20)$$

Now, to observe the impact on equilibrium family size of various price and income changes, several hypothetical cases can be analyzed.

Case 1. The Couple Perceives a Rise in the Present Value of Nonlabor Income. For example, if the couple were to receive an unexpected inheritance from a hitherto unknown maiden aunt, the rise in potential income could be represented as:

$$\frac{dK}{dV} = -\frac{A_{13}}{A}, \quad (21)$$

the value of which depends upon whether or not child rearing is a "normal activity." In consumer theory those commodities of which more is bought as the consumer's income rises, all other things being held constant, are termed "normal goods." Economists from Gary Becker onward have argued that children are also normal goods in this technical sense—that is, for the representative couple, a rise in nonlabor income should result in a rise in optimal family size.

---

[u]Remember that the inner product $(w \cdot T)$ of two vectors is a scalar. K^* is the equilibrium number of children.

This expectation runs counter to much of the empirical evidence,[10] and is not required by the economic theory of the consumer; however, a convincing case can be made for the normality of children and this is done in Appendix A to this study. We proceed under the assumption that child rearing is indeed a normal activity, and the comparative static results of this section are based upon that assumption.[v] The normality assumption requires that equation (21) be positive, implying that a rise in nonlabor income will lead to a rise in the fertility of the representative couple.[w]

Case 2.   The Couple Perceives a Change in the Expected Price of a College Education.   Because education may be an element in the couple's production function for children, the perceived price of a child (P) may change, and this may alter the representative couple's optimum family size. From the total differential we have:

$$\frac{dK}{dp_e} = \left[\lambda(A_{11}/A) + K^*(A_{13}/A)\right] \frac{\partial P}{\partial p_e} \tag{22}$$

where p_e is the expected price of a college education.[x] The partial derivative $\dfrac{\partial P}{\partial p_e}$ represents the couple's perception of the impact of a change in the price of a college education on the price of a child. Since it depends upon the production function for children, the impact of this price change depends importantly upon the degree of substitutability among inputs in the childrearing process.[y] The remainder of expression (22)

[v]Children may well be "normal commodities" even in the face of the cross-section and time series evidence that fertility and various measures of income are negatively correlated. See Section 3 of this chapter and Chapter Six for further discussion.

[w]Willis (op. cit., p. S44) argues that if the wife does not work during the entire life cycle, a rise in exogenous income will increase the shadow price of child services which will offset the positive income effect described above. However, his result requires the lifetime resource allocation framework described earlier as well as other dubious assumptions, specifically the assumption that children are "time intensive" relative to other activities.

[x]Note from equation (8) that P, the perceived price of a child, is a function of the market prices of inputs into child rearing, p_e being one of them. Note also that the other two terms of equation (20) drop out of (22) because $\dfrac{\partial V}{\partial p_e} = 0$ and $\dfrac{\partial (w \cdot T)}{\partial p_e} = 0$.

[y]If the family size decision were envisioned as a complete lifetime resource allocation (as in Willis, op. cit.), the impact of the change in p_e on the prices of other consumption activities would also have to be considered. However, in this formulation the fertility decision is conceived to be a budget division between child rearing and remaining uncommitted purchasing power. Formally this means that $\dfrac{\partial P_N}{\partial p_e} = 0$, and that at the first stage decision, all potential inputs into alternative activities are perfect substitutes. This is not implausible, especially when small changes in input prices are at issue. Note also that if a market commodity is not utilized in child rearing then the direct effect $\dfrac{\partial P}{\partial p_j} = 0$, and the indirect effect on potential income $\dfrac{\partial P_N}{\partial p_j}$ is also assumed to be negligible.

represents the effect of a given change in price upon the couple's optimal family size. This price effect is composed of a substitution effect, $\lambda(A_{11}/A)$, which is required to be negative because of the second order conditions for a constrained maximum of the utility function,[11] and an income effect, $K^*(A_{13}/A)$, which also must be negative because of the assumed normality of the child rearing activity.

Consequently, a rise in the perceived price of a child should have a negative impact on the representative couple's optimal family size. Therefore, the fertility response of a couple to the rise in the price of an input into child rearing will depend upon two factors: the magnitude of the change in P induced by the change in the market input price, and the strength of the combined income and substitution effects, these effects being independent of the particular input under consideration. In Section 4 we examine some of the implications for aggregate fertility policy suggested by the comparative static analysis of price effects.

Case 3. Passage of the Equal Rights Amendment to the U.S. Constitution Leads to a Rise in the Wife's Expected Wage Stream.   From equation (2) we have:

$$\frac{dK}{dw_w} = \left[\lambda(A_{11}/A + K^*(A_{13}/A)\right]\frac{\partial P}{\partial w_w} - (A_{13}/A)\frac{\partial(w \cdot T)}{\partial w_w}, \tag{23}$$

where w_w is a subvector of the total wage vector and the expression $\frac{\partial(w \cdot T)}{\partial w_w}$ represents the rise in potential wage income brought about by the rise in the wife's expected wage rates. Clearly this partial derivative will be positive in the present example. In this case a rise in the price of an input into child rearing has two effects—a negative price effect and a positive income effect. The overall effect of the wage change is ambiguous and again depends importantly upon the degree of substitutability perceived to exist between a mother's time in child care and other substitutes such as babysitters, day care centers, father's time, and so on. If parents do not consider these alternatives to be good substitutes for a mother's time, the negative price effect may well predominate and the optimal family size of the couple will decline. On the other hand, if the mother's time is perceived to be highly substitutable, family size may rise as a result of the rise in her expected wages.

Summary
Section 2 has presented and explored the implications of an analytical model of fertility for a representative couple. This model is firmly rooted in the tradition of the microeconomic theory of consumer behavior; however, even though this section has emphasized economic variables,

prices, wages, and income, it must be reemphasized that the allocative behavior described here is ultimately shaped by noneconomic forces operating directly upon the joint utility function and indirectly upon the price of a child. In this section the social context of the fertility decision has not been emphasized, except to note that the perceived production function for children may be strongly influenced by social and institutional pressures. In the following section the microeconomic decision model presented here is firmly anchored in the social and cultural framework described in Chapter One and the presentation of the model will then be complete.

The discussion of this section has focused attention on factors that potentially influence the fertility decision of individual couples yet which have rarely been discussed in the sociodemographic literature on fertility or, indeed, in much of the current economic fertility literature. For example, this model suggests that the couple's perceived production function for children plays an important role in determining the price of a child and in determining the degree to which changes in input prices into child rearing might affect the demand for children.

The model provides a formal version of the notion held by many that the cost of children ought to be an important determinant of the demand for them. Moreover, the concept of potential income is introduced as a measure of income relevant to the long range fertility decision. Finally, the model suggests ways in which parents may respond to changes in the perceived values of prices, wages, and income relevant to the fertility decision. These responses may prove to be quite important with respect to aggregate policy designed to alter birth rates. The implications of the model for population policy are explored more thoroughly in Section 4 of this chapter.

3. DIFFERENTIAL FERTILITY AND A STRATEGY FOR ESTIMATION

If all couples in the population possessed identical utility functions and identical perceived production functions for children, the demand equation (17) could be estimated directly if the requisite data on price and income were available. The estimated price and income elasticities would then represent the overall effect of changes in underlying input prices, wages, and nonlabor income on the demand for children. However, the body of sociodemographic research surveyed in Chapter One suggests quite strongly that there are differential social, psychological, and institutional factors that systematically affect the demand for children in addition to the impact of price and potential income. These differences would be manifested in two ways: (1) in the individual couple's utility function, and (2) in the perceived price of children.

For example, preferences for children may vary systematically by socioeconomic status. Women with college degrees are often characterized as possessing lower relative preferences for children versus other activities because of the wider span of interests fostered by education. Factors such as this would make the estimation of the simple demand function in equation (17) inappropriate, and a new demand function:

$$K = K^r(P, I) \qquad (24)$$

would have to be substituted. In this demand function, the indicator r represents those noneconomic factors which affect the demand for children and which vary systematically over the population of couples.

Noneconomic factors may affect the demand for children in two ways: (1) by altering the quantity of children demanded for any given level of P and I and (2) by altering the response of different couples to changes in P and I. These latter interaction effects can, if undetected, seriously distort the interpretation of price and income effects estimated from data. In particular, cross-section estimates of the "income elasticity" of demand for children may not, in fact, be measuring a pure income effect; rather, they may be measuring a mixture of income effects which vary with the preference structures of the couples involved. Consequently, the negative or U-shaped relation between fertility and income which has so often been remarked in the sociodemographic literature may not be inconsistent with the hypothesis that children are normal "goods." In Chapter Six a number of attempts are made to assess the impact of various possible interaction effects.

In addition, social factors might systematically affect the couple's perception of the opportunity cost of a child. Our representation of the couple's perceived production function for children explicitly allows for the impact of social norms on the options perceived to be available to the couple. If these normative factors are systematically related to the couple's potential income, failure to include explicitly a measure of the opportunity cost of children will seriously bias attempts to measure the income elasticity of demand for children. Most of the sociodemographic work cited in Chapter One attempts to measure the impact of income on fertility without any regard to the offsetting impact of systematically related perceptions of the price of children. If the demand equation:

$$K = Q(I) \qquad (25)$$

is estimated, given that the true demand equation is:

$$K = K(P, I),^z \qquad (26)$$

the omission of P will tend to bias estimates of the income elasticity in

---

[z]Neglecting for the moment the possibility that preferences for children are also related to income.

(25) downward, the strength of the bias being directly related to the strength of the correlation between P and I.[12] Consequently, the low values of the zero order correlations commonly reported in the literature are not sufficient to lead one to conclude (as has Judith Blake) that "the theory of economic demand for consumer durables does not . . . appear to be a reasonable model for reproductive motivation."[13] Rather, it should be recognized that the relation between income and family size embodies a complex set of relationships which, to be understood, will require the application of analyses considerably more elaborate than those hitherto utilized.

The approach taken in this study is to construct the entire behavioral model of fertility, including not only the derived demand equation for children that is the result of each couple's attempt to maximize long run welfare, but also a set of equations designed to explain the noneconomic determinants of the opportunity cost of a child and of potential income. In this sense the demand for children is placed in the social and psychological context represented by Figure 1–1 in Chapter One.

The model actually estimated in the following chapters (see Figure 2–1) is a simplified version of that framework. It pictures the demand for children as depending upon potential income, the opportunity cost of children, and a set of sociodemographic factors acting as proxies for the taste variables represented by r in equation (24). Moreover, both I and P are also pictured as depending upon various sociodemographic factors, this formulation representing the hypothesis that noneconomic factors play a major role in the determination of the expected price of a child. Indeed, ample evidence is provided in Chapters Three and Four to demonstrate that expenditures on children are strongly associated with a couple's long range income, and that social factors—primarily education and occupation—are responsible for differences in the perceived cost of a child.[aa]

The deterministic model of Figure 2–1 is recursive: a couple's preexisting preference structure, its preconceived notions of the price of a child and its potential income are all determinants of the demand for children. Likewise, the empirical estimation of the model proceeds in the same manner: first, estimates of the time cost and money cost of a child are constructed (Chapters Three and Four) and the components of potential income are derived (Chapter Five). Then the demand equation for

---

[aa]Although the data will demonstrate the positive correlation between expenditures per child and long range income, this will not be enough to argue the superiority of the recursive structure promoted here over Gary Becker's formulation of the quality–quantity tradeoff. Either approach is consistent with a positive correlation between expenditures per child and potential income.

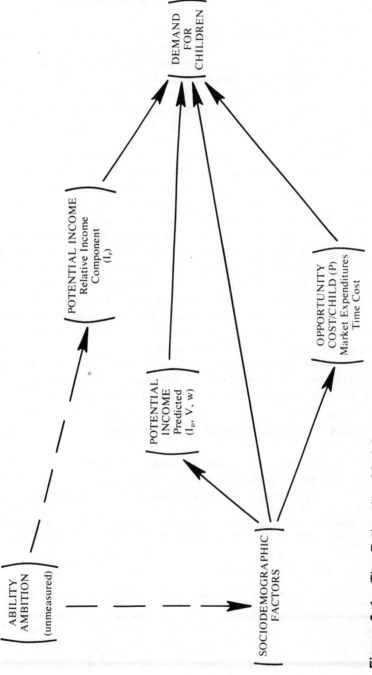

Figure 2–1. The Estimation Model

children (24) is estimated (Chapter Six) using the constructed proxies for price, *P,* and potential income *(I).*[bb]

This elaborate estimation procedure is necessitated by the almost total lack of information available about the perceived cost of child rearing. Chapters Three and Four represent perhaps the most complete estimate of the opportunity cost of a child by income group yet derived for the United States; however, as will become apparent, the constructed measures of time and money expenditure are less than ideal proxies for each couple's true expectations of the opportunity cost of child rearing.

It is a fundamental hypothesis of this study that parents from varying potential income groups perceive systematically varying prices for their children. That is, couples with high potential income expect, because of normative pressures and taste differentials, to spend on the average more per child than do couples at the lower end of the economic spectrum. This does not mean that high status couples are technically less efficient in producing satisfaction from children than are low status couples,[cc] since child rearing is, after all, a nonmarket activity the psychic returns from which are neither marketable nor measurable.[14] Moreover, the differentials in the price (or opportunity cost) of a child across couples are due to differentials both in the input prices faced by various couples and in the quantity and quality of various inputs utilized in child rearing. However, it should again be emphasized that *P* is not a decision variable; couples here are pictured as making fertility decisions based on preconceived notions of the opportunity cost of a child, and the quality-quantity tradeoff proposed by Becker is not at issue.[dd]

4. POLICY IMPLICATIONS OF THE THEORY

Although the present study is not primarily concerned with the feasibility of various policy approaches to the alteration of aggregate fertility rates, the model does illustrate rather clearly the avenues open to gov-

[bb]In Figure 2–1 potential income *I* is composed of two components, predicted potential income (I_p) and relative potential income (I_r). Potential income is the sum of these two components:

$$I = I_p + I_r = w \cdot T + V + I_r.$$

See Chapter Five, Section 3 for a discussion of the reasons behind this altered empirical specification.

[cc]This was suggested by a reviewer of an earlier version of this study.

[dd]Note also that the ex post nature of the expenditure and time allocation data utilized to estimate *P* will prohibit the generation of numerical estimates of the comparative static effects of input price changes on the demand for children. Estimation of these effects will have to await the appearance of new data sets designed expressly to measure them.

ernmental policy. In the absence of direct coercion[ee] a number of policy approaches remain available for the manipulation of fertility.

1. Direct attempts might be made to alter preferences relating to child rearing versus other activities. These efforts might range from the simple provision of better information about the resource cost of children to the more overt forms of persuasion and propaganda. Essentially, this means altering the elements of the collection of social-psychological factors influencing fertility in equation (24). Two questions emerge with respect to this line of policy: Will it work? Is it desirable from a political point of view? In spite of the considerable volatility of American fertility rates in the last 40 years there is virtually no evidence available which suggests that governments can effectively alter aggregate fertility rates through persuasion and propaganda. With respect to the second question, the answer is equally unclear. The degree to which government policy in this area should move past the mere provision of information into an attempt to change individual attitudes and social norms has been the subject of an intense debate that has highlighted issues of individual liberty, social justice, and environmental policy.[15]

2. Government policy might be aimed at the alteration of the production function for children through attempts to change group norms or individual preferences regarding what parents conceive to be necessary inputs for child rearing. Again, the emphasis would appear to be upon methods of persuasion and propaganda, although legislative measures might be taken to require that certain types of inputs are or are not provided. Obviously, policies of this type are intended to alter P, the perceived price of a child.

3. Another approach to changing P would be the alteration of the prices of inputs into child rearing so as to produce fertility responses of the type illustrated in Section 2. This set of policy alternatives may prove to be particularly attractive in the political and social climate characteristic of the United States. Indirectly coercive though they would be, these policies would not attack directly the perceived right of every American couple to have exactly the number of children desired without interference from the government.[ff]

[ee]E.g., the licensing of pregnancies, addition of chemical contraceptives to water supplies, mandatory abortion, etc., all of which have seriously been proposed as population control measures.

[ff]Government policies often have intended and unintended consequences and this is likely also to be true of many social welfare policies that will affect fertility. For example, federally subsidized day care centers might well benefit both working and nonworking mothers, which is desirable, while at the same time their concomitant effect might be to lower P and thus increase fertility, which may not be desirable. Student loan programs might also increase fertility while enabling more children to receive education. Which of the conflicting goals will have priority is a political problem the resolution of which may be especially difficult.

It should be apparent from this brief discussion that there are many policy avenues open for use, not all of which are economic in nature. It is the advantage of a decision model of fertility such as the one presented in this chapter that the whole spectrum of possibilities is presented in a unified context; moreover, the model describes precisely the sorts of data needed to assess the potential success of any of the policy alternatives available. To date, the data necessary to describe the quantitative impact of alternative policies on aggregate fertility have simply been unavailable, and this situation must be rectified if a proper understanding of the policy choices open to the government is ever to be achieved.

5. RELATION TO THE LITERATURE

Precursors
Even though many years have passed since it first appeared, Gary Becker's original theory of fertility continues to dominate a large share of the current research on the economics of family size.[16] Although he was not the first to advance the proposition that economic analysis is relevant to family size decision, Becker set the frame of reference from which subsequent discussions have proceeded.[17] He proposed a model based on orthodox consumer theory in which the husband and wife, acting jointly, attempt to maximize a utility function (Becker's notation):

$$U = U(x, y, p)$$

subject to an income constraint:

$$\alpha p x + \pi y = I,$$

given x the quantity of children, p an expenditure measure of the "quality" of x, y an index of other goods, I money income, α a parameter shifting the cost of each quality of x by the same percentage,[gg] and π the price of y. Becker insisted—and his followers still insist—that p, the "quality" of a child, is a decision variable along with family size. In his formulation the couple is pictured as choosing not only the optimal number of children but also the optimal expenditure per child. As is obvious, this view of the fertility decision constrasts with theory presented earlier in this chapter. Becker's view of the quality–quantity tradeoff remains an essential feature of virtually all the subsequent research associated with the University of Chicago and the National Bureau of Economic Research.[hh]

[gg]The parameter α plays no role in the theoretical development of Becker's static model.

[hh]An interesting exception is a paper by Yoram Ben-Porath,[18] which displays a

Becker's model contains other features that have subsequently been discarded or modified, often as a result of new insights by Becker himself. First, Becker argued that all parents face the same prices for inputs utilized in child rearing; however, development of the household production models forced the recognition that, at the very least, the price of parental time varies systematically with the education and occupation of the husband and wife.[19] Moreover, as was suggested in Section 2, couples may also perceive different prices for certain other market inputs because of the existence of differential subsidies and price discrimination. It does not appear, therefore, that Becker's original argument can be maintained at any level.

Second, Becker paid insufficient attention to the time frame within which the fertility decision takes place. However, his later excursions into the theory of household production and into the theory of human capital formation resulted in the development of revised fertility models in which closer attention was paid to the relation between nonmarket and market activities and to the long term nature of the family size decision vis-à-vis other allocation decisions. The subsequent fertility models of Becker's students and associates (the "Chicago-NBER group"), as well as my own, have benefited considerably from Becker's analytical creativity during the mid 1960s.

Other precursors of my model include James Duesenberry, Bernard Okun, and Alexander Gershenkron,[20] who were early critics of a too facile transfer of economic theory to a field they perceived to be dominated by noneconomic considerations; and Deborah Freedman, who in a short paper sketched out a theory suggesting that the opportunity cost of child rearing (*P*) is influenced by social and institutional considerations and presented some interesting empirical results to support that hypothesis.[21] In some important respects the present theory is an extension and formalization of that insight.

In 1969 Richard Easterlin attempted to reconcile in a comprehensive manner the apparent conflicts between the sociological and microeconomic approaches to fertility.[22] Although he did not attempt to present an explicit model, Easterlin's insights and point of view motivate much of the theoretical structure of the present model. In particular, he is acutely aware of the special role that differential tastes may play in the analysis of the fertility decision and of the need to account for them explicitly.

In addition to Freedman's 1963 paper, a handful of early attempts were made to test statistically various aspects of the consumer approach to fertility. Notable among these with respect to the present study were

curiosity about and an openness to the impact of noneconomic determinants of fertility generally missing in the work of other members of the Chicago NBER group.

papers by Mincer, Stafford, and Freedman and Coombs.[23] Mincer argued that the rearing of children by a mother entails an "opportunity cost"[ii] that affects family size and must be accounted for if statistical misspecification and bias are to be avoided. Using data from the 1950 Survey of Consumer Expenditures, he attempted to incorporate a proxy for time cost in his regressions by including a measure of the wife's full time earnings. The results were as might be expected: family size and wife's earnings were negatively related. Given the simultaneity of wife's labor force participation and family size at a given point in time, too much should not be made of Mincer's empirical results; his true contribution lay in alerting the profession to the necessity for explicit consideration of time costs in the analysis of fertility. This insight was later to be formalized and made into an explicit feature of the subsequent economic models of fertility.

Frank Stafford observed the current family size of graduate students in various disciplines and attempted to determine the degree to which it varied with respect both to current and expected future income. His results, although they relate more to timing than to completed fertility, suggest that long range measures of income have an important role to play in the analysis of fertility.

Ronald Freedman and Lolagene Coombs utilized data from the 1961 Detroit Area Survey and two subsequent reinterviews to examine various aspects of the relation between economic variables and fertility. They found that long range income expectations appear to play a role in fertility expectations of the white wives interviewed, and that wives who perceived their current income as "adequate" expected more children and were building their families more rapidly than others. Moreover, they found significant negative relationships between fertility expectations and desired expenditures of time and money for competing purposes; these findings were highly suggestive that a resource allocation model of fertility, properly formulated, might yield significant insights about the family size decision.

Finally, a critique of Becker's initial study by Judith Blake was important in motivating the present study.[24] Blake provided a comprehensive attack both upon Becker's theory and upon his rather casual attempts at empirical verification. Her paper was a valuable addition to the literature in that it expressed a sociologist's misgivings and misunderstandings about the value of microeconomic theory as applied to fertility research.

Indeed, this chapter (as well as Chapter One) is an attempt to present an economic theory of fertility in a social context—something which

---

[ii]Mincer's "opportunity cost" is analogous to "time cost" as defined in this study.

Blake argued very effectively that Becker did not do. Her main theoretical objections to Becker's theory centered around his almost total disregard of the social context of reproduction. She argued forcefully that differences in social status affect both parental perceptions and their freedom to separate their children's living standards from their own; moreover, Blake went to some lengths to emphasize the institutional constraints on parenthood that restrict a couple's ability to make a family size decision independently of the social milieu within which it exists.

The Current Literature

Most of the recent writings on the economics of fertility rely upon one or more of the precursors mentioned above; however, the impact of Gary Becker's 1960 paper has been by far the most widespread. The tangible manifestation of his influence is most easily found in the two special supplements to the *Journal of Political Economy,* which appeared in March 1973 and March 1974. In these two volumes students and colleagues of Becker have extended and refined the original Becker model with such vigor that this "Chicago-NBER" approach must be regarded as currently the dominant view of reproductive behavior within the economics profession. On balance, I believe that the current preeminence of the Chicago-NBER model is unwarranted and in the next few pages I outline some of the major areas of disagreement between that model and the approach taken in this chapter.[jj]

The Search for a Positive Income Effect. Since Becker first hypothesized that the impact of income on family size should, other things being equal, be positive, economists have spent considerable effort searching for that elusive result.[26] For any given couple, I believe that the assumption of a positive income effect is plausible and, indeed, this assumption is made in the comparative static analysis of Section 2; moreover, a strong theoretical case can be made for this assertion, as is demonstrated in some detail in Appendix A. However, it is not sufficient that the comparative static impact of income on family size be positive in order to observe a positive relation between income and family size in the cross-section.

Economic theory has nothing to say about the structure of preferences across the income distribution, and, if income and preferences are

---

[jj]While there are a number of versions of the Chicago-NBER model, most of them are alike with respect to the following characteristics: (1) the models represent fertility as a lifetime static optimization decision; (2) joint maximization of utility by husband and wife is the rule; (3) the explicit child quality versus quantity tradeoff assumption is retained; (4) very little theoretical attention is paid to noneconomic determinants of family size.[25]

positively correlated, we should not be surprised to observe a negative relation between income and family size across the socioeconomic spectrum even though children are "normal goods" in the technical sense. Likewise, we should not expect that because income and fertility are negatively correlated in the cross-section, a cēteris paribus rise in income will reduce the number of children demanded. Parents may well react to income changes as predicted by economic theory even though the cross-sectional relation is negative. In any case, a comprehensive theory of fertility ought to be able to explain the negative relation between income and fertility in the cross-section even in the face of a strong presumption that children are normal goods. Section 3 presents such a theory based on sociological arguments; the Chicago-NBER theories are not particularly enlightening in this regard.

Expenditures on Children versus "Child Quality." Followers of Becker have expanded upon his notion that the fertility decision involves a quantity-quality tradeoff.[27] Becker originally meant by "quality" an index of expenditures on children: ". . . let me hasten to add that 'higher quality' does not mean morally better. If more is voluntarily spent on one child than another, it is because the parents obtain additional utility from the additional expenditures and it is this additional utility which we call higher 'quality.' "[28] However, in the household production framework subsequently adopted, quality is no longer a measure of inputs into children; it is now "produced" by means of a production function that is identical across couples. Child quality thus becomes an output of home production, the production level of which is determined simultaneously with optimal family size. Unfortunately, child quality is unmeasurable; indeed, as Peter Lindert notes ". . . the outputs here are psychic returns from home activities (interaction with children) that cannot be marketed, and thus cannot be measured. To compare child-service outputs is to compare utiles."[29] Nor is it sufficient to express child quality as an aggregate of narrowly defined personal characteristics such as height, beauty, intelligence, temperament, etc. As I have argued elsewhere,[30] even if it were possible to measure these characteristics objectively, the weights utilized to construct the aggregate index of child quality must be derived from the couple's preference orderings of the various characteristics, and there is no guarantee that the couples will agree in ranking them. Therefore, it is not possible to construct an unambiguous empirical measure of child quality.

There are, therefore, strong methodological objections to the notion of child quality as the output of a home production process; moreover, this notion of child quality as an output distorts the original intention of Becker to underscore the similarity between the family size decision and the decision to purchase a consumer durable. Becker was making the point that, as income rises, consumers tend to purchase not only increased *amounts* of consumer durables but higher *quality* consumer durables as well. With respect to expenditures on children he is surely correct: as the following two chapters will demonstrate in some detail, the value of resource expenditures on children does rise appreciably with potential income. However, this fact alone does not justify treating child rearing as simply another consumption activity.

Parenthood is a fundamentally important activity in the American culture. Child rearing involves the exercise of duties and responsibilities which are in large measure dictated by society at large and more specifically by the social and cultural group within which a couple resides. To persist in making the simple analogy between the fertility decision and the purchase of a consumer durable is to distort the true value of the microeconomic analysis of fertility, which is to explain family size decisions as they occur within the social and cultural context of American life.

The model presented in this chapter demonstrates that specific attention can be paid to these noneconomic factors while making full use of the suggestive framework of consumer theory. For example, the perceived price of a child is shown to depend specifically upon social and cultural factors; moreover, it is argued to be a fundamental determinant of completed family size and, therefore, a potentially important policy variable. Because Becker views the quality of a child as a joint decision variable, the price of a child as perceived by parents has no analytical or policy status, and a potentially important variable is essentially ignored in the Chicago-NBER analyses.

The Life Cycle, Work-Leisure Decisions, and Simultaneity. Another aspect of Becker's pathbreaking theoretical efforts has been the development and refinement of life cycle models of human capital accumulation.[31] The human capital approach tends to emphasize both the interrelatedness of such diverse activities as marriage, education, child rearing, and labor force participation, and the life cycle context within which these various behaviors take place. The Chicago-NBER models have tended to adopt this life cycle approach, and one of the theories (that of Robert Willis [32]) has managed to exploit fully the implications of this assumption. Willis postulates a one period lifetime optimization framework within which the husband and wife, at the outset of marriage, choose not only the optimal quantity and quality of children, but also determine the lifetime labor force participation of the wife.

The notion that the fertility decision, lifetime consumption decisions, and lifetime labor force behavior are jointly determined has a certain amount of merit, especially if the object of analysis is the *dynamic* allocative behavior of couples over time; however, too much emphasis can be placed on this simultaneity. For example, no one would dispute the assertion that the desire for children is generally connected with the decision to marry; nevertheless, it is inconsistent with available evidence to contend that age at marriage and *completed* fertility are jointly decided. Certainly it is not necessary that the two decisions be made simultaneously; the range of desired family sizes is small enough to provide the average couple with ample opportunity to determine and produce its optimal family size even if no decisions are made until well after marriage. There are, of course, many reasons why age at marriage and actual completed fertility are strongly related, but these reasons (premarital pregnancy, longer exposure to risk within marriage) lie largely outside the domain of the perfect control decision models characteristic of the Chicago-NBER group.

Likewise it is difficult to justify the imposition of a lifetime labor force behavior on couples at the outset of marriage, in spite of the analytical simplifications thereby achieved. Early in the life cycle couples must decide and achieve their desired fertility for biological reasons, but there is no evidence that these fertility decisions are accompanied by labor force participation decisions that extend over the life cycle. The approach taken in this chapter is that the fertility decision does not require that the husband and wife make final labor force participation decisions even though subsequent participation may be profoundly influenced by the presence of children in the family.[kk]

An Assessment of the Chicago-NBER Theory

By now it should be evident that there are some significant problems associated with the Chicago-NBER framework. Assessment of its contribution to the study of fertility is complicated by the scarcity of attempts to fully work out its theoretical implications. Despite the recent accumulation of literature which at least nominally conforms to the Chicago-NBER framework,[33] there is a paucity of attempts to explore the theoretical implications of the model. Indeed, only Willis has managed to carry out a thorough analysis,[34] and his work contains enough questionable features to bring his comparative static conclusions into doubt.

1. Assumptions. Willis makes the curious assumption that parental resources are used only to produce child quality; none is associated with

___

[kk]See Chapter Three for a discussion of the impact of children upon the labor force participation of husband and wife.

the production of *N,* the number of children. Since quality per child is produced by means of a linearly homogeneous production function, Willis's formulation does not allow for any biologically or institutionally determined minimum standard of living for the child. These minimums, if they exist, are part of the parental preference structure; however, Willis makes no attempt to consider whether these minimum standards do exist or whether they might vary systematically across the population.

Another assumption of crucial importance to Willis's theoretical argument is the assumption that children are "time intensive" relative to other consumption activities. This does not mean that child rearing takes more parental time than do the alternative activities; it means that the *ratio* of time to market inputs, in physical units, is higher in the production of child services[ll] than in the production of alternative activities. No attempt besides an appeal to its inherent plausibility is made to justify this assumption; however, it is a questionable assumption at best: (1) How can one compare "factor intensities" in physical units in a multifactor world in which the sets of factors utilized in alternative home consumption activities may be radically different? (2) Even if children do require large quantities of parental time, is it plausible to assert that they require relatively more time than alternative activities such as reading for pleasure, athletic activities, and so on? A very strong case can be made for the opposite assumption, that children are less time intensive than many competing activities. The factor intensity assumption comes about because Willis has adopted a theoretical framework developed by Ronald Jones to analyze the structure of a simple two-factor, two-good general equilibrium model of a competitive economy.[35] Whether this adoption is appropriate or not is open to serious question.

2. Methodological Procedures. In the course of a long and very involved derivation of comparative static properties, Willis takes some steps analytically that are open to debate. Prominent among these is his use of special assumptions to produce a "finding" and his subsequent restatement of the "finding" without the proper qualification.[mm] Most

---

[ll]"Child services" are defined as the product of numbers of children (*N*) and quality per child (*Q*). Since the production of *N* is resource-free, the assumption that child services are time intensive is equivalent to the assumption that the production of *Q* is time intensive.

[mm]At one point in his argument Willis produces a result by assuming a biased preference structure (p. S27) and later restates the finding (p. S29) without mentioning that it depends upon a very special assumption about tastes. At another point some of the mathematical argument is based upon a direct fiction employed in order to make the analysis tractable; however, the results of this analysis are later summarized with no attention to the impact of this pretense upon the substantive conclusions (pp. S27–S30, S55–S56).

curious, however, is Willis's adoption of a two-stage procedure to produce the comparative static conclusions. The first stage results, which are essential to the development, are generated by the minimization of an expression for "full income" subject to a production possibilities constraint. However, the first order conditions for a minimum which are presented and utilized in the paper are incorrect because the necessary convexity conditions do not obtain.[nn] This would appear to invalidate the procedure entirely.

From this discussion it should be clear that there are problems inherent in the Chicago-NBER approach that may substantially reduce its usefulness as a description of human fertility. It makes use of a number of assumptions and formulations that are open to debate; it tends to ignore the noneconomic determinants of fertility; and it has not produced behavioral hypotheses of particular interest. Indeed, the focus of much of the Chicago-NBER literature has been confined to an assessment of the impact of income on fertility. However, of more interest from a behavioral and policy point of view is the impact of price changes on fertility behavior; and on this matter the Chicago-NBER group is generally silent.

6. SUMMARY

This chapter completes the development, begun in Chapter One, of an integrated socioeconomic theory of fertility. In the previous chapter it was argued that fertility decisions are actually resource allocation decisions and require analysis as such. However, these resource allocation decisions take place in a social and cultural environment that may profoundly affect them, and Chapter One describes the ways in which these noneconomic elements of the decision environment may influence the fertility decision.

Chapter Two presents the detailed development of the analytical model. First, an analysis of an individual couple's fertility decision is presented. This analysis, although firmly based in the orthodox theory of consumer behavior, attempts to take account of some of the special factors that distinguish fertility decisions from standard consumption problems normally studied by economists. Foremost among the differences is the irreversibility of the family size decision and the necessity of a major commitment of resources early in the life cycle. Once the

---

[nn]Willis proposes (pp. S24–25, S30) to minimize the function $I = \pi_c C + \pi_s S$ subject to the production possibilities function $\phi(C, S, H, \kappa, T) = 0$. However, ϕ is concave to the origin and minimization of I will lead to a corner solution, not the interior solution stated by Willis. In fact the first order conditions advanced by Willis, $\phi_c/\phi_s = \pi_c/\pi_s$, will lead to a relative maximum, not minimum.

necessary modifications in the basic consumer theory have been made, it is possible to judge the comparative static effects of changes in various economic variables, prices of inputs, wage rates, and nonlabor income.

In Section 3 the theory is extended to account for group differentials in fertility. It is argued that noneconomic factors might dominate, leading to cross-sectional relationships between fertility and income that would appear, at first inspection, to conflict with the microeconomic theory of fertility but that are in fact consistent with it. Given a socioeconomic theory of differential fertility, it is then possible to specify the empirical model to be tested in the following chapters.

Policy implications of the microeconomic model are assessed in Section 4. The price (or opportunity cost) of a child is emphasized as being a policy variable of potentially major importance in efforts to influence the aggregate birth rate. However, policy approaches acting upon noneconomic determinants of fertility were also reviewed and the case made that, to be useful for policy analysis, a theory of fertility should be comprehensive enough to allow comparison of all competing policy approaches, both economic and noneconomic in nature.

The chapter concludes with an attempt to place the current model into the context of previous economic theories of fertility. In particular, the models of the Chicago-NBER group were contrasted with that of the present study so that the reader might better understand the differences in theoretical emphasis between the two approaches.

The remaining chapters of this study are devoted to an empirical analysis of the model presented in this chapter. The following two chapters are devoted to the construction of an empirical proxy for *P,* the price of a child. This effort is made especially difficult since *P* has never been directly measured, and the proxies constructed from disparate sources can only crudely approximate a couple's perceptions of the cost of a child. We will find that *P* varies considerably with a couple's potential income, a finding that lends direct support to the theories advanced in Section 3 of this chapter.

Finally, Chapter Six presents the statistical estimates of the demand for children represented by equation (24) in this chapter. Chapter Six thus draws upon the theory of Chapters One and Two and the statistical work of Chapters Three through Five.

CHAPTER TWO

1. Gary S. Becker, "A Theory of the Allocation of Time," *Economic Journal* LXXV (299) (September 1965): 493–517; and Kelvin J. Lancaster, "A New Approach to Consumer Theory," *Journal of Political Economy* LXXIV (2) (April 1966): 132–175.

2. See Alan Deardorff and Frank Stafford, "Labor Supply in Labor-Leisure and Household Production Models" (unpublished), Ann Arbor, Mich.: University of Michigan Department of Economics, October 1973; Robert A. Pollak and Michael L. Wachter, "The Relevance of the Household Production Function and Its Implications for the Allocation of Time," *Journal of Political Economy* LXXXIII (2) (April 1975): 255–77; Reuven Hendler, "Lancaster's New Approach to Consumer Demand and Its Limitations," *American Economic Review* LXV (1) (March 1975): 194–199.

3. See Thomas J. Espenshade, "Adapting Consumer Theory to the Fertility Decision" (unpublished), Florida State University, 1973 for a similar point of view.

4. See, for example, James M. Henderson and Richard E. Quandt, *Microeconomic Theory,* New York: McGraw-Hill, 1971, Chapter 3, Sections 1 and 5.

5. Robert J. Willis, "A New Approach to the Economic Theory of Fertility Behavior," *JPE Supplement, 1973,* pp. S14–S64.

6. Suggestive of the impact that children have on other parental activities is the article by Ronald Freedman and Lolagene Coombs, "Childspacing and Family Economic Position," *American Sociological Review* 31 (5) (October 1966): 631–648.

7. Reuben Gronau, "The Effect of Children on the Housewife's Value of Time," *JPE Supplement, 1973,* pp. S168–S199.

8. Jacob Mincer and Solomon Polachek, "Family Investments in Human Capital: Earnings of Women," *JPE Supplement, 1974,* pp. S76–S108.

9. For variants on the concept of potential income, see Richard Easterlin, "Towards a Socioeconomic Theory of Fertility," in *Fertility and Family Planning: A World View,* S.J. Behrman, Leslie Corsa, Jr., and Ronald Freedman, eds., Ann Arbor: University of Michigan Press, 1969; Peter H. Lindert, "Remodelling the Household for Fertility Analysis," Madison, Wis.: Center for Demography and Ecology Working Paper 73–14, May 1973, pp. 3-10–3-12; and Dennis N. DeTray, "Child Quality and the Demand for Children," *JPE Supplement, 1973,* p. S73.

10. See Chapter One, Section 2.

11. See R.G.D. Allen, *Mathematical Economics* (2d ed.), London: Macmillan, 1964, pp. 658–660.

12. Henri Theil, "Specification Errors and the Estimation of Economic Relationships," *Review of the International Statistical Institute* XXV (1957): 41–51.

13. Judith Blake, "Income and Reproductive Motivation," *Population Studies* XXI (3) (November 1967): 205.

14. Peter Lindert, "The Relative Cost of American Children," Madison, Wis.: Graduate Program in Economic History Discussion Paper EH 73–18, p. 34.

15. Paul Demeny, "The Economics of Population Control," in *Rapid Population Growth,* prepared by the National Academy of Sciences, Baltimore: The Johns Hopkins Press, 1971, pp. 199–221; David Friedman, *Laissez-Faire in Population: The Least Bad Solution,* New York: The Population Council, 1972; A.E. Kier Nash, "Going Beyond John Locke? Influencing American Population Growth," *Milbank Memorial Fund Quarterly* XLIX (1) (January 1971): 7–31;

Arthur J. Dyck, "Population Policies and Ethical Acceptability," in *The American Population Debate,* Daniel J. Callahan (ed.), Garden City, N.Y.: Doubleday Anchor, 1971; Judith Blake, "Population Policy for Americans: Is the Government Being Misled?" in Callahan, *op. cit.;* Bernard Berelson, "Beyond Family Planning," *Science* 163 (February 7, 1969): 533–543.

16. Gary S. Becker, "An Economic Analysis of Fertility," in Universities—National Bureau of Economic Research, *Demographic and Economic Change in Developed Countries,* Princeton: Princeton University Press, 1960. See also the accompanying comments by James Duesenberry and Bernard Okun.

17. Other approaches to the economics of family size can be found in Harvey Leibenstein, *Economic Backwardness and Economic Growth,* New York: John Wiley, 1957, pp. 159–170, and in Bernard Okun, *Trends in Birth Rates in the United States Since 1870,* Baltimore: Johns Hopkins Press, 1958.

18. Yoram Ben-Porath, "Economic Analysis of Fertility in Israel: Point and Counterpoint," *JPE Supplement, 1973,* pp. S202–S233.

19. Becker, "A Theory of the Allocation of Time," *op. cit.,* pp. 509–510.

20. Duesenberry, *op. cit.;* Okun, *op. cit.;* Alexander Gershenkron, "Review of *Demographic and Economic Change in Developed Countries,*" *Journal of the American Statistical Association* 56 (296) (December 1961): 1006–1008.

21. Deborah Freedman, "The Relation of Economic Status to Fertility," *American Economic Review* LIII (3) (June 1963): 414–426.

22. Richard A. Easterlin, "Towards a Socioeconomic Theory of Fertility," in *Fertility and Family Planning: A World View,* S.J. Behrman, Leslie Corsa, Jr., and Ronald Freedman, eds., Ann Arbor: University of Michigan Press, 1969.

23. Jacob Mincer, "Market Prices, Opportunity Costs and Income Effects," in *Measurement in Economics,* Carl Christ, ed., Princeton: Princeton University Press, 1965; Frank P. Stafford, "Student Family Size in Relation to Current and Expected Income," *Journal of Political Economy* 77 (Part 1) (July/August 1969): 471–477; Ronald Freedman and Lolagene Coombs, "Economic Considerations in Family Growth Decisions," *Population Studies* 20 (2) (November 1966): 197–222.

24. Judith Blake, "Are Babies Consumer Durables?" *Population Studies* 22 (1) (March 1968): 5–25.

25. See also Harvey Leibenstein, "An Interpretation of the Economic Theory of Fertility: Promising Path or Blind Alley?" *Journal of Economic Literature* XII (2) (June 1974): 457–479; Julian L. Simon, *The Effects of Income on Fertility,* Chapel Hill, N.C.: Carolina Population Center, 1974; Easterlin, *op. cit.;* Warren C. Robinson and David E. Horlacher, "Population Growth and Economic Welfare," *Reports on Population/Family Planning,* No. 6, New York: The Population Council, February 1971.

26. See Willis, *op. cit.;* and Gary Becker and H. Gregg Lewis, "On the Interaction Between the Quantity and Quality of Children," *JPE Supplement, 1973,* pp. S279–S288.

27. Willis, *op. cit.;* and De Tray, *op. cit.*

28. Becker (1960) *op. cit.,* p. 211.

29. Peter Lindert, "The Relative Cost . . . ." *loc. cit.*

30. Boone A. Turchi, "The Demand for Children: An Economic Analysis of

Fertility in the United States," unpublished PhD dissertation, University of Michigan, 1973, pp. 100–102; see also, Pollak and Wachter, *op. cit.*, pp. 273–76.

31. See Gary S. Becker, *Human Capital*, New York: National Bureau of Economic Research, 1964.

32. *Op. cit.*

33. See the *JPE Supplement, 1973;* Glenn G. Cain and Adriana Weininger, "Economic Determinants of Fertility: Results from Cross-Sectional Aggregate Data," *Demography* 11 (2) (November 1973): 205–223; Maurice Wilkinson, "An Econometric Analysis of Fertility in Sweden, 1870–1965," *Econometrica* 41 (4) (July 1973): 633–642.

34. Dennis N. DeTray, *op. cit.* also attempts a derivation; however, his efforts are inconclusive.

35. Ronald W. Jones, "The Structure of Simple General Equilibrium Models," *Journal of Political Economy* LXXIII (6) (December 1965): 557–572.

Chapter Three

The Time Cost of Children

1. INTRODUCTION

The largest single input into the child rearing process is parents' time. Although self-evident to any parent this basic fact has until recently been underemphasized in the economic literature on fertility. In the sociological literature the enormous time requirements of child rearing are generally recognized, but there has been little if any attempt to incorporate time costs formally into a model of fertility. This chapter presents quantitative estimates of the time required to raise children from birth to age eighteen. As the model of child rearing presented in Chapter Two suggests, failure to incorporate the time costs of child rearing into a demand model will result in serious specification error.[1] Also suggestive of the large claim that children place on the parents' time is the voluminous literature on labor force participation of married women cited in Chapter One.

The model of Chapter Two assumes that parents, in deciding on their completed family size, make estimates of the time that will be spent in child rearing during the eighteen years that the child is resident in the family. These estimates do not have to be very precise to carry a large impact in the fertility decision; the mother of one preschool child will spend approximately 3,700 hours in child care during the six preschool years, and a mother of three children spaced two years apart will average 6,000 hours of child care by the time her oldest child reaches age six. Women with any child rearing experience at all will be fully aware of the sizable time requirement of an additional child.

Since the time available to parents is a scarce resource it has a value that must be included in the cost of child rearing. This involves both the estimation of parents' expectations regarding time to be spent in child

75

rearing and the discovery of the value placed on that time by the husband and wife. Ideally both these measures might be obtained directly, say from a personal interview; however, our data do not permit this, and indirect measures of time spent in child rearing are substituted instead. The absence of direct measures also limits severely our ability to describe the production function for children.

Consequently resort must be made to data sources which give information on the actual time use behavior of parents with children of differing ages. Can data on actual behavior be safely substituted for the desired information on projected time costs? Obviously it will not be possible to determine how much error is introduced by this procedure until at least some of the proper data are collected; however, we might expect that the danger of using the actual behavior data is not great for two reasons: first, parents do not typically make a final decision about family size until they have had at least some experience in rasing young children.[2] Second, the parents can observe the experience of older couples of similar socioeconomic status and develop an idea of the time requirements of older children. In any case, the time estimates are not made in a complete void and it would not appear unreasonable to expect that the estimates and the actual experience of older couples are generally similar.

Even if actual child care behavior is accepted as a reliable proxy an additional problem remains. Data on parents' actual child care behavior are not available and we are forced to rely on a fairly crude substitute, parental time spent on "housework." The data analyzed in the body of this chapter come from two surveys conducted by the Survey Research Center of the University of Michigan in 1965 and 1970.[a] In both instances a goal of the study directors was to examine the productive use of time by individuals and ". . . to explain and interpret differences within this country in the extent to which families work, plan ahead, accept change, avoid risk, and keep a high and rising, but realizable, set of goals."[3] To fit their own analytical purposes the study directors devised several different measures of time use: regular housework, mar-

---

[a]Survey Research Center Study number 721, herein referred to as the Productive Americans survey; and Survey Research Center Study number 768, referred to as the Family Economics survey. Both these surveys as well as the others used in this study are conducted under a complex sample design known as cluster sampling. This method reduces enormously the cost of conducting social surveys, but at the cost of reduced efficiency. Standard errors estimated using formulas appropriate to simple random samples will, in general, understate the true standard error of the sample value. See James N. Morgan, Ismail A. Sirageldin, and Nancy Baerwaldt, *Productive Americans* (Ann Arbor, Mich.: Institute for Social Research, 1966, Appendix A). See also, Leslie Kish, "Confidence Intervals for Clustered Samples," *American Sociological Review* 22 (April 1957): 154–165; and Leslie Kish, *Survey Sampling* (New York: John Wiley, 1965).

ket work, irregular work, volunteer work, time spent commuting, etc. None of these is entirely satisfactory for the study of child care behavior. The arbitrary division of time into segments such as housework, leisure, volunteer work, and so on has little basis in theory. Better yet would be information on time spent in a range of consumption activities, one of which would be child rearing.

Nevertheless, the Survey Research Center classifications of time use are a marked improvement of the standard practice in the economics profession of dividing time into two components: market work and leisure. The conceptual difficulties involved in making use of arbitrary taxonomies of different types of time use are clearly illustrated with reference to child rearing. Many of the tasks ordinarily involved in bringing up children are manifestly not leisure,[4] but they are, nevertheless, elements of an activity that is undertaken not for financial remuneration (market work) but for psychic gain (i.e., for consumption). Some of the time inputs into child rearing provide satisfaction directly while others provide it only indirectly through the growth and maturation of the child. Both of these elements, however, are inputs into the child rearing process and contribute to the opportunity cost of children. Use of a category such as housework as the basis on which to estimate the inputs into child rearing runs the risk of missing altogether those aspects of the process that result directly in pleasure to the parents.[5] In the empirical sections to follow, this problem should be kept in mind. Use of housework as a proxy for child rearing activities is likely to result in underestimates of the time actually involved in the act of bringing up children. Nevertheless, housework and child rearing are intimately connected, as will shortly become apparent.

The following sections discuss the necessity for the formation of potential income groups to aid in analysis, the development of an estimation model of time allocation to children, the problems introduced by simultaneity, and finally, present quantitative estimates of the direct and indirect time costs of children.

2. POTENTIAL INCOME GROUPS

An important hypothesis of the fertility model of Chapter Two is that the perceived and actual cost of child rearing rises with the potential income of a couple—that is, the income elasticity of cumulative expenditures on child rearing is positive. Since we need to derive cumulative estimates of money and time expenditures on children it is necessary to synthesize our estimates from the experience of many different cohorts of parents.

The major problem involved in the use of the synthetic cohort technique is the identification of features by which we can group couples in terms of potential income. The method to be used in this chapter and especially in Chapter Four is to assign each couple to a potential income group based on the education and occupation of the husband. Each potential income group will contain couples of all ages and it will therefore be possible to derive cumulative estimates of time and money expenditures on children.

Use of current occupation and education to assign a couple to a position in the long range income distribution represents at best an imperfect solution to the problem of assessing each family's income potential and status grouping over time. Occupations reported at the date of survey may change as the husband ages, or may have been radically different when the husband was younger. We need each couple's assessment of their long range income and status potentials at the time of the fertility decision, but we have only the couple's actual position at the time of interview. If occupation and education never changed, use of them to form the potential income groups would be unexceptionable; however, occupation is especially likely to change as a man ages. For example, a young husband may currently be classified as a clerical or sales worker and yet have a high probability of becoming a managerial worker in the future. Use of current occupation alone as a guide to classification will result in significant measurement error.

In addition, the occupation classifications used in the sample surveys encompass jobs at a wide range of income levels. Table 3–1 lists sixteen occupational-educational subgroups and ranks each subgroup by its mean total expenditure on current consumption, which is closely related to mean family income for the subgroup. The table refers to the Bureau of Labor Statistics' Survey of Consumer Expenditure, which is a prime data source for the money expenditure estimates found in the following chapter; however, the grouping principle applies to the Survey Research Center surveys utilized in this chapter.

We observe that there are striking differences in family income among persons classified in the same occupational group. For example, professional and technical workers with at least some education past high school rank second on the scale of mean total expenditure on current consumption while those with a high school education or less rank sixth. Self-employed businessmen with a high school diploma or above rank fourth while those with less than a diploma rank eleventh.

Clearly, use of the husband's education is warranted in order to obtain more homogeneous income groupings. Education is less likely to change over time than is occupation and use of the education variable as an additional classification factor leads to greater homogeneity within potential income groupings. The sixteen occupation-education subgroups are grouped to form six potential income groups as designated in the last column of Table 3–1. These potential income groups will represent our

Table 3–1. Characteristics of the Occupational-Educational Subgroups in the Bureau of Labor Statistics' Survey of Consumer Expenditure

Category	Number of Cases	Rank by Mean Total Expenditure	Potential Income Group[a]
Professional and technical, non-farm			
High school or less	211	6	2
More than high school	771	2	1
Managers and officials			
High school or less	361	3	1
More than high school	296	1	1
Self-employed businessmen			
0–11 grades	267	11	4
High school and above	273	4	2
Clerical and sales workers			
High school or less	526	8	3
More than high school	278	5	2
Craftsmen and foremen			
0–11 grades	861	9	3
High school and above	712	7	2
Operatives and kindred workers			
0–8 grades	478	13	5
9 grades and above	737	10	4
Unskilled laborers and service workers			
0–8 grades	324	15	6
9 grades and above	379	12	4
Farmers, farm managers, and ranchers			
0–8 grades	599	16	6
9 grades and above	532	14	5

[a]Group number 1 has the highest mean total expenditure, group 6 the lowest.

approximation of each couple's position in the distribution of lifetime income and socioeconomic status, but the possibility of error inherent in a classification scheme such as this should continually be kept in mind. In the absence of information about a couple's expectations or past experience the potential income group is a useful categorization of couples by long range income.[6]

3. AN ESTIMATION MODEL OF TIME ALLOCATION IN THE FAMILY

A Model From Consumer Theory

Since direct estimates of parental time required in child rearing are not available, we must estimate the time requirement on the basis of indirect methods. Given data on parental time allocations, it is possible to estimate these time requirements based on a model from consumer theory. Since it is the pure impact of children on parental time allocation that we are pursuing, rather than the impact of other social and economic variables, major emphasis will be placed on the former; however, the estimates to be derived for other explanatory variables are those relevant to a short run consumer theory model.[b]

Assume that a couple, viewed during a particular period, is faced with the optimal allocation of the husband's and wife's time. They must choose among a set of consumption activities Z_i $(i = 1, n)$ each of which is produced by a production function of the form:

$$Z_i = G_i(x_i, t_{w_i}, t_{h_i})\ i = 1, n,$$
(1)

where x_i is a vector of market purchased commodities, t_{w_i} is wife's time spent in activity i, and t_{h_i} is husband's time spent in activity i. Note that the couple's choice is constrained by the possible existence of children in the family at the start of the period.[c] This constraint may be represented as:

$$\psi^s(\bar{K}, t_{w_k}, t_{h_k}, x_k) = 0$$
(2)

where $\bar{K}$ is an indicator of family size and age composition of the children.

Then, the couple's problem is to maximize its joint utility function:

$$U = U(Z_1, \ldots, Z_n) = U[G_1(\cdot), \ldots, G_n(\cdot)]$$
(3)

subject to the overall time constraints for the period

$$T = \sum_{i=1}^{n+1} t_{w_i} + T_w \quad \text{(wife)}$$
(4)

$$T = \sum_{i=1}^{n+1} t_{h_i} + T_h \quad \text{(husband)}$$
(5)

[b]In this formulation a short run single period utility function is the object of maximization. The problem might also be formulated in life cycle terms, if it is believed that the underlying behavior is primarily governed by life cycle considerations. However, given the data available for the present study, the empirical estimating equations for the two approaches appear to be virtually identical. See Gilbert R. Ghez and Gary S. Becker, "The Allocation of Time and Goods Over the Life Cycle," Report No. 7217 (Chicago: Center for Mathematical Studies in Business and Economics, University of Chicago, April 1972) for an example of the alternative approach.

[c]Of course, one of the new consumption activities that can be undertaken is the addition of a child to the family in the current period.

The money expenditure constraint:[d]

$$\sum_{i=1}^{n+1} p \cdot x_i = w_w T_w + w_h T_h + V, \tag{6}$$

and the child constraint represented by equation (2). T_w and T_h are the time spent at work by the husband and wife, V is nonlabor income, w_w and w_h are the wage rates of husband and wife, T is the total time available, and p is a vector of prices of market inputs.

Given that constraints (4) and (5) can be combined with (6), the optimization problem resolves to the maximization of the Lagrangian:

$$L = U\big[G_1(\cdot), \ldots, G_n(\cdot)\big] - \lambda\Big[\sum_{i=1}^{n+1} p \cdot x_i$$
$$- w_w(T - \sum_{i=1}^{n+1} t_{w_i}) - w_h(T - \sum_{i=1}^{n+1} t_{h_i}) - V\Big]$$
$$- \gamma\big[\psi^s(\bar{K}, t_{h_k}, t_{w_k}, x_k)\big]. \tag{7}$$

Once the first order conditions for a maximum are found they may be solved simultaneously to find the derived demand equations for parents' time and money resources:

$$t^*_{w_i} = t_i(p, w_w, w_h, V, T, \bar{K}), \quad i = 1, n+1$$
$$t^*_{h_j} = h_j(p, w_w, w_h, V, T, \bar{K}), \quad j = 1, n+1 \tag{8}$$
$$x^*_l = x_l(p, w_w, w_h, V, T, \bar{K}), \quad l = 1, n+1.$$

Equation system (8) represents the reduced form of a system of simultaneous equations expressing the demand for each of the inputs into all of the consumption activities. Time spent at work is a residual. Note that the production process ψ^s is not necessarily the same process as ϕ^s in Chapter Two. Parents' expectations may differ significantly from their actual behavior in child rearing; however, the estimates of inputs in child rearing developed in this and the following chapter are based on the assumption that expectations conform rather closely to the observed behavior of others of similar occupational and social status and that actual behavior is a good indicator of the parents' perceived production functions.

---

[d]An implicit assumption underlying this model is that net borrowing during the period is zero. In this short run context it is possible to make borrowing an endogenous factor, but the short run constraints on borrowing are current assets and liabilities, current wage rate, and expected earnings capacity, which depend in turn on the education, occupation, and age of the couple, variables included in the following analysis for other reasons (see text following). Consequently omission of borrowing and lending does not affect the empirical specifications to be specified below.

A Model That Fits the Data

The model just discussed presumes that we know all the consumption activities available to the couple and the production functions and prices of all the inputs. It allows us (theoretically) to perform comparative static analyses to observe how input proportions change as factor prices are altered, thus providing information on the degree of substitutability between husband and wife time inputs or between time and money inputs. This information is of special interest; for example, one of the principal assumptions underlying current political agitation for a national system of day care centers is that parental time and nonparental time are highly substitutable in the rearing of children. The ideal data discussed in Section 1 would allow us to draw conclusions about the substitutability of inputs; the data that are actually available do not.

Time use is classified much more crudely than the above model requires, and the classifications do not allow us to devise a model based on the idea of a consumption activity. Data regarding money expenditures on children are not included in the Survey Research Center data sets and consequently the possibilities of substitution of time for money cannot be assessed. As a result, the model actually presented for estimation will differ rather considerably from the model just presented.

The couple's time allocations will be represented by seven variables that are mutually determined during the course of the decision period:

1. The wife's regular housework in hours annually.
2. The husband's regular housework.
3. The wife's annual hours of market work.
4. The husband's annual hours of market work.
5. Annual hours of housework obtained from outside the home.
6. The wife's annual hours of "leisure" (a residual).
7. The husband's annual hours of leisure (also a residual).

These seven variables are the endogenous members of the system. The first four, which are at the center of our interest, can be represented by structural equations of the form:

$$HW = \beta_o + \Sigma \beta_k r_k + \Sigma \alpha_j y_j + e, \tag{9}$$

where, for example, (9) is the structural equation for wife's housework (HW), each y_j represents another of the endogenous variables, the r_k represent a subset of exogenous variables of the system (from equation (8)), and e is an error term.

In the sections that follow we will assess the impact of children of the husband's and wife's regular housework and on their market work and, later, attempt to determine the degree to which social and cultural variables interact to produce differences in child rearing behavior from group to group. Since time cost is a function of the parents' wage rates, cost differences may emerge even if child care behavior is identical for all groups; however, differences in actual time spent may either increase or reduce these time cost differentials among the potential income groups.

4. DETERMINANTS OF WIFE'S HOUSEWORK

Introductory Comments
In this and the following sections the impact of children on the time allocation of the husband and wife will be analyzed. Because children constitute only one of the factors influencing the parents' time allocation, the estimation model adopted must treat other influences. These other influences will be discussed briefly but the primary center of interest remains the assessment of the impact of children. The endogenous variables of the system are presented in Section 3, but some additional discussion of the predetermined variables in the system is warranted.

Variables in the system are considered exogenous if, during the time period under consideration, their magnitude is not subject to the control of the husband and wife. Thus, for any given year the number of children present, the education of the husband and wife, their wage rates, their income from nonlabor sources, etc., are considered to be predetermined. Obviously, whether a variable may legitimately be considered exogenous to the system depends upon the length of the time period under consideration and the time frame of the optimizing behavior of the husband and wife.

Most of the exogenous variables in the system estimated below would be considered endogenous to a system that takes the life cycle of the individual or married couple as the frame of reference. Given the appropriate longitudinal data, it would be possible to formulate the model such that many of the variables here considered to be exogenous could be incorporated into the system fully. For our purposes, however, we assume that the couple allocates the time available subject to the constraints posed by the presence of children, and the family's education, tastes, and available wage rates.

The Impact of Children
Tables 3–2 and 3–3 present regression results derived from subsamples of the Productive Americans and Family Economics surveys re-

Table 3-2. Determinants of Wife's Time Spent in Regular Housework—Productive Americans Sample
(Dependent Variable: Annual Hours of Regular Housework, Wife)

Independent Variables	Regression (1) 2SLS		Regression (2) OLS	
	Coefficient	Standard Error	Coefficient	Standard Error
Intercept	1022	472	1722	240
Other members 18+	137	101	74	62
Number and Spacing of Children				
Preschool only				
1	829	200	530	161
2	1473	222	1044	177
3+	1750	376	1261	300
Preschool—grade school				
2	1201	234	866	184
3+	1413	193	1052	146
Preschool—high school				
2	685	496	308	399
3+	1627	199	1331	161
Grade school only				
1	564	197	426	158
2	735	203	483	162
3+	867	263	583	210
Grade school—high school				
2	630	182	571	146
3+	758	168	550	136
High school only				
1	198	157	290	124
2	290	227	133	176
3+	538	471	426	373
Education of wife				
0–5	193	401	−124	287
6–8	360	151	256	115
9–11	123	114	52	88
High school	—	—	—	—
HS and nonacademic training	−5	132	28	104
College, 1–3	−334	182	−105	110
College, College +	−711	233	−370	130
Nonlabor income (×100)	1	1	0	1
Age of wife	5	6	2	4
Number of rooms in dwelling	−4	49	28	26
Religion of head				
Catholic	197	106	106	76
Non-Catholic	—	—	—	—
Head's mean hourly wage rate	28	36	−3	19
Market work: wife (estimated, ×100)	16	31	—	—
Housework: extrafamilial (estimated, ×100)	17	15	—	—

Table 3-2. Continued

Independent Variables	Regression (1) 2SLS		Regression (2) OLS	
	Coefficient	Standard Error	Coefficient	Standard Error
Market work: wife (×100)	—	—	−46	4
Housework: extrafamilial (×100)	—	—	−23	11
Mean of dependent variable	2143		2143	
N	1076		1076	
R^2			0.30	

Source: Productive Americans Survey sample tape (SRC study No. 721), Survey Research Center, University of Michigan. Date of survey: 1965, data relate to 1964. Criteria for selection of subsample: (a) head is married, spouse present; (b) his race is caucasian; (c) his maximum age is 60; (d) he is not retired or unemployed.

spectively. Each table contains two regressions numbered consecutively which present the results using two-stage least squares and ordinary least squares.[e] Each equation contains variables representing the number and ʻage distribution of the children in the family, the number of adults (aged 18 or over) besides the husband and wife currently residing in the family, the education of the wife, nonlabor income, religion, size of dwelling unit, head's wage rate, and selected endogenous variables.

Children are represented by an elaborate dummy variable system that has some rather marked advantages over a simple metric representation of the number of children in a given age group. Use of the dummy variable system allows us (1) to assess the marginal impact of the addition of a child of a given age, and (2) to assess the impact of different age distributions on the wife's housework. Of course use of this system implies a reduction in degrees of freedom that could in some instances be unacceptable; however, sample sizes are sufficient in the present instance to permit the consumption of considerable degrees of freedom.

As an aid in interpreting the regressions, assume that we are considering a family with two children of grade school age; the wife (age 33) has a college education; the husband earns $4.00 per hour and is Catholic; the family lives in a four-room home and receives $2,000 annually in nonlabor income; the wife neither works nor hires outside labor, and there are no other adults in the family. Then, to compute the number of hours of housework predicted by regression (1), Table 3-2, we add the

[e]Given a perfectly specified model, two-stage least squares (2SLS) may be shown to have large sample properties that make it superior to ordinary least squares (OLS). However, when multicollinearity or misspecification are present, the superiority of 2SLS estimators over OLS estimators is called into question. Consequently, both estimates are presented here for comparison. See a recent econometrics textbook for a discussion of the finite sample properties of 2SLS and OLS estimators—for example, John Johnston, Econometric Methods (New York: McGraw-Hill, 1972, pp. 408–420).

Table 3–3. Determinants of Wife's Time Spent in Regular Housework—Family Economics Survey
(Dependent Variable: Annual Hours of Regular Housework, Wife)

Independent Variables	Regression (3) 2SLS		Regression (4) OLS	
	Coefficient	Standard Error	Coefficient	Standard Error
Intercept	−95	228	381	76
Other members 18+	34	91	31	41
Number and spacing of children				
Preschool only				
1	671	215	884	82
2	772	350	998	104
3+	1331	570	1760	159
Preschool—grade school				
2	809	286	887	117
3+	1090	311	1144	100
Preschool—high school				
2	822	428	942	196
3+	1179	256	1002	103
Grade school only				
1	513	286	532	133
2	583	275	451	127
3+	1010	365	719	164
Grade school—high school				
2	667	222	476	97
3+	1068	246	645	90
High school only				
1	341	202	251	89
2	667	315	416	135
3+	961	817	326	364
Education of wife				
0–5	−293	472	−18	198
6–8	151	192	98	88
9–11	250	150	110	58
High school	—	—	—	—
HS and nonacademic training	−99	162	−40	70
College, 1–3	−309	193	−82	76
College, College +	−782	263	−361	87
Nonlabor income (×100)	−3	2	−1	1
Age of wife	29	75	19	2
Number of rooms in dwelling	−4	48	86	15
Religion of head				
Catholic	385	197	90	52
Non-Catholic	—	—	—	—
Head's mean hourly wage rate	−58	35	−21	9
Market work: wife (estimated, ×100)	7	23	—	—
Housework: extrafamilial (estimated, ×100)	424	234	—	—

Table 3–3.   Continued

Independent Variables	Regression (3) 2SLS		Regression (4) OLS	
	Coefficient	Standard Error	Coefficient	Standard Error
Market work: wife (×100)	—	—	−30	3
Housework: extrafamilial (×100)	—	—	−24	7
Mean of dependent variable	1791		1791	
N	1486		1486	
R^2			0.41	

Source: OEO Family Economics Study sample tape (SRC study No. 768); Survey Research Center, University of Michigan. Date of survey: 1970, data relate to 1969. Criteria for selection of sample, see source to Table 3–2.

product of each variable and its estimated coefficient to find the total number of housework hours predicted for the wife. In our example the calculation is:

$$HW = 1022 \times INTERCEPT + 137 \times 0 + 735 \times KGS2 - 711 \times EW7 + 1 \times$$
$$YNL(\times 100) + 5 \times AW - 4 \times SIZ + 197 \times RE + 28 \times$$
$$WH + 16 \times MW + 17 \times HM,$$
$$= 1022 + 0 + 735 - 711 + 2 + 165 - 16 + 197 + 112 + 0 + 0$$
$$= 1506 \text{ hours.}^f$$

Since the couple has two children of grade school age, the dummy variable KGS2 equals 1 and the other 14 dummy variables equal zero. If the couple had one child of preschool age and another in grade school, the term 735 × KGS2 would be replaced by the term 1201 × KPG2. Note that each of the coefficients on the dummy variables representing family size represents the total impact of the children in that family, not the average impact per child. Thus, in regression (1), one preschool child is associated with 829 hours of housework, while two preschool children are associated with 1,473 hours, or 736.5 hours per child.

Each of the four regressions demonstrates the profound impact that the presence of children has on the housework performed by the mother; however, while the interrelationships among the coefficients of each regression are generally similar, there is some variation in absolute

[f]The symbols in the equation are interpreted as follows: KGS2 represents two children of grade school age; EW7 represents educational attainment of a college degree or better; YNL represents nonlabor income; AW is wife's age; SIZ is the number of rooms in the dwelling unit; RE represents religion; WH is the husband's hourly wage; MW is annual hours of wife's market work; HM represents hours of housework obtained from outside the family; KPG2 represents two children, one preschool and the other grade school.

levels among the coefficients of the different regressions. If the estimating equations were well specified, and if multicollinearity were not too severe, the 2SLS estimates would appear to be preferable.

Multicollinearity is a problem, however, due to the error introduced because of the lack of precise empirical equivalents of underlying theoretical variables. We cannot, therefore, assert with any confidence that the 2SLS estimates are superior to the OLS estimates. Furthermore, since prior estimates of the time requirements of children do not exist, we cannot rely on prior opinion to choose among the four estimates of the impact of children.[g] All the regressions have produced plausible estimates and in the absence of an adequate choice criterion, I propose to use a simple average of the four coefficient sets as the basis upon which to construct estimates of the opportunity cost of child rearing.

Table 3–4 presents the mean of the four regression estimates for each of the fifteen dummy variables representing family size. Since the variance among the four estimates is not particularly large, use of the mean figures appears to be less arbitrary than selection of one of the regressions only. Most of the following comments will be addressed to Table 3–4, but the overall strength of the family size coefficients in each of the four regressions should be noted. In most instances the absolute value of the regression coefficients is considerably larger than the standard error of the estimated coefficients. This is further evidence that family composition has a profound impact on the wife's time allocation, perhaps unmatched by any other factor.[7]

Tables 3–2 to 3–4 demonstrate the sizable impact of children on the wife's time resources. As expected, preschool children require by far the most attention on the part of the wife. A mother with at least one preschool child can expect to spend a minimum of 700 additional hours in housework each year. For larger families with at least one child under age six, additions to housework can climb to over 1,500 hours. Once children enter school, however, their impact on the wife's housework declines to a range of 500 to 800 hours annually. Finally, as the youngest child turns thirteen, net additions to housework decline to a range of 265 to 563 hours annually, depending on family size.

Clearly, then, the time cost of child rearing is an important factor in the overall cost of child rearing. Even for those parents who discount future time expenditures at a high rate, the large amount of care required

[g]My own inclination is to trust the OLS estimates rather more than the 2SLS estimates. Since the instrumental regressions used in the calculation of the 2SLS estimates do not appear able to explain much of the variance in the endogenous variables (R^2's on the instrumental regressions explaining wife's market work and the family's purchase of housework are in the range of 0.16 to 0.07) the instrumental variables used in place of the actual endogenous variables would seem to introduce more error than they reduce.

Table 3–4. Mean Impact of Children on Wife's Housework

Number and Spacing of Children	Annual Hours of Housework Attributed to Children
Preschool Only	
1	728
2	1072
3+	1525
Preschool—Grade School	
2	940
3+	1175
Preschool—High School	
2	690
3+	1284
Grade School Only	
1	508
2	563
3+	794
Grade School—High School	
2	586
3+	756
High School Only	
1	270
2	265
3+	563

Source: These values are the arithmetical means of the coefficients of the four regressions found in Tables 3–2 and 3–3.

by preschool aged children cannot help but be a factor in the fertility decision. Note also that the decline in housework accompanying the growth of the family may be more than offset by increased claims on parental time for such child care activities as assisting with school work, PTA, Scouts, transportation and so on that are hardly captured by the housework measure.

The coefficients also suggest that the marginal impact of children declines as family size increases. In all three age categories mean housework per child declines as family size increases (Table 3–4) and the greatest decline is associated with the transition from one to two children in the age group. The transition from two to three or more children is considerably less pronounced and indicates that an only child may generate considerably more attention from the mother than does a child in a larger family.

The marginal declines in time spent per child may or may not signal the presence of economies of scale in child rearing; for mothers of preschool children the decline in expenditure per child more likely represents the presence of a global constraint on time available, rather than an increased efficiency in child care. Indeed, if the mother of the previous example (drawn from regression 1) has two preschool children, she will be spending 2,244 hours annually on regular housework and addition of a third child will raise annual housework to 2,521 hours, or approximately seven hours per day. However, part of the child rearing burden is shifted from the mother to the children themselves as they provide entertainment and diversion for each other. To the degree that family size increases promote this shift to less expensive "labor" it is possible to argue that larger families do in fact bring economies of scale in production.

Differences in the age distribution of the children also affect the mother's housework. As can be observed from Table 3–4, two-child families with at least one preschool child require the most housework time, but the age of the oldest child is negatively associated with hours of housework: two preschool children require 1,072 hours, one preschool and one grade school child require 940 hours, and a preschooler and high school require 690 hours. At least part of this decline is probably due to the systematic differences in the age of the youngest child; on the average, the youngest child in a family of two preschool children is most likely younger than the preschool child in families in which the oldest child is in grade school or high school.

For larger families with three or more children a wider age spacing leads to increased housework by the wife. Women with three or more preschool children spend on the average 1,525 additional housework hours annually, while those families exhibiting the spacing preschool—grade school find the mother's housework time increased by 1175 hours and families with the preschool—high school spacing show an increase of 1,284 hours. Most likely this result is an artifact of the dummy variable system. Families containing both preschool and high school age children are likely to be the largest in the sample and therefore the larger time requirement in this group is likely the result of larger average family size.

For the families in which the youngest child is in grade school, we do not find a consistent relationship between spacing and housework; for two-child families an older child in high school indicates slightly more housework, while for larger families wider spacing leads to slightly less housework. These results do not allow a general judgment as to how spacing affects housework for a given number of children, but there is at least some evidence that wider spacing promotes lower housework per child.

However, even if wide age spacing were to promote lower annual time expenditures, it does add to the cumulative time cost of children. As is evident from the regressions, the time spent on a child depends on the number and spacing of the children in the family, and in order to discuss the cumulative expenditure of time on a child it is necessary to specify the number and the spacing of the children.

Table 3–5 and Figure 3–1 illustrate the cumulative time spent in child rearing for one-, two-, and three-child families. Children are assumed to be spaced at two-year intervals, and annual hours spent in child care related housework are presented for each year that a child remains in the family. For a three-child family it is estimated that the wife devotes 18,389 hours of child care during the 22 years that children are residing in the family. For a two-child family cumulative time spent in child rearing falls to 12,946, and for the one-child family cumulative child care amounts to 9,274 hours. Thought of in these terms, the commitment of time implied by the decision to have children is truly impressive. For

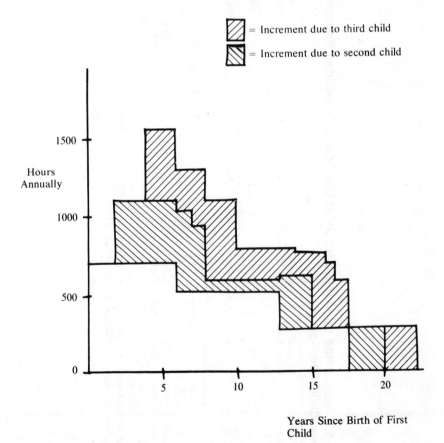

Figure 3–1. Annual and Cumulative Hours of Child Care Associated Housework for Wives in One-, Two-, and Three-Child Families

Table 3–5. Annual and Cumulative Hours of Child Care Associated Housework for Wives in One-, Two-, and Three-Child Families[a]

Event Year	First Child Born	Second Child Born		Third Child Born			First Enters School		Second Enters School		Third Enters School		First Enters Grade 8	
	0	1	2	3	4	5	6	7	8	9	10	11	12	13
3 children	728	728	1072	1072	1525	1525	1275b	1275b	1075b	1075b	794	794	794	796b
2 children	728	728	1072	1072	1072	1072	980b	900b	563	563	563	563	563	586
1 child	728	728	728	728	728	728	508	508	508	508	508	508	508	270

Event Year	Second Enters Grade 8		Third Enters Grade 8						Third Finishes High School	Total hours	Mean/Child	Incremental
	14	15	16	17	18	19	20	21	22			
3 children	756b	756b	716b	563	265	265	270	270	270	18,389	6130	5443
2 children	586	265	265	265	265	270				12,946	6473	3672
1 child	270	270	270	270	270					9,274	9274	

[a]Birth interval selected arbitrarily at two years for the two and three child families.
[b]Adjustments made for aging of children within an age group.

example, if we value the wife's time by the wage rate she might earn in market work[h] we find that a college woman working at an average wage of $4.05 will have invested $74,475 in the three-child family presented in Table 3–5, or an average of $24,820 per child. The time cost of a two-child family for the same woman would be $52,431 and the cost of an only child would be $37,560. For another woman with the same families and an eighth grade education, the cumulative time costs would be $35,123, $24,727, and $17,713 for the three-, two-, and one-child families respectively.[i]

The costs of child rearing are thus demonstrated to be substantial for *any* woman but especially for those women of advanced education. Since American marriages exhibit substantial homogamy with respect to education and social origin,[8] high status men tend to marry women of comparable education and background and the tendency for the cost of children to rise with the husband's income potential is reinforced. The positive association of potential income and time cost is independent of differences in child rearing practices that may exist.

Of particular interest is the incremental time cost of the third child. Despite the recent upturn in proportions of white wives expecting to remain childless or to have only one child, the vast majority continue to expect two or more children.[j] Consequently, the decision whether or not to have the third child represents for most couples the first major decision point regarding completed fertility. In our example (Table 3–5) the addition of a third child increases cumulative child related house-work by 5,443 hours. Although this is a sizable increase, mean time expenditure per child declines from 6,473 hours in the two-child family to 6,130 hours per child.

Note that 48 percent of this incremental time expenditure is incurred during the first six years of the child's life, a circumstance which has two implications: first, since the impact of an additional child is felt almost immediately, differences in time orientation among couples would not appear to be significant in assessing the marginal time cost of the third child. In either case the 2,600 hours of housework required during the six years subsequent to the third child's birth suggest that time costs will loom importantly in the decision to have another child. Second, it should be observed, however, that in our example over 61 percent of these

[h]As noted in Section 1, use of the wage rate to value a woman's time may lead to an underestimate of the true opportunity cost of children.

[i]Computed at a mean wage of $1.91 per hour (1969, see Chapter Five).

[j]In June 1974 85.4 percent of all white wives aged 18 to 39 expected to have two or more children; this is a decline from the 90.7 figure reported for all wives in 1967. See U.S. Bureau of the Census, *Current Population Reports,* Series P-20, No. 269, "Prospects for American Fertility: June 1974" (Washington, D.C.: U.S. Government Printing Office, September 1974, Tables 2 and 3).

2,600 hours will be incurred during the period in which there is at least one other preschool child present.

To the extent that the mere presence of a preschool child is sufficient to foreclose other opportunities for market work or nonmarket activities, the value of these particular 1,600 hours in alternative pursuits may be considerably below what it would have been in the absence of other preschool siblings. Indeed, for some women the value of this time in alternative pursuits might approach zero, a circumstance that would markedly reduce the incremental cost of the third child. Therefore, although addition of the third child signifies a large and immediate time commitment to child rearing, the impact of this commitment on the fertility decision depends very much on the subjective value that parents place on the opportunities foregone.

However, note that the effect of increasing the interval between second and third births from two to four years is (1) to increase the incremental cost of the third child's first six years by 318 hours, and (2) to reduce the proportion of the total increment (ca. 2,930 hours) occurring while other preschool siblings are present to 16 percent or 470 hours. Thus, although the incremental cost of the third child's first six years rises by only about 12 percent due to longer spacing, the perceived impact of the additional child may be considerably greater because of the child's consumption of time, for which a high opportunity cost in terms of foregone activities exists.

This example provides at least a partial explanation of the well documented tendency for the probability of an additional birth to fall sharply after the youngest child in a family has entered school. When a wife is in the business of mothering two preschool children, addition of a third child may pose a quantitative but not qualitative change in her activities and opportunities. However, once she has almost succeeded in changing her primary occupation to "mother of grade school children" the perceived marginal opportunity cost of an additional child may become markedly higher, even though the incremental cost in terms of hours does not rise very much due to wider spacing.

In the following section we observe that the presence of a preschool child—not the number of preschool children—appears to be the controlling factor in a wife's participation in market work, a consideration that would appear to lend support to this discussion of spacing patterns.

Clearly, the timing and spacing patterns chosen by couples may depend on a number of considerations specific to a given family. If, for example, a wife wishes to retain a job and advance professionally during the preschool years, she may opt for a longer interval between births so that nonfamilial activities may be pursued, even at the cost of a considerably higher cumulative time cost for child rearing. However, if minimization of cumulative time spent in child rearing is a goal, close spacing would appear to be the proper approach, both in terms of minimizing the amount of time that preschoolers are at home and in terms of total time cost.[k]

The Impact of Other Socioeconomic Factors

As the behavioral model of time allocation presented in Section 3 suggests, children represent only one of the factors influencing a wife's housework. Each of the other explanatory variables included in the regressions will be briefly discussed here as an aid to interpreting their theoretical role in the analysis.

Other Members 18 or Older. Since many families have older children or other family members present, it is necessary to account for their influence on the wife's housework. Other adults living in the family unit may either help or hinder the wife's housework efforts, and there is no a priori reason to expect either effect to predominate. The regressions, however, indicate that the presence of other adults in the household serves to increase the wife's housework on the average. To the extent that these other adults are actually the children of the parents who are living at home, this net increase in housework can be considered an addition to the time cost of child rearing; however, the data do not allow us to distinguish between own children and other adults. In none of the regressions is the standard error of the estimated coefficient small enough to allow us to reject the null hypothesis at any reasonable level of significance. In fact, inclusion of this variable is important mainly as a means of purging the coefficients on the other family size variables of possible effects operating through the presence of adults.

Wife's Education. The dummy variable system representing the effect of the wife's education is intended as a proxy for both economic and noneconomic effects. Education acts here as a proxy for the woman's market wage and current stock of human capital; associated with wage differentials are two effects that may be offsetting. The first effect, the substitution effect, should lead to a reduction in housework as wages rise. If housework is an input into various nonmarket consumption activities, we would expect to see a substitution of market goods and services for a wife's time as her education (and potential wage) increase.

---

[k]Of course the preschool years may have certain qualities desired by mothers who might, therefore, opt for a longer spacing to enjoy them more fully. The measures of time spent in child rearing utilized in this study are not of much help in analyzing this facet of the child rearing experience.

On the other hand, an income effect is also operating that induces a shift of wife's time from market labor to nonmarket opportunities. These two effects are offsetting and theory does not tell us which effect should predominate.

In addition, it has been argued that a wife's tastes and attitudes towards housework vary with education.[9] Well educated women are characterized as having available a wider set of alternative uses for their time, with the result that they are less prone to housework than their less educated contemporaries. If this taste differential actually exists we would expect it to reinforce the substitution effect postulated above. The four regressions provide some evidence that the combined taste-substitution effect does predominate. In both samples well educated women perform considerably less housework than do their less educated contemporaries, and, although standard errors are generally large, the progression of the coefficients is reasonably regular[1] suggesting a negative relationship between housework and education.

Husband's Wage and Nonlabor Income. Variables measuring the husband's wage rate and the family's nonlabor income are introduced in an attempt to account for the other economic influences operating on the wife's time allocation.[m] Due to the unsatisfactory analytical nature of the housework variable, it is difficult to predict the effect of these two variables. The total effect of an increase in the husband's wage rate and/or nonlabor income on the wife's nonmarket time should be positive, but the effect on housework may well be negative as market goods and services are substituted for the wife's time inputs. The regression results are mixed, with the signs of the coefficients in Table 3-3 uniformly negative while those in Table 3-2 vary; however, the standard error of only one of the eight coefficients is less than twice the absolute value of the coefficient.

Wife's Age. This variable is included in the regressions to capture age and generational differences net of differences in education, income, and size of family.[n] Regressions from both of the samples indicate that age of wife has a positive effect on housework but again standard errors are large in all but regression (4).

---

[l]The exception if the coefficient on the variable "Education: 0–5 years." This category contains so few cases, however, that sampling error may preclude any meaningful inference.

[m]See Section 3 above.

[n]In a cross-section sample such as this, age and cohort are identical and the variable is measuring a combined (net) effect.

Number of Rooms in House and Religion of Head. The size of a family's dwelling should affect the amount of housework performed by the wife; however, since size of family and number of rooms are correlated the net effect of housing size was not expected to be large. In the 2SLS regressions the coefficients are small (−4 in each regression) and accompanied by large standard errors. The OLS regressions produce positive coefficients but only the coefficient in regression (4) is accompanied by a relatively small standard error. The religion variable was included to determine whether wives of Catholic husbands behave differently with respect to housework. Catholics are alleged to possess a stronger orientation to family life than are non-Catholics, an orientation encouraged by the Church as the following quotation suggests:

> . . . When you enter marriage, you dedicate yourselves to the service of new life. Conjugal love is by its nature productive and creative, seeking to extend and fulfil itself in a child. . . . It follows that anything which interferes with your partnership in parenthood offers a threat to your happiness. . . . During the childbearing and child rearing period the wife's energy and interest must be focused on the home if she is to perform her task adequately.[10]

The data suggest that wives of Catholic husbands[o] do engage in more housework than other wives; the coefficients from the four regressions range from 90 to 385 hours annually with the ratio of coefficient to standard error ranging from 1.39 to 1.95. Confirmation of a Catholic–non-Catholic behavior differential is not possible with these results, but they are suggestive and worthy of further study. In particular we will attempt to assess the degree to which child care behavior differs among Catholic and non-Catholic families. We might suspect that Catholic mothers do spend more time in child care than do non-Catholic mothers, in line with the teachings of the Church. If this is the case, then the time costs of rearing children are higher for Catholics and this higher cost might serve to reduce the Catholic–non-Catholic fertility differential. A test of the religious interaction will be reported in Section 7 below.

Wife's Market Work and Nonfamilial Housework. Both a wife's market work and the family's receipt of housework from outside the family should be negatively associated with the wife's housework. In both the OLS regressions the estimated coefficients have the expected minus

---

[o]Religion of the wife was unavailable in either of the two surveys, and our speculations about religious differentials are subject only to the partial analysis based on the husband's religion.

signs and are accompanied by relatively small standard errors. House-work from outside would not appear to be a very good substitute for the wife's efforts, with 100 hours of nonfamilial housework resulting in a reduction of only 24 hours of wife's housework. Likewise, 100 hours of market work by the wife serves to reduce her housework by only 30 to 46 hours annually.[p] The 2SLS regressions appear to be completely unreliable with regard to these two variables. The signs of the estimated coefficients are all positive and three of the four are accompanied by large standard errors. The fourth coefficient, on nonfamilial housework (regression (3)), is accompanied by a smaller standard error but suggests, implausibly, that 100 hours of extrafamilial housework results in the net addition of 424 hours to the wife's housework.

Summary

The regressions of Tables 3–2 and 3–3 illustrate the central role of children in the determination of the housework of a wife. The hypotheti-cal wife of the example at the beginning of this section finds her house-work increased by 735 hours annually due to the presence of two children of grade school age. The same woman with two preschool children averages close to 2,000 hours of housework per year, the equivalent of a full time job. These regressions allow us to construct estimates of the cumulative time spent in child rearing (Table 3–5 and Figure 3–1) that incorporate spacing and timing differences. The cumula-tive time cost for a child is seen to be quite large, varying from 6,000 to 9,000 hours depending on family size and spacing. Thus, in terms of resource commitment at least, the analogy of children as consumer durables would not appear to be misplaced.

5. DETERMINANTS OF WIFE'S MARKET WORK

The Impact of Children

The presence of children in a family has just been shown to be responsible for a major reallocation of mother's time toward housework and, by inference, other child rearing activities.[q] As a part of this reallocation there is also a shift in the amount of the mother's time devoted to market work and other nonmarket activities; however, in the

---

[p]When husband's housework was included in a previous regression 100 hours of husband's housework resulted in a decline of only eight hours in wife's housework. Since the standard error on this coefficient was quite large the variable was dropped from the regression.

[q]This section has benefited considerably from the comments of Peter Lindert, who, nevertheless, should not be held accountable for the contents.

absence of institutional impediments to time allocation it is the value of the time actually spent in child rearing that constitutes the time cost of children. This value depends, of course, on the psychic valuation that the wife places on her time—that is, upon the "shadow price" of her time. But, since the wife has the option of entering the labor market at a given wage, the shadow value of her time will never be below the wage rate at the margin.[11]

This, however, presupposes that the labor market is competitive so that entry and exit are free and wages and hours worked are flexible. In this environment, the mother of children (especially preschoolers) would be able to supply just the correct number of hours so as to reach an optimal allocation of her time. However, if the requirements of child rearing compel her to seek part time employment or work in the off hours, she may be unable to work the desired number of hours at the wage rate for which she is qualified. Thus, because of labor market imperfections the mother of small children may be forced to work at a lower wage than a childless woman of equal qualifications, or she may spend more time out of the labor force altogether than she would have in the absence of these rigidities. In either case, these labor market imperfections raise the opportunity cost of the time devoted to child rearing because of the constraints imposed on the allocation of nonchild rearing time.

An accurate measure of the shadow price of the wife's time would include her assessment of the impact of these rigidities on the value of time spent in child rearing. Unfortunately, such a measure does not exist and we are continually forced back to the wife's expected market wage as a measure of the value of her time. Granted that the measure is crude, it still gives the best empirical approximation available in the absence of direct information.

However, we can attempt to get at least an idea of the impact of children on the wife's market work net of their direct claim on her time. To do this we estimate the structural equation for wife's market work and include wife's housework as a predictor in the equation. If children are strongly associated with the wife's housework as they appear to be, then we expect the coefficients on family size to be small in the absence of institutional rigidities in the labor market. The coefficients on the family size variables in Tables 3–6 and 3–7 do not support this expectation. Especially with regard to preschool children these coefficients are large and significant, and it might be concluded that children have a separate impact on the wife's market work independent of their direct child care requirements.

The regression coefficients on the family size variables do not exhibit the regularity found in the analogous coefficients in regressions (1) through (4). For example, in regression (8) a wife with two children, one in high school the other preschool, experiences a net contribution of −501 hours by the children to her market work, while a wife with three or more children experiences a net contribution of −201 hours. These coefficients may reflect differences in economic need—a larger family may require that the wife work—but inclusion of income and wage variables in the regression is designed to control for this possibility.

The lack of regularity of this type should not be disturbing, however, since for market work it is the presence of at least one child of a given age rather than the number of children which may exercise the most important influence on the wife's work behavior. Thus, if the regression coefficients for the variables representing the presence of at least one preschool child are averaged over the four regressions, we find that the presence of a preschool child reduces the wife's work by approximately 460 hours per year or by 9.2 hours per week. The same procedure shows that in families with a youngest child of grade school age, the average reduction in wife's market work is 233 hours per year or 4.6 hours per week. For families in which the youngest child is thirteen or older the average work reduction is 51 hours per year or one hour per week.

Initially, then, the presence of young children in the family inhibits the participation of the wife in market work by approximately nine hours per week. Certainly this is not implausible: the average wife with two preschool children spends close to 40 hours per week in regular housework and the addition of nine hours of market work, while it would make her a very busy woman, does not represent an exorbitant demand on her time. As the children enter school, providing the wife with discretionary time during the day, work lost as a result of children drops to four or five hours per week. Finally, as the children enter high school their presence in the family constitutes no hindrance on the wife's work efforts. Indeed, high school children may provide a positive incentive for the wife to work: the signs on all four of the coefficients attached to the variable "high school only, one child" are all positive as are the signs on the coefficients of the variable "other members 18 and older." We might speculate that as the children reach college age, the wife is induced to undertake some work in order to defray their college expenses.[12]

The interpretation placed on the family size coefficients of regressions (5) through (8) suggests that in addition to the direct time cost involved, child rearing possesses another cost, market opportunities lost because of imperfections and rigidities in the labor market. This serves to raise the value of time spent in child rearing over what it would be in the absence of these rigidities; however, given the difficulties associated with valuing time empirically, no attempt will be made to adjust our time value estimates to account for the labor market imperfections effect.

This is not to say that the market time effect is unimportant; sociologists and psychologists have often suggested that one of the psychic costs of child rearing is the feeling of isolation experienced by the mothers of young children, feelings that might loom large in the preference structure and that might be drastically reduced or eliminated were the labor market flexible enough to accommodate the demand for part time market work exhibited by these women.

The Impact of Other Socioeconomic Factors

The other explanatory variables included in regressions (5) through (8) are generally similar to those contained in the first four regressions and will be discussed only briefly.

The economic variables "wage of husband" and "nonlabor income" exhibit the expected signs, although magnitudes vary between the two samples. The effect of nonlabor income on wife's market work is negative and small, as economic theory would lead us to expect; and the effect of the husband's wage rate is also negative, as expected. Wife's education, acting as a proxy for her potential wage, is subject to opposing forces. The substitution effect would be expected to be negative—i.e., an increase in the wife's wage should, holding real income constant, result in an increase in work effort. On the other hand, the income effect should be positive, resulting in a reduction of work effort as the potential wage rises.

Confounding the picture is the possibility mentioned in Section 4 that women with different educational backgrounds have different attitudes towards work. The regression results do not clarify the picture: the dummy variables representing education exhibit coefficients in the Productive Americans sample (Table 3–7) that are weakly consistent with the idea that the substitution effect (or the substitution effect and a differential taste pattern) predominate. The results for the Family Economics survey demonstrate no consistent pattern (Table 3–6).

The two other exogenous variables "religion of husband" and "age of wife" display conflicting results. Wife's age appears to have a negative impact on work effort in the Productive Americans sample while the coefficients of the two Family Economics regressions conflict in sign. Religion enters with a negative sign in the Productive Americans regressions and with a positive sign in the Family Economics regressions. Standard errors are large on these coefficients.

The signs associated with two of the endogenous variables are as might be predicted. Increased purchases of housework from outside are associated with increased market work by the wife, and reductions in housework are associated with increases in market work. Husband's

Table 3-6. Determinants of Wife's Time Spent in Market Work—Family Economics Survey
(Dependent Variable: Annual Hours of Market Work, Wife)

Independent Variables	Regression (5) 2SLS		Regression (6) OLS	
	Coefficient	Standard Error	Coefficient	Standard Error
Intercept	95	105	625	69
Other members 18+	111	45	69	37
Number and spacing of children				
Preschool only				
1	−411	118	−58	78
2	−763	189	−321	96
3+	−893	300	−199	148
Preschool—grade school				
2	−504	165	−139	106
3+	−667	206	−313	92
Preschool—high school				
2	104	235	238	179
3+	−355	234	−142	93
Grade school only				
1	−46	146	71	121
2	−279	152	−113	114
3+	−383	210	−114	148
Grade school—high school				
2	−94	130	35	88
3+	−213	172	−116	80
High school only				
1	96	104	168	80
2	66	168	118	122
3+	−294	410	−209	327
Education of wife				
0–5	−161	228	−260	178
6–8	4	99	−1	79
9–11	90	80	77	52
High school	—	—	—	—
HS and nonacademic training	196	76	246	62
College, 1–3	−32	104	63	68
College, College +	−174	184	46	79
Nonlabor income (×100)	−3	1	−1	1
Age of wife	−5	5	9	2
Religion of head				
Catholic	129	107	92	47
Non-Catholic	—	—	—	—
Head's mean hourly wage rate	−25	18	−26	8
Housework: wife (estimated, ×100)	−26	18	—	—

Table 3–6. Continued

Independent Variables	Regression (5) 2SLS		Regression (6) OLS	
	Coefficient	Standard Error	Coefficient	Standard Error
Market work: head (estimated, ×100)	58	8	—	—
Housework: extra-familial (estimated, ×100)	134	114	—	—
Housework: wife (×100)	—	—	−24	2
Market work: head (×100)	—	—	8	2
Housework: extra-familial (×100)	—	—	45	6
Mean of dependent variable	670		670	
N	1486		1486	
R²			0.21	

Source: See Table 3–3.

market work displays conflicting signs in the two samples. The coefficients are positive in the Family Economics regressions and negative in the Productive Americans regressions. Theory does not provide us with an expectation as to the correct sign of this particular variable.

A Note on Multicollinearity
By now the reader has noted a degree of instability in the coefficients in regressions (1) through (8). Much of this instability may be attributed to multicollinearity which is rather severe in these regressions. In fact under the Haitovsky criterion [13] the null hypothesis, "determinant of the correlation matrix of independent variables equals zero," cannot be rejected even at significance levels below 0.01. This multicollinearity arises for at least two reasons: (1) variables are included in the regressions that are themselves highly correlated (e.g., housework and family size in regressions (5) through (8)); and (2) some of the variables provide poor measures of the underlying phenomena they are supposed to represent and in fact overlap considerably with other included variables that ostensibly are representing different phenomena. For our purposes the multicollinearity is not too serious; the dummy variables representing family size remain reasonably stable even in the face of the near singularity of the matrix of independent variables. But, as mentioned previously, the presence of such a high degree of multicollinearity does detract from the advantages possessed by 2SLS in the estimation of simultaneous equations.

Table 3–7. Determinants of Wife's Time Spent in Market Work—Productive Americans Survey
(Dependent Variable: Annual Hours of Market Work, Wife)

Independent Variables	Regression (7) 2SLS		Regression (8) OLS	
	Coefficient	Standard Error	Coefficient	Standard Error
Intercept	2373	570	2216	170
Other members 18+	17	58	27	44
Number and Spacing of Children				
Preschool only				
1	−599	132	−403	115
2	−937	149	−532	128
3+	−1004	250	−510	216
Preschool—grade school				
2	−744	152	−419	133
3+	−812	127	−421	105
Preschool—high school				
2	−674	326	−501	284
3+	−690	137	−266	117
Grade school only				
1	−342	129	−189	113
2	−601	133	−418	114
3+	−624	173	−403	149
Grade school—high school				
2	−152	118	21	104
3+	−450	108	−243	94
High school only				
1	157	100	225	88
2	−303	142	−224	125
3+	−292	304	−115	266
Education of wife				
0–5	−617	246	−512	204
6–8	−163	112	−47	83
9–11	−133	74	−92	62
High school	—	—	—	—
HS and nonacademic training	−2	86	9	74
College, 1–3	114	121	90	79
College, College +	179	173	97	93
Nonlabor income (×100)	0	1	0	0
Age of wife	−9	4	−8	3
Religion of head				
Catholic	−52	74	−20	54
Non-Catholic	—	—	—	—
Head's mean hourly wage rate	−130	31	−85	14
Housework: wife (estimated, ×100)	8	10	—	—
Market work: head (estimated, ×100)	−33	18	—	—
Housework: extrafamilial (estimated, ×100)	87	90	—	—

Table 3–7. Continued

Independent Variables	Regression (7) 2SLS		Regression (8) OLS	
	Coefficient	Standard Error	Coefficient	Standard Error
Housework: wife (×100)	—	—	−23	2
Market work: head (×100)	—	—	−12	3
Housework: extra-familial (×100)	—	—	10	7
Mean of Dependent Variable	615		615	
N	1076		1076	
R²			0.26	

Source: See Table 3–2.

6. DETERMINANTS OF HUSBAND'S TIME USE

Although the mother typically bears the brunt of the time cost of child rearing the father's role may not be minor. The father of preschool children may also spend a significant amount of time caring for his children, but if this is so, the data available here do not provide convincing evidence. Table 3–8 contains two regressions from our model that are designed to explain the market work and housework performed by the husband. Of immediate interest is the allocation between his market work and housework: the average husband spends 2,350 hours per year at market work and only 166 hours in regular housework. Thus he spends three hours per week in housework while the average wife spends slightly over 40 hours.[14] The results reported in Table 3–8 are not particularly noteworthy and only a short discussion of each regression will be presented here.

Husband's Housework

Regression (10) is the model's structural equation for husband's regular housework. As evidenced by the R² of 0.07 the equation is not very successful in explaining husband's housework. The coefficients on the dummy variables representing family size are particularly disappointing, especially compared to the regressions explaining wife's time allocation. Only one of the fifteen coefficients is accompanied by a standard error less than half in absolute value, and this coefficient is attached to a category represented by only seven families in a sample of 1,076. Otherwise we note that, disregarding standard errors, husband's house-

Table 3–8. Determinants of Husband's Time Allocation

Independent Variables	Market Work, Husband Regression (9)		Housework, Husband Regression (10)	
	Coefficient	Standard Error	Coefficient	Standard Error
Intercept	2837	72	317	67
Other members 18+	−21	37	−37	16
Number and Spacing of Children				
Preschool only				
1	−115	86	−8	43
2	62	97	46	47
3+	380	178	109	80
Preschool—grade school				
2	218	109	29	50
3+	268	79	58	39
Preschool—high school				
2	252	250	408	107
3+	68	96	14	44
Grade school only				
1	51	97	−31	42
2	101	96	6	42
3+	163	127	29	56
Grade school—high school				
2	205	89	32	39
3+	176	801	12	35
High school only				
1	64	71	1	33
2	31	109	−50	47
3+	166	232	−54	100
Education of head				
0–5	567	118	−62	52
6–8	−260	69	−24	31
9–11	−106	64	−16	28
High school	—	—	—	—
HS and nonaca-demic training	58	68	22	29
College, 1–3	−26	73	11	31
College, College +	147	72	74	31
Nonlabor income (×100)	4	0	0	0
Age of head	—	—	3	1
Religion of head				
Catholic	—	—	34	20
Non-Catholic	—	—	—	—
Head's mean hourly wage rate	−145	12	−25	5
Housework: wife (×100)	—	—	−2	1
Market work: head (×100)	—	—	−6	1
Housework: extra-fami-lial (×100)	—	—	3	3

Table 3–8. Continued

Independent Variables	Market Work, Husband Regression (9)		Housework, Husband Regression (10)	
	Coefficient	Standard Error	Coefficient	Standard Error
Housework: husband (×100)	−30	7	—	—
Market work: wife (×100)	−6	3	—	—
Mean of Independent Variable	2350		166	
N	1076		1076	
R²	0.20		0.07	

Source: See Table 3–2.

work tends to increase as the number of children increases for those families with preschool or preschool and grade school children. The increments to father's housework are not large, however. In addition, the presence of high school children or other adults would appear to correspond to a reduction in the husband's housework.

Why is family size not more strongly correlated with the husband's housework? It would appear that the basic cleavage in the husband's and wife's marital roles affects what is termed housework for each spouse. Since the primary responsibility for child care tends to be the wife's, her duties contain much more of the sort of task that is commonly termed housework. For the husband, on the other hand, the time spent in child care may be much more heavily concentrated in activities which are not housework, e.g., actual play with the children. Thus the housework variable may do a poor job of measuring the time spent in child care by the husband because of differences in the composition of that child care time. Again, it should be noted that the housework variable likely understates the time that a mother spends with her children also, but since a higher proportion of her child care time is spent in housework the results are still rather vivid. In any case, we have another example of the desirability of having a better measure of child care time than regular housework.

Other interesting aspects of regression (10) are: (1) the negative wage effect that is expected, (2) the positive relation between the husband's education and the housework he performs, and (3) the general lack of substitutability between a husband's housework time and the wife's housework, the husband's market work, and housework obtained from outside the household. The positive relation between a husband's education and housework may be representative of the loosening of sex role stereotypes at higher status levels,[15] while the lack of substitutability reminds us of just how strong those roles remain.

Husband's Market Work

Regression (9) appears to do better in explaining the husband's market work, partly because it is a better measure of the actual phenomenon than is husband's housework and, as a result, is more susceptible to accurate reporting. Again, the coefficients on the family size variables are not terribly impressive; most are accompanied by sizable standard errors. We might note, however, that larger families in each age group appear to result in a net increase of market work in the range of 100 to 400 hours per annum. There does not appear to be any trend with the age of children.

Husband's wage is associated with a coefficient of −145 hours per dollar wage, an indication that the income effect predominates. Non-labor income, however, is associated with a positive, albeit small, coefficient. The coefficients on the education variables, while exhibiting some small standard errors, do not follow an orderly progression.

The time cost of children with respect to the husband's time allocation is not represented in the following chapters. The regressions in Table 3–8 provide little incentive for the systematic inclusion of the husband's time cost component. As mentioned, at least part of the problem is the unsatisfactory nature of the housework variable as a measure of the husband's efforts in child care. Undoubtedly the husband incurs a direct time cost as the children are raised, but in most cases this effort is dwarfed by the time spent by the mother. As more suitable data are collected the husband's share of the time cost of child rearing can be calculated with a precision that will warrant its inclusion in measures of the time cost of children.

7. INTERACTION EFFECTS

Since a mother's child care efforts can be measured only indirectly, we cannot determine from regressions (1) through (4) if social and economic differentials lead to differences in child care behavior. That is, the regressions embody the assumption that parents are homogeneous with respect to child care behavior. We have reason to believe, however, that couples differ with respect to the amount of time they spend in child care, and in this section three possible interactions are analyzed.

It has been noted above that even if parents from different social and economic groups spend the same amount of time in child care the time cost of children will vary depending on the education of the wife. If women from different groups do in fact behave differently, these time cost differences may be increased or reduced. Using the Productive Americans data, we will assess possible differences in child care behavior with respect to three criteria: the family's religion, the wife's education, and the family's potential income group.

The method to be used—the analysis of covariance—has been described elsewhere,[16] but a brief description of the rationale underlying it may be useful. By pooling all the cases in the Productive Americans sample we implicitly assume that the effect of children upon the housework of the wife is uniform for all families. This assumption may in fact be incorrect and it may be possible to explain more of the variance in wife's housework by explicitly accounting for the interaction of family size and another variable, say religion.

The analysis of covariance provides us with a means of determining whether or not there is significant interaction; it relies on the same set of assumptions that apply to analysis of variance and correlational analysis.[17] However, a feature of the present data set reduces the power of the covariance analysis to indicate intergroup differences: since family size is specified through the use of fifteen dummy variables, division of the sample results in numerous cells with very few cases, and the resulting coefficients on family size are therefore unstable due to sampling variation. Comparisons of child care behavior among the groups can, consequently, be only tentative; nevertheless, some suggestive findings do emerge.

Wife's Education

A common hypothesis in the sociological literature on fertility is that higher education gives a woman a broader set of options and different tastes regarding allocation of her time. In this section we attempt to determine if a wife's education interacts with the other explanatory variables in determining housework. The sample is first divided into three educational groups: women with education past high school, women with a high school diploma, and women with less than a high school diploma. Separate regressions are performed on each group and the residual sum of squares from this method is compared with the residual sum of squares from regression (2) to determine if the reduction in the residual sum of squares from the separate regressions is large enough to reject the hypothesis that the underlying structure is the same for all three groups.

The first panel of Table 3–9 presents the residual and incremental sums of squares along with the mean square error. The appropriate F-statistic is, at the 95 percent confidence level, $F_{0.05}(37,1010) \geq 1.41$, in

Table 3–9. Analysis of Covariance for Three Interactions

Source	Sum of Squares	df	Mean Square
Single equation	$.11078655 \times 10^{10}$	1047	$.10581332 \times 10^{7}$
Education of wife			
Separate equations	$.10738392 \times 10^{10}$	1010	$.10632071 \times 10^{7}$
Incremental	$.34026334 \times 10^{8}$	37	$.91963064 \times 10^{6}$
Potential income group			
Separate equations	$.10170119 \times 10^{10}$	989	$.10283234 \times 10^{7}$
Incremental	$.90853636 \times 10^{8}$	58	$.15664420 \times 10^{7}$
Religion of head			
Separate equations	$.10633856 \times 10^{10}$	1020	$.10425349 \times 10^{7}$
Incremental	$.44479895 \times 10^{8}$	27	$.16474035 \times 10^{7}$

order to reject the null hypothesis that there is no difference in residual variation between the two methods. For the education interaction the actual test statistic is $F_{ED.\ WIFE} = 0.86 < 1.41$; therefore, we cannot reject the null hypothesis. These data do not support the idea that child care behavior varies with the wife's education, but the data here tested are certainly not strong enough to allow us to dismiss the possibility of interaction entirely, especially in view of the results for differences due to potential income group, which follow.

Potential Income Group

A couple's potential income group is indicative of its long range position in the income distribution and can thus be expected to be a close proxy for socioeconomic status. Chapter Four details how money expenditures on children vary with respect to a couple's potential income and in this section we seek to determine if the influence on a wife's time allocation to housework is materially affected by the couple's position in the income distribution.

Again the sample is divided into three parts: the first part contains potential income group 1; the second, groups 2 and 3; the third, groups 4, 5, and 6. The second panel of Table 3–9 presents the pertinent data for the second analysis of covariance: with 58 degrees of freedom in the numerator and 989 in the denominator, the requisite F-value at the 95 percent level is approximately 1.33. The F-statistic calculated from the table is $F_{PIG} = 1.52$. We are, therefore, able to reject the hypothesis of complete homogeneity among the potential income groups.

The next question is, of course, whether the heterogeneity is manifested in the family size coefficients. Table 3–10 presents the regression coefficients on the family size variables from the three separate regressions.[r] Evidently, sampling error is beginning to obscure any systematic differences in child care behavior among the potential income groups. The number of cases associated with each dummy variable becomes in some instances quite small, as noted in the table for some of the more extreme examples.

Three more regressions were computed using a different specification for children in order to determine if it is possible to obtain an idea of at least the gross differences in child care behavior. In place of the dummy variable system, three interval variables representing the number of children 0 to 4.9 years, 5 to 12.9 years, and 13 to 17.9 years respectively are substituted. The coefficients attached to these variables represent mean housework per child in the given age group. They are very sensitive to actual differences in family size since the marginal housework time allocated to children declines rapidly in large families. The

[r]The other coefficients are omitted for clarity; they exhibit no consistent differences.

Table 3–10.   Family Size Coefficients for Two Interactions[a]

	Religion		Potential Income Group		
Variable	Non-Catholic	Catholic	Group 1	Groups 2 and 3	Groups 4–6
Number of children (dummy variables)					
Preschool only					
1	635[c]	176[c]	706[c]	402	600[c]
2	1089[c]	769	175	1113[c]	1473[c]
3+	1260[c]	1135[b]	870[b]	798[b]	2431[cb]
Preschool—grade school					
2	1124[c]	−154[b]	1785[c]	308	530
3+	781[c]	1298[c]	1202[c]	914[c]	1075[c]
Preschool—high school					
2	170[b]	332[b]	−290[b]	565[b]	429[b]
3+	1298[c]	1368[c]	1490[cb]	1329[c]	1240[c]
Grade school only					
1	465[c]	76[b]	404[b]	−108	1230[c]
2	546[c]	323	228	411	1237[cb]
3+	675[c]	175[b]	638[b]	678[c]	293[b]
Grade school—high school					
2	488[c]	936[c]	434	347	1015[c]
3+	539[c]	549	623[c]	334	800[c]
High school only					
1	244	462	239	360	205
2	152	149[b]	−230[b]	275	134
3+	136[b]	769[b]	0[b]	515[b]	295[b]

[a]Other variables in regressions omitted from this table.
[b]Less than ten cases in this category.
[c]The absolute value of this coefficient is twice its standard error.

coefficients on these variables are presented immediately below; the superscript c indicates that the coefficient is twice its standard error:

	Group 1	Groups 2 and 3	Groups 4–6
Preschool Children	327[c]	142[c]	166[c]
Grade School Children	267[c]	−23	−18
High School Children	−21	95	−8

These coefficients provide at least some indication that Group 1 mothers devote more time per child than do mothers in the other groups. However, mean family size is considerably smaller in Group 1 than in the other two parts representing Groups 2 through 6. Standard deviations of the variables also increase markedly, indicating that family sizes in the latter two regression groups are considerably larger than those in Potential Income Group 1. We cannot, therefore, infer differential child care behavior in the three groups holding family size constant, and thus we are left with the possibility that couples in potential income groups may exhibit differential child care behavior. We do not attempt to incorporate this into the analysis to follow, but future research efforts might profitably be directed to the detection of differences by economic status.[18]

Religion of the Husband

In Section 4 it was suggested that Catholic mothers might spend more time with their children than non-Catholics, and we see that the analysis of covariance suggests that there is a religious interaction. Whether or not this interaction is due to differences in child care behavior is problematical, but again the presence of an interaction of any type is an indication of the desirability of future research.

The last panel of Table 3–9 presents the analysis of covariance for the religious interaction. The sample was divided according to religious denomination of the head of household into Catholic and non-Catholic segments. The F-value required for rejection of the null hypothesis is $F_{0.05}(27, 1020) \geqslant 1.49$ while $F_{RELIGION} = 1.58$. Again the null hypothesis may be rejected; however, sampling variability stands in the way of a determination whether child care behavior is a source of the heterogeneity. The coefficients from the two regressions are presented in Table 3–10; note how many of the cells possess less than ten cases.

8. SUMMARY

In this chapter we have derived estimates of the cumulative time spent in child rearing by a mother during the eighteen years from birth to graduation from high school. Although the actual amount of time spent per child varies with birth order and spacing, the cumulative time spent per child averages close to 6,300 hours for moderate size families of two or three children. This figure does not include any of the time spent by the husband in child rearing activities because the available variable, housework, appears to be poorly suited to the measurement of these activities.

Children, especially those of preschool age, were also shown to have a marked impact on market work performed by the mother. It was estimated that preschool children were responsible for a net reduction in the mother's market work of nine hours per week. For children between the ages of six and thirteen the reduction in market work declines to four or five hours per week. However, it is incorrect to count time reallocated from market work as part of the time cost of child rearing. To the extent that this reallocation is a result of labor market rigidities, a case can be made that the value of time spent directly in child rearing is higher than it otherwise would be. However, time lost from market work but not utilized in child rearing is spent in other utility producing activities and cannot, therefore, be considered part of the opportunity cost of child rearing.[s]

Finally, several tests were performed in an attempt to determine if child care behavior varies systematically by religious denomination, the wife's education, or the husband's potential income group. Some support was found for differentials by religion and potential income group, although inadequate data preclude the construction of alternate estimates. Differentials in child care behavior should be subject to further exploration, especially as socioeconomic decision models of fertility are elaborated.

Even if these differentials are disregarded, the time cost of a child varies with the potential wage of the wife. Furthermore, since American

----

[s]A study recently prepared for the U.S. Commission on Population Growth counts all time lost from market work because of children as part of the cost of child rearing. Assuming that a mother is kept out of the labor force from the child's birth to age fourteen, the "average" mother of two children will lose $66,800 in wages. At the implied wage rate of $2.08 the same mother of two will incur a direct time cost of $26,927.68, which is only 40 percent of the Commission estimate. Moreover, the Commission report vastly overestimates the actual time lost from work by a mother of two, which is approximately 2,440 hours over the twenty years that children are in the family. Thus, adding both direct time cost and "lost" market time, we still arrive at a total time "cost" of children of only $32,002.88, which remains only 48 percent of the Commission estimate. It would therefore appear that the Commission study vastly overestimates the true time cost of children due to conceptual as well as empirical shortcomings. See Ritchie H. Reed and Susan McIntosh, "Costs of Children," in U.S. Commission on Population Growth and the American Future, *Economic Aspects of Population Change*, Elliott R. Morss and Ritchie H. Reed, Eds., Vol. II of Commission Research Reports (Washington, D.C.: U.S. Government Printing Office, 1972, pp. 337–350).

marriages exhibit substantial homogamy with respect to education and social origin, we expect to find a positive elasticity of opportunity cost with respect to a couple's potential income. In fact, for one of the surveys used in the test of the complete model in Chapter Six, the elasticity of opportunity cost per child with respect to the couple's potential income is 0.60.[t] Thus, part of the model of Chapter Two would appear to be substantiated: opportunity cost and long range income do in fact appear to be positively correlated. Once the elasticity of money expenditure with respect to potential income is determined we will be well situated to assess the impact of rising costs on the demand for children.

In this chapter a profile of time expenditures on children has been constructed that will allow the calculation of the time component of the opportunity cost of child rearing specified in the estimation model of Chapter Two. The discounted present value of time expenditures on children is computed in Chapter Five and is subsequently employed in Chapter Six as the determinants of the demand for children are statistically analyzed. In the following chapter the other major element of the opportunity cost of child rearing—money cost—is estimated for each potential income group, and preparations are thus complete for the estimation of the demand model of Chapter Two.

CHAPTER THREE

1. This point has been previously argued by Jacob Mincer using an estimation model considerably less comprehensive than the model presented in Chapter Two. See Jacob Mincer, "Market Prices, Opportunity Costs and Income Effects," in Carl Christ, ed., *Measurement in Economics,* Princeton: Princeton University Press, 1965, p. 107.

2. Ronald Freedman, L. Coombs, and L. Bumpass, "Stability and Change in Expectations About Family Size: A Longitudinal Study," *Demography* 2 (1965): 262.

3. James N. Morgan, I.A. Sirageldin, and N. Baerwaldt, *Productive Americans,* Ann Arbor, Mich.: Institute for Social Research, 1966, p. 2.

4. Becker, *op. cit.* (1965), quoting Sebastian de Grazia, offers this definition: Leisure is a state of being in which activity is performed for its own sake or as its own end (p. 503).

5. See also Pollack and Wachter, *op. cit.* on the analytical problems associated with jointness in the production of children and other household activities.

6. For a related approach to this problem see Robert Willis, "A New

[t]The survey cited is the 1967 Survey of Economic Opportunity. See Chapter Five for an explanation of the way opportunity cost and potential income were calculated for each family.

Approach to the Economic Theory of Fertility Behavior," *JPE Supplement, 1973:* S48–S53.

7. See also Wendy Lee Gramm, "The Demand for the Wife's Non-Market Time," *Southern Economic Journal* 41(1) (July 1974): 124–133; and Arleen Leibowitz, "Women's Allocation of Time to Market and Non-Market Activities: Differences by Education" (unpublished Ph.D. dissertation), Columbia University, 1972.

8. See, for example, Zick Rubin, "Do American Women Marry Up?" *American Sociological Review* 33 (1968): 750–760; and Bruce Warren, "A Multiple Variable Approach to the Assortative Mating Phenomenon," *Eugenics Quarterly* 13 (1966): 285–290.

9. See James N. Morgan, I.A. Sirageldin, and N. Baerwaldt, *Productive Americans,* Ann Arbor, Mich.: Institute for Social Research, 1966, p. 111; and J. Richard Udry, *The Social Context of Marriage,* Philadelphia: J.B. Lippincott, 1966, pp. 365–366.

10. John L. Thomas, S.J., *The Family Clinic* (1958), pp. 130–131, as quoted in Judith Blake, "Income and Reproductive Motivation," *Population Studies* 21(3) (November 1967): p. 197.

11. See Robert Willis, *op. cit.,* pp. S33–34.

12. For a discussion in support of this hypothesis see John B. Lansing, Thomas Lorimer, and Chikashi Moriguchi, *How People Pay for College,* Ann Arbor: Survey Research Center, University of Michigan, 1960, pp. 69–72.

13. Yoel Haitovsky, "Multicollinearity in Regression Analysis: Comment," *Review of Economics and Statistics* LI (4) (November 1969): 486–488.

14. See Reuben Gronau, "The Effect of Children on the Housewife's Value of Time," *JPE Supplement, 1973,* pp. S168–S201.

15. Udry, *op. cit.,* p. 366.

16. See Franklin M. Fisher, "Tests on Equality Between Sets of Coefficients in Two Linear Regressions: An Expository Note," *Econometrica* 38(2) (March 1970): 361–366, and the references therein cited. See also, Johnston, *op. cit.,* pp. 192–207.

17. See D.V. Lindley, *Introduction to Probability and Statistics: Part 2, Inference,* Cambridge, Eng.: Cambridge University Press, 1965, pp. 104ff.

18. C. Russell Hill and Frank P. Stafford, "The Allocation of Time to Preschool Children and Educational Opportunity," *Journal of Human Resources* 9 (Summer 1974): 323–341; Leibowitz, *op. cit.;* Peter Lindert, "The Relative Cost of American Children," Madison, Wis.: University of Wisconsin Graduate Program in Economic History Discussion Paper No. 7318, p. 19.

Money Expenditures on Children

1. INTRODUCTION

Aside from direct time expenditures, the second major element of the cost of children is the value of market purchased goods and services utilized in child rearing. These goods and services are combined with parental time to produce the consumption activity "child rearing" described in Chapter Two. This chapter focuses on five major market inputs into child rearing in an attempt to assess both the magnitude of money expenditures on children as well as the variations in money expenditure per child among the different potential income groups.[a] The items chosen, food, clothing, housing, education, and recreation, do not represent an exhaustive list of market inputs into child rearing; however, they may account for as much as 75 to 80 percent of all money expenditures on children.[1] Indeed, they may represent an even higher proportion of the expenditures expected by young couples who lack extensive experience in child rearing.

As with Chapter Three, the purpose in this chapter is to develop estimates of the cost of children by potential income group that can be directly applied to the behavioral model of fertility developed earlier. Ideally, of course, we would prefer to have direct information regarding the parents' own perceptions of the production function for children; however, data limitations force the use of actual expenditure data. This means both that we will again be assuming that actual behavior corresponds to expected behavior, and that only the outcomes of the implicit optimizing process involved in allocating expenditures to children will be

[a]These groups are defined and described in Section 2, Chapter Three. In 1960–61 the mean annual family income after taxes for each of the six groups was: (1) $9,413, (2) $7,275, (3) $6,280, (4) $5,936, (5) $5,418, (6) $4,349.

observed. This second implication indicates further that the ex post measures of the cost of children that are developed will not allow the analysis of substitution possibilities in the production of children. Consequently, we will not be able to determine the true quantitative impact on the cost of child rearing of a change in an input price except under the assumption of zero substitutability among inputs. Future microeconomic studies of fertility will have to develop much better descriptions of the production function for children if the responsiveness of fertility to changes in economic variables is to be understood.

Prior Contributions

An extensive literature exists detailing the consumption patterns of households.[2] These patterns are studied through data provided by household surveys as well as through the aggregate statistics derived from the national income and product accounts. In most of the research in this area the focus of concern has been on the income elasticity of expenditure on different items or classes. Demographic composition of the household has been introduced into these analyses mainly to eliminate bias in the estimates of income elasticity. Some of these studies, however, have attempted to estimate the proportion of expenditure accounted for by various members of the family. Two of the better known attempts are those by Henderson[3] and by Dublin and Lotka.[4] Recently, Henderson's methodology has been adapted by Espenshade to estimate the cost of children in the urban United States, and Peter Lindert has collected data from a number of sources in order to estimate the long term change in the relative cost of American children.[5] Moreover, recent work on welfare standards has brought about estimates of budgets for urban families[6] and the Consumer and Food Economics Research Division of the United States Department of Agriculture has been active in assessing the impact of children on expenditures in various consumption categories.[7]

These studies, especially the recent work by Espenshade and Lindert, serve as useful comparison pieces to the estimates derived below, but the present study has certain requirements that make the estimation of new cost data mandatory. The primary requirement is for cost data by potential income group, a categorization not available from any of the previously mentioned sources. Indeed, most of the cost estimates from these sources are presented in tabular form for "typical" families of "moderate" income and family size—descriptions that are not useful for the present study.

Since we are interested in the long range expenditures on children, and since the data are available only in the form of cross-sectional surveys, we are again forced to synthesize the experience of a single cohort from the behavior of many cohorts. To the extent that behavior changes between cohorts, estimates so derived may be seriously misleading. Easterlin,[8] for example, has postulated that the "baby boom" resulted at least in part from the fact that parents most responsible for it had been reared during the 1930s in a period that provided them with a singular set of attitudes about consumption and family size. He suggests that these attitudes are cohort specific and will not be present among the younger couples now entering the most fertile ages.

This could be troublesome, because in order to estimate the cumulative cost of children, we must make the assumption that expenditure behavior on children is reasonably similar across cohorts. If, however, distribution of expenditures on an item such as children's clothing over the socioeconomic spectrum is markedly different for two cohorts, attribution of the expenditure behavior of the older cohort to the behavior of the younger may lead to serious problems of measurement and interpretation. The problem, of course, stems from the lack of data on parents's projections of expenditures on children. Lacking these, the assumption that intercohort expenditure patterns are similar for parents of comparable social and economic position is virtually unavoidable.

Estimates of expenditure on children will be based mainly on the Bureau of Labor Statistics "Survey of Consumer Expenditure" (SCE) conducted in 1960–61 on a national sample of households. This survey examined in detail the annual consumption expenditures of 13,728 consumer units and provided along with these expenditure data limited information on the socioeconomic and demographic composition of each unit.[b] Criteria for selection of consumer units from the survey for this analysis included: (1) head of household was a white male; (2) his wife and own children *only* were present; and (3) he possessed an identified civilian occupation. Cases selected for analysis numbered 7,605 families. Data from other surveys are also utilized in the analysis of housing and education expenditures, and will be described in the appropriate sections. In Section 7 the estimates developed below will be compared to other recent attempts to measure the cost of children.

Estimation of Cumulative Expenditures on Children

The hypothesis to be tested in the following sections is that expenditures per child vary with the potential income group of the couple.

---

[b]Some critics have argued that the quality of the SCE cannot be very high, considering that respondents are required to exhibit substantial recall regarding budget allocations. Indeed, the data are coded in dollars *and cents* on the survey tape! The reader will agree from personal experience no doubt that the accuracy of such responses is problematic. See Houthakker and Taylor, *op. cit.*, Chapter 6.

Statistically, therefore, we must determine if the data allow us to reject the hypothesis that expenditure per child is homogeneous with respect to potential income group. As in Chapter Three we are again testing for interaction between long range income and expenditure per child.

For three of the expenditure items—food, clothing, and recreation—separate regressions are calculated for each of the six potential income groups. The regressions again employ a dummy variable representation of the children in the family that allows us to assess the impact of family size and age distribution on marginal expenditures on children.[c] The estimating equation is of the form:

$$E_i = \alpha_i + \beta_{i1}C_1 + \beta_{i2}C_2 + \ldots + \beta_{i16}C_{16} + e_i \quad (i = 1, 3)$$

where E_i represents money expenditure on the ith expenditure item, the C_j are the dummy variables representing children, and e_i is the error term. Since only those families of husband, wife and their own children are analyzed, the constant term α_i represents the expenditure on parents. Essentially then this regression equation allocates expenditures completely among all members of the family.

When all six regressions are performed, the resulting matrix of estimated coefficients

$$
\begin{matrix}
\beta_{i1}^{1} & \beta_{i2}^{1} & \ldots & \beta_{i16}^{1} \\
\beta_{i1}^{2} & \beta_{i2}^{2} & \ldots & \beta_{i16}^{2} \\
& \cdot & & \cdot \\
& \cdot & & \cdot \\
& \cdot & & \cdot \\
\beta_{i1}^{6} & \beta_{i2}^{6} & \ldots & \beta_{i16}^{6}
\end{matrix}
$$

allows us to assign cumulative expenditures on children in each of the potential income groups. Analyses of covariance may then be performed to determine if there are significant differences in expenditures on children among the six groups.

For two of these expenditure categories—food and recreation—estimation of expenditures on children is complicated by the fact that only family expenditures on the items are recorded. Use of the regression specification just described may lead to downward biased estimates of expenditure per child. The source of the bias and its effects on the estimates is examined in Appendix B.

Price and Income Changes

The allocation of resources among competing items of consumption is dependent upon tastes, relative prices, and real income. The relative

[c]Note that because of differences in data format the dummy variable system utilized in this chapter is somewhat at variance with that utilized in Chapter Three.

share of food expenditures in the family's budget is, for example, expected to decline as the family's real income rises because the income elasticity of expenditure on food is low. These considerations become relevant to the present study because the cost of child rearing is estimated from various surveys conducted at different times. Both the cost of housing and educating a child are estimated from surveys taken as much as nine years after the SCE. Estimated costs can be standardized on a base year through the use of price deflators supplied by the Office of Business Economics, but the changes in consumption due to changes in relative prices cannot be corrected. Thus the price of clothing relative to that of food may have risen in the period 1960 to 1969 but since the cross-price elasticities are unknown it is not possible to adjust for changes in consumption expenditure on different commodity groups due to changes in relative prices.

In addition, the rise in real income over the period results in shifts in the composition of total expenditure. Since income elasticities of expenditure differ, we would expect those commodity groups with low elasticities to account for a lower proportion of total expenditure in 1969 than in 1960. Therefore, since the income elasticity of expenditure on food is less than that of clothing, we would expect the ratio of food expenditures to clothing expenditures calculated from 1960–61 data to be too high for families in 1969, ceteris paribus. No attempt will be made to account for differing composition of expenditure due to changes in relative prices and real income, and the reader should remember that the relative weights assigned to the different expenditure items are only approximate.

2. FOOD EXPENDITURES ON CHILDREN

The food that a child consumes during his eighteen-year residence in the family constitutes a major cost of child rearing. It is particularly difficult to maintain separate food consumption standards in the family because provision of a different quality meal for children entails an additional preparation. As Duesenberry notes, "Children may eat a different menu from their parents, but if so, it is because they *like* peanut butter sandwiches."[9] We therefore expect to observe similar food consumption patterns among parents and their children. We also expect to observe a rise in food expenditure as we move from the lowest potential income group to the highest. The rise need not be substantial; numerous studies have demonstrated an income elasticity of expenditure on food of considerably less than unity.[10]

All the studies concerned with estimation of the cost of raising children have attempted to assign food costs. Most of these studies assign an "adult equivalent" value to children of different ages and compute the expenditures on food as a proportion of adult expenditures. For example, Dublin and Lotka produce estimates of the annual food expenditure on children in which a child progresses from 0.48 to 1.02 equivalent adults as he matures from birth to ages sixteen and above.[11] A procedure such as this can be misleading: even if food consumption follows the pattern postulated in the equivalent adult system, there is no guarantee that expenditure on food is proportional to the physical quantity of food consumed.

It is to be expected that there are substantial economies of scale inherent in food consumption both in terms of quantity discounts on purchased foodstuffs and in terms of changed methods of food preparation within the family. Larger families might engage more extensively in bulk buying and home production of food, and they may substitute direct labor in the form of gardening, canning, and freezing for money expenditure on convenience foods as the size of the family grows. Thus it is likely that expenditure estimates based on physical consumption data will overstate the money cost of food for children.[d] As the data to be presented below tend to confirm, marginal expenditures on food decline with family size.

Another method of assigning food costs is that used by Jean L. Pennock.[12] Using U.S. Department of Agriculture (USDA) food plans [13] she has assigned annual food expenditure per child on a normative basis. The procedure is somewhat arbitrary: expenditures are assigned on the basis of food plans that provide "well balanced" diets, not on the basis of an observed consumption pattern well balanced or not. Furthermore, the assumption is made that the child is fed according to a "low cost level" budget as defined by the USDA.

There are at least three reasons why this procedure is not adequate for our purposes. First, the assigned expenditure is based on what ought to be, not what actually is: there is nothing to guarantee that American families actually follow a well balanced diet as defined by the USDA. Second, the existence of economies of scale is apparently not considered in the calculation of total food expenditures, a point that parents may well consider when making family size decisions. Third, imposition of a low cost diet plan negates the whole point of searching for expenditure differences between potential income groups. Granted, these are not expected to be large, but they may well exist and it is a primary goal of this chapter to search for them.

As described in Section 1, the SCE sample has been divided into six potential income groups and a separate regression has been estimated for

---

[d]Part of this decline in dollar expenditure on food may be offset by the increased time cost of food preparation. This is an example of the substitution of time inputs for dollar inputs in the rearing of children.

each. Table 4–1 presents the results of these regressions. Included as regressors are dummy variables indicating every possible combination of family structure. The dummy variables represent children of three different age groups as well as different age distributions.[e] To interpret the table consider as an example a family with two grade school aged children which is a member of Potential Income Group 3. From column 3 of Table 4–1 we can write the following regression equation for this family:

$$E_{food} = 1162 + 465.$$

For this particular family all the dummy variables except that one signifying two grade school aged children are equal to zero. The dummy variable representing "2 children, grade school" is equal to one. Therefore, total estimated expenditure on food for the family is simply the sum of the intercept term (food consumption attributed to the husband and wife) and the coefficient of the relevant dummy variable (food consumption of two grade-school-age children). If the particular family contained only one grade-school-age child, the coefficient *465* would be replaced with the coefficient *234* in the table. Finally, if the family was composed of three or more children who ranged in age from preschool to adult (18 or over), total family expenditure on food would be 1162 + 494 = 1656.

The single most striking aspect of Table 4–1 is the almost uniform impact of the first child on total food expenditure in the family. At first glance, row 1 of the table (one child, preschool) would lead us to the implausible conclusion that the cost of feeding the first child is negative. More likely, however, is the possibility that the arrival of the first child results in basic changes in the food consumption practices of the husband and wife. Before the arrival of a child the couple may, especially if the wife works, eat more meals in restaurants and utilize high priced convenience foods for home consumption. With the arrival of the child the wife is more likely to be at home and to spend more time in food preparation. As a result, total money expenditures may well fall, reflecting the shift to home consumption and preparation and the concomitant shift from money expenditure to (nonmarket) time expenditure in the preparation of meals, even though the cost of feeding a child is positive.

The regression results lend mixed support to the idea of economies of scale in food consumption. If there are economies of scale associated with family size, food expenditure on two children in a given age group might be expected to be less than twice expenditure on one child. For example, from the previous example we have a ratio of expenditure: *2 children, grade school/1 child, grade school* = 465/234 = 1.44, indicating

[e]Note that due to the manner in which age of children was coded on the original SCE source tape it is not possible to construct a category "high school—adult." Families with children in this category are included in the "grade school—adult" classification.

Table 4-1. Allocation of Food Expenditures: Six Potential Income Groups

Dependent Variable: Annual Food Expenditures in Dollars

Independent Variable	(1)	(2)	(3)	(4)	(5)	(6)
			Regression Coefficients for Six Potential Income Groups			
1 child, preschool	-158	-215ᵃ	-215	-228ᵃ	-399ᵃ	90
2 children, preschool	-148ᵃ	81	-22	-73	-235ᵃ	192[a]
3+ children, preschool	-15	270[a]	260[a]	167[a]	40	296[a]
2 children, preschool—adult	119	335[a]	352[a]	306[a]	316[a]	372[a]
3+ children, preschool-adult	502[a]	593[a]	494[a]	508[a]	416[a]	568[a]
1 child, grade school	164	231[a]	234[a]	131	260[a]	204
2 children, grade school	376[a]	356[a]	465[a]	289[a]	326[a]	584[a]
3+ children, grade school	399	658[a]	167	783[a]	588	160
1 child, high school	335[a]	461[a]	369[a]	347[a]	305[a]	188[a]
2 children, high school	920[a]	785[a]	563[a]	365[a]	446[a]	440[a]
3+ children, high school	661[a]	734[a]	613[a]	238	295	241
1 child, adult	651[a]	482[a]	127	343[a]	-53	218
2 children, adult	456[a]	527[a]	587[a]	563[a]	370[a]	224[a]
3+ children, adult	882[a]	1140[a]	1428[a]	712[a]	980[a]	970[a]
2 children, grade school—adult	633[a]	612[a]	460[a]	365[a]	466[a]	458[a]
3+ children, grade school—adult	882[a]	829[a]	619[a]	831[a]	478[a]	566[a]
Intercept	1480	1194	1162	1128	1004	754
R²	0.22	0.25	0.21	0.23	0.18	0.22
N	1428	1474	1387	1383	1010	923

Source: Bureau of Labor Statistics, Survey of Consumer Expenditure sample tape (1960–61). Criteria for inclusion in the analysis: (1) head is white; (2) head is male; (3) only head, wife and own children present; (4) head possesses an identified civilian occupation.

ᵃDenotes that the estimated coefficient is at least twice its standard error.

.he money expenditure on food for two children is considerably less than twice that for one child.

Demographic considerations make the use of this expenditure ratio somewhat less than perfectly satisfactory. Presumably, as a child ages his requirement for food increases. Thus two children in a given age group may exhibit differing food requirements, and the declining cost of preparing a given quantity of food may be obscured by the increasing consumption of the older child. This problem would seem to be especially acute in the preschool age group where food requirements increase rapidly as the child ages. In addition, the coefficients from which these ratios are derived are subject to considerable sampling variability, as reference to the small number of cases in some of the cells (Table 4–2) will attest.

In spite of these difficulties, formation of these ratios within the homogeneous age groupings may provide some idea of the existence of declining marginal expenditures.[f] Comparison of one- and two-child families in Table 4–1 indicates that food expenditures on two children are less than twice as high as those on one child in fourteen of 24 cases. If preschool children are omitted the proportion with a ratio less than two rises to twelve in eighteen cases. Comparison of one-child and three- or-more-child families yields an overwhelming number of cases in which the expenditure ratio is less than three. There is, therefore, some support for the notion that marginal food expenditures decline with family size.

In order to determine whether food expenditures on children vary by potential income group, an analysis of covariance was performed and is presented in the first panel of Table 4–3. The value of the F-statistic needed to reject the hypothesis that the potential income groups are homogeneous with respect to food expenditures on children is (at the 99 percent level) somewhat less than 1.47. The F-value computed from Table 4–3 is 3.65, which allows us to reject the null hypothesis. Thus even in the food category, where it might be expected that expenditure differences are the smallest, we find significant variations among the potential income groups.

With the regression coefficients of Table 4–1 as a basis, mean annual expenditure per child and cumulative mean expenditure per child can be calculated for the six potential income groups. These calculations are presented in Table 4–4. Note that although there is a decline in expenditures across the potential income groups it is not uniform but rather U-shaped. This is especially true for preschool and grade school children, for whom expenditure per child is highest in Potential Income Group 6.

[f]It seems best to omit entirely the groups composed of children of more than one age group, as the problems of differences in demographic composition become excessive.

Table 4-2. Distribution of Cases—Six Potential Income Groups (SCE)

Independent Variable	Group Number					
	(1)	(2)	(3)	(4)	(5)	(6)
1 child, preschool	45	48	28	42	18	5
2 children, preschool	130	150	85	144	42	26
3+ children, preschool	142	122	74	111	63	31
2 children, preschool—adult	63	73	66	67	31	22
3+ children, preschool—adult	267	243	229	211	185	119
1 child, grade school	35	50	51	44	25	23
2 children, grade school	47	51	26	35	21	10
3+ children, grade school	9	11	3	10	3	3
1 child, high school	63	65	89	64	58	66
2 children, high school	39	47	22	21	27	17
3+ children, high school	4	5	9	2	4	2
1 child, adult	13	12	15	11	8	11
2 children, adult	52	60	81	65	60	72
3+ children, adult	10	8	16	11	15	19
2 children, grade school—adult	42	53	78	61	40	32
3+ children, grade school—adult	160	172	149	152	155	126
No children	307	453	366	332	255	339
N	1428	1474	1387	1383	1010	923

Source: See Table 4-1.

Table 4–3. Analysis of Covariance for Three Expenditure Items

Source	*Sum of Squares*	*df*	*Mean Square*
Food expenditures			
Single equation with dummies for income group	$.243 \times 10^{10}$	7584	$.320 \times 10^6$
Separate equations	$.234 \times 10^{10}$	7509	$.312 \times 10^6$
Incremental	$.856 \times 10^8$	75	$.114 \times 10^7$
F = 3.65			
Clothing expenditures			
Single equation with dummies for income group	$.153 \times 10^9$	7584	$.202 \times 10^5$
Separate equations	$.146 \times 10^9$	7509	$.195 \times 10^5$
Incremental	$.678 \times 10^7$	75	$.904 \times 10^5$
F = 4.63			
Recreation Expenditures			
Single equation with dummies for income group	$.489 \times 10^9$	7584	$.645 \times 10^5$
Separate equations	$.459 \times 10^9$	7509	$.611 \times 10^5$
Incremental	$.302 \times 10^8$	75	$.403 \times 10^6$
F = 6.59			

Only among children of high school age is there a reasonably uniform decline across the groups.

To obtain a rough idea of the responsiveness of expenditures per child to the parents' income, elasticities have been calculated using the double-log regression of the form $E = a + bY$, where E is the natural logarithm of cumulative expenditure per child on a commodity and Y is the logarithm of the family's cumulative total consumption expenditure over the eighteen years that a child remains in the family. For food expenditures the results are:

$$E_{food} = 5.69 + 0.24Y \quad R^2 = 0.24.[g]$$
$$(0.22)$$

The estimated income elasticity of 0.24 confirms that although food expenditure per child does vary over the potential income groups, the differences are not great.

[g]Since the coefficient of determination (R^2) is derived from grouped data, it does not represent explained interfamily variance of cumulative food expenditure. It is included here only for purposes of comparison with the double-log regressions of the succeeding sections.

Table 4–4.   Mean Annual and Cumulative Food Expenditure Per Child

Age of Child	Potential Income Group Number					
	(1)	*(2)*	*(3)*	*(4)*	*(5)*	*(6)*
Mean annual expenditure						
Preschool[a]	172[b]	167	176	153	158	186
Grade school[c]	223	238	232	153	219	242
High school[d]	370	386	294	238	254	212
Cumulative expenditure						
1960–61 prices	4444	4589	4151	3173	3747	3865
Adjusted to 1969 prices	5500	5679	5137	3927	4637	4783

Source: Table 4–1.

[a]Means in this row computed by division of the coefficient in row 4, Table 4–1 by two.

[b]This figure is the simple average of the two means in columns (2) and (3) of this table.

[c]Means in this row are the weighted averages of coefficients in rows, 6, 7 and 15 of Table 4–1 (e.g., 223 = 0.33[164 + 0.5(376 + 633)]).

[d]Means in this row are the weighted averages of coefficients in rows 9, 10 and 15 in Table 4–1 (e.g., 370 = 0.33[335 + 0.5(920 + 633)]).

3.   EXPENDITURES ON CHILDREN'S CLOTHING

The data available for analysis of expenditures on children's clothing provide the sole opportunity to analyze information pertaining specifically to children. The dependent variable for the regressions contained in Table 4–5 is "annual clothing expenditure for children aged zero to seventeen." As might be anticipated, the regression results are considerably more vivid than those of the previous section; the general level of explanation is much higher with the lowest coefficient of determination equal to 0.46. In addition, only four of the estimated coefficients are accompanied by standard errors more than half as large.[h] Furthermore, as reference to the second panel of Table 4–3 illustrates, we are able decisively to reject the hypothesis that families in the various groups are homogeneous with respect to clothing expenditure on children. The *F*-statistic equals 4.63, considerably higher than is necessary to reject the null hypothesis.

For grade-school-age children and older, average expenditure per child declines as family size increases. For preschool children declines in average expenditure per child are not as consistent when family size

[h]Indicated in the table by brackets. Note that the estimated intercepts are very close to zero since the dependent variable relates only to children.

Table 4-5. Allocation of Clothing Expenditure—Six Potential Income Groups[a]
Dependent Variable: Annual Expenditures on Children's Clothing in Dollars

Independent Variable	Regression for Group Number:					
	(1)	(2)	(3)	(4)	(5)	(6)
1 child, preschool	52	[38]	[42]	51	[28]	[43]
2 children, preschool	96	90	88	83	61	58
3+ children, preschool	144	166	155	126	115	103
2 children, preschool—adult	218	224	194	198	172	189
3+ children, preschool—adult	364	307	290	293	274	265
1 child, grade school	175	180	157	137	123	112
2 children, grade school	263	234	218	236	185	216
3+ children, grade school	394	397	201	344	232	148
1 child, high school	293	259	288	223	190	166
2 children, high school	529	432	413	354	328	255
3+ children, high school	436	544	519	429	316	213
1 child, adult	—	—	—	—	—	—
2 children, adult	—	—	—	—	—	—
3+ children, adult	—	—	—	—	—	—
2 children, grade school—adult	391	342	292	302	268	236
3+ children, grade school—adult	408	365	346	339	312	238
Intercept	0	0	1	1	4	0
R²	.50	.53	.52	.50	.46	.52
N	1428	1474	1387	1383	1010	923

Source: See Table 4-1.

[a]Brackets indicate that the absolute value of the coefficient is less than twice its standard error.

increases from one to two children. Again, demographic factors may be
behind these results. Families with only one preschool child may be
assumed to have a child at the young end of the age group since a
majority of couples plan to have a second child before the oldest
reaches five years of age. Families with two children might have one
very young child and one child aged four or above. If clothing costs
increase markedly as the child approaches six years of age, the economies derived from reuse of the first child's clothes might be offset
by the increased requirements of the oldest child.

Table 4–6 presents estimates of mean annual expenditure per child
for each of the three age groups as well as cumulative expenditures.
Cumulative expenditures for clothing the average child range from
$3,439 in Group 1 to $2,132 in Group 6 (1969 prices). The estimated
income elasticity of expenditure per child is given by the regression:

$$E_{clothing} = 0.24 + 0.67Y \quad R^2 = 0.92$$
$$(0.10)$$

4. RECREATION EXPENDITURES ON CHILDREN

Since many recreation expenditures on children normally encompass
those items considered to be luxuries, we would expect to find a high
income elasticity of expenditure across potential income groups. Recreation as defined in the SCE consists of expenditures on radio, television,

Table 4–6. Mean Annual and Cumulative Clothing Expenditure Per Child

Age of Child	Potential Income Group Number					
	(1)	*(2)*	*(3)*	*(4)*	*(5)*	*(6)*
Mean annual expenditure						
Preschool[a]	50	42	43	46	29	36
Grade school[b]	154	148	133	128	108	110
High school[c]	279	237	248	200	177	147
Cumulative expenditure						
1960–61 prices	2772	2474	2428	2172	1813	1718
Adjusted to 1969 prices	3439	3070	3013	2695	2249	2132

Source: Table 4–5.

[a]Means in this row are weighted averages of coefficients in rows 1 and 2, Table 4–5 (e.g.,
50 = .5[52 + .5(96)]).

[b]Means in this row are weighted averages of coefficients in rows 6 and 7, Table 4–5 (e.g.,
154 = .5[175 + .5(263)]).

[c]Means in this row are weighted averages of coefficients in rows 9 and 10, Table 4–5 (e.g.,
279 = .5[293 + .5(529)]).

phonograph equipment, and musical instruments as well as other items such as paid admissions to spectator events, costs of participant sports, club dues, and hobbies. Especially relevant to children, annual expenditures on pets and toys are also included. This definition of recreation is, however, faily restrictive: it does not include vacation and other recreational travel expenses, which are accounted for elsewhere; nor does it include expenditures on bicycles, boats, motorcycles, or motor scooters, which are accounted for under categories dealing with transportation. On the whole, then, recreation expenditures are probably more strictly defined here than would be optimal for our purposes, with some of the miscellaneous expenditure categories including items that more properly belong here. Consequently, expenditures on recreation are probably somewhat underrepresented in our calculations of the total money expenditure on children, although it is not clear that our estimate of the income elasticity of expenditure is biased by these omissions.

Table 4-7 presents the regression results for recreation expenditures on children. As is immediately apparent, children do not account for a great deal of the variation in total family expenditures on recreation: the coefficient of determination never rises above 0.11 and is much lower in most of the regressions. In addition, less than half the estimated coefficients are accompanied by small standard errors. The coefficients for preschool children are particularly small and unstable, and as a result I have arbitrarily set mean annual expenditure on preschool children to zero in the calculations reported in Table 4-8. Instability of the regression coefficients notwithstanding, we may safely reject the hypothesis that recreation expenditures per child are the same in the various potential income groups. The final panel of Table 4-3 presents the analysis of covariance for recreation expenditures and the resulting F-statistic ($F_{recreation} = 6.59$) allows us to reject the null hypothesis.

Cumulative expenditure on recreation per child (Table 4-8) rises quite sharply over the potential income groups. The regression estimate of the elasticity of expenditure yields:

$$E_{recreation} = -11.21 + 1.56Y \quad R^2 = 0.93$$
$$(0.21)$$

The estimated elasticity of 1.56 confirms the prior opinion that recreation expenditures per child are responsive to income differentials. In absolute value they are not large when compared to other expenditures such as food, clothing, and housing but their importance in the fertility decision might be considerably underrepresented because of our lack of information about the couple's perceived production function for children. Many of these recreational items may represent important expenditures to parents who are determined to provide their children with certain advan-

Table 4-7. Allocation of Expenditures on Recreation—Six Potential Income Groups
Dependent Variable: Annual Total Expenditure on Recreation

			Regression for Group Number			
Independent Variable	(1)	(2)	(3)	(4)	(5)	(6)
1 child, preschool	-5	-26	-2	11	-65	-44
2 children, preschool	2	0	0	19	-21	40
3+ children, preschool	-27	19	63[a]	46	5	7
2 children, preschool—adult	-2	51	75[a]	80[a]	-3	68[a]
3+ children, preschool—adult	80[a]	60[a]	88[a]	74[a]	61[a]	40[a]
1 child, grade school	129[a]	128[a]	80[a]	55	39	6
2 children, grade school	160[a]	95[a]	136[a]	100[a]	82[a]	39
3+ children, grade school	218[a]	43	1	98	-93	-50
1 child, high school	65	97[a]	131[a]	61[a]	19	69[a]
2 children, high school	120[a]	106[a]	45	104[a]	108[a]	104[a]
3+ children, high school	151	153	107	-3	32	38
1 child, adult	278[a]	46	-49	81	-72	55
2 children, adult	98[a]	129[a]	119[a]	138[a]	63[a]	13
3+ children, adult	124	144[a]	666[a]	238[a]	264[a]	200[a]
2 children, grade school—adult	163[a]	90[a]	74[a]	128[a]	52	76[a]
3+ children, grade school—adult	218[a]	127[a]	137[a]	126[a]	73[a]	118[a]
Intercept	314	236	168	170	140	90
R^2	.06	.04	.11	.05	.07	.07
N	1428	1474	1387	1383	1010	923

Source: See Table 4-1.
[a]The absolute value of these coefficients is at least twice as large as their associated standard errors.

Table 4–8. Mean Annual and Cumulative Recreation Expenditure Per Child

Age of Child	Potential Income Group Number					
	(1)	*(2)*	*(3)*	*(4)*	*(5)*	*(6)*
Mean annual expenditure						
Preschool	0	0	0	0	0	0
Grade school[a]	104	88	74	53	40	13
High school[b]	69	65	64	59	33	53
Cumulative expenditure						
1960–61 prices	1070	937	834	664	446	355
Adjusted to 1969 prices	1333	1168	1039	827	555	442

Source: Table 4–7.

[a]Means in this row are weighted averages of coefficients in rows 6 and 7, Table 4–7 (e.g., 104 = .5[129 + .5(160)]).

[b]Means in this row are weighted averages of coefficients in rows 9, 10 and 15, Table 4–7 (e.g., 69 = 0.33[65 + .5(120 + 163)]).

tages that they themselves never enjoyed. Without direct information about the parents' aspirations for their children it is difficult to know if the quantitative importance of the present estimates is a proper representation of parental perceptions.

5. HOUSING EXPENDITURES ON CHILDREN

Introduction

The arrival of a child generally signifies the requirement of additional living space for the family. Whether the family actually acquires additional space is, of course, subject to a host of factors including the supply of housing and the family's income position; however, it is extremely difficult to segregate children, and the quality of their housing will presumably approximate that of their parents. It is, for example, difficult to imagine a family's children living in crowded conditions while the parents are not. The cost of housing children is one of the major cumulative expenses in child rearing. Pennock [14] has estimated that cumulative expenditure (in 1969 prices) per child may average as high as $6,840, and although the range reported below is considerably less than this figure, the cost of housing a child remains a major item of expense.

Since housing is a joint consumption item, its availability or nonavailability may have a major impact on the family size decision. In Sweden, West Germany, Hungary, and other European countries, the inelastic supply of housing is thought to be a major factor behind delayed marriages and small families.[15] Inelastic housing supply gives rise to two situations that are suspected to be antinatalist in effect: (1) rationing of housing, resulting in long waiting lines and late marriage, and/or (2) extremely high prices for the available housing stock in the absence of rent control. Failure to build a certain type of housing (e.g., three- or four-bedroom apartments) might well influence couples to keep their family size down.

In the United States, where the supply of housing has historically been more responsive to consumer demand, our interest centers on differential expenditures for housing services. Space of a given quality is an input into the child rearing process and we would expect expenditure on it to vary with the socioeconomic status of the couple. The relevant variable for our purpose is actual expenditure for housing services during the eighteen years that the child is in the family. We are not, therefore, interested in that portion of allocations to housing that is intended merely for asset accumulation.[i]

There are two dimensions to the entity "housing services." The first is quantity, which can be measured in a number of ways such as number of rooms, total floor space, lot size, and so on. Limitations of available data force the selection of number of rooms as the dependent variable in the analysis that follows. The second dimension is the quality of housing, which can be measured as price per unit area or other measure of quality. Below, quality is measured as cost per room.

The actual measurement of housing services for renters is not a difficult task, since rent payments can be considered as the monthly payment for housing services. This is, of course, only the case from the point of view of the renter; from society's point of view, the monthly rent payment is composed of allocations for housing services, taxes, depreciation, profit, and so forth. Our concern, however, is with the point of view of the individual family for whom the monthly rent payment is strictly a payment for services received.

Home ownership presents a different problem. The monthly outlay of the homeowner consists not only of a payment for housing services, but a savings component that represents acquisition of an asset. In a perfectly competitive world, it would not, in principle, be difficult to compare housing services derived from owned and rental housing. The housing market, however, is far from perfect; an imperfect capital market restricts the quality range of housing that is open to purchase and

---

[i]Asset accumulation is, of course, an important part of the life cycle models of consumption and labor force participation employed by members of the Chicago-NBER school. Whether or not it is important for the fertility decision depends upon the degree to which child rearing affects net asset accumulation as opposed to distribution of assets within the couple's portfolio. There is virtually no information available on this question, as far as I am aware.

also precludes full participation in the housing market by low status families.[16] Geographical separation of owned and rental housing further isolates the two markets, not to mention the institutional barriers to home ownership that exist in suburbs and ethnic enclaves. The result is that identical monthly outlays for housing may signify wide differences in quantity or quality received.

If our main interest were in the situation at a given point, we could avoid the problem by considering owners and renters separately.[17] Our concern, however, is the long term experience of families from different income groups as they proceed through the child rearing cycle. Over time the typical family may both rent and buy depending on its demographic composition and the current income position of the head. We would expect, for instance, that high status families tend to buy homes earlier than do low status families and that they provide more room for younger children than do low status couples. In order to assess the cost of children at different ages, it is necessary to know something about the amount and quality of housing that they occupy at different ages. Therefore the differential incidence of renters in the potential income groups should be recognized as being germane to the analysis.

Data and Measurement of Housing Costs

Data from two sources have been utilized to measure two aspects of differential housing expenditure on children: (1) the differential impact of children on the quantity of housing (number of rooms) consumed, and (2) the differential impact of children on the quality of housing consumed. In this manner our understanding of the effect of children on housing expenditure will be considerably more complete than it would be if only total expenditures were observed.

The data are derived from the 1965 Productive Americans Survey and the 1970 Family Economics Survey, both conducted by the Survey Research Center of the University of Michigan.[j] Both surveys contain identical questions concerning the quantity of housing consumed by a family, but their measures of expenditure on housing differ. Quantity is measured as number of rooms used by the family and the quality of housing is measured by the construct "annual cost of housing per room." For renters, annual cost per room is defined as annual rent plus total expenditure on utilities plus amount saved on additions and repairs. For homeowners, annual housing cost is defined as 6 percent of 1970 house value (whether paid or foregone) plus property taxes, annual

[j]These surveys are described in Chapter Three. Data relate to 1964 and 1969 respectively.

utilities, and amount saved on additions and repairs.[k] Measures of housing cost are derived solely from the 1970 Family Expenditure Survey.

In the estimates that follow, cost per room for each potential income group is measured simply as the mean housing cost per room for the group as a whole. This measure presents two problems that should be mentioned. First, it does not allow us to assess the impact of parity on housing quality.[l] It is well established that total expenditure on housing declines with family size if income is controlled.[18] The average impact on quality for different age groups is illustrated in Table 4–9, where the dollar reduction in annual cost per room is presented for four different potential income groups.[m] The presence of adults results in the greatest reduction per person followed by children aged 0 to 5, children aged 13 to 17, and children aged 6 to 12.

The regression coefficients (which are the values reported in the table) appear to be relatively unstable and it is not clear how much reliance should be placed on them. Since the coefficients are similar in size and relatively small, we will ignore intragroup quality changes and utilize the potential income group averages (last row of Table 4–9) in the calculations that follow. It is not clear that the inaccuracy thereby introduced is greater than would be produced by an attempt to correct for differences in parity.

The second problem with this measure is that the marginal cost of housing children might be below the average cost of housing as a whole. It might be argued, for instance, that the type of space required by children is the cheapest to build and that the marginal cost of an additional bedroom will be less than the average cost. David, however, finds that there are few if any economies of scale in owner occupied housing and that cost per room is approximately constant in relation to number of rooms. He does find evidence of economies of scale in renter

[k]The commonly applied rule of thumb is that house value is approximately equal to 120 times monthly rent, but this rate of transformation appears to be essentially arbitrary. See Margaret Reid, *Housing and Income* (Chicago: University of Chicago Press, 1962, p. 43), and James N. Morgan, "Housing: The Relation of Quantity to Quality (cost to number of rooms) and the Relation of Housing Consumption (costs) to Income," February 1971 (mimeographed).

[l]In a personal communication, Beverly Duncan suggests that the impact of children on the cost of housing is not uniform. The first child represents completely new requirements as to amenities and location while succeeding children have a minor impact. Perhaps so, but it is also possible that family size influences housing adjustments. The two-child family has available a greater range of housing options than does the four-child family. For example, a couple with two children may be able to afford the higher costs of educating a child in a central city, while the couple with four children may be forced to move to a suburb to obtain comparable education for their children.

[m]Because of the small sample (only 1,960 cases), four of the six potential income groups were combined into two new groups. Groups 3 and 4 compose the new Group 3, and Groups 5 and 6 compose the new Group 4.

Table 4–9. Change in Annual Housing Cost Per Room (in Dollars) Caused by the Addition of a Person in a Specified Age Group[a]

Age Group	Potential Income Group				Row Average
	(1)	*(2)*	*(3)*	*(4)*	
Children 0–5	−16	−18[b]	−3	−19	−14
Children 6–12	−5	−12[b]	−8	17	−2
Children 13–17	−27[b]	−20[b]	−5	17	−9
Adults 18+	−28[b]	−36[b]	−44[b]	−40	−37
Average cost per room	418	349	313	253	333

Source: Productive Americans Survey sample tape (SRC study #721), Survey Research Center, University of Michigan; Office of Economic Opportunity, "Family Economics Survey," (SRC study #768), Survey Research Center, University of Michigan. Date of Survey: 1965 (Productive Americans); 1970 (OEO). Criteria for selection of subsample; (a) Head married, spouse present; (b) Age of head, 20–49; (c) Race of head, white; (d) Occupation and education of head reported.

[a]The values in the table are the coefficients of variables listed in the left-hand column in a regression that also included as explanatory variables age of head, disposable family income, and dummy variables representing date of survey, religion of head, and whether own or rent. In each regression, the unit of observation is the family.

[b]These coefficients were greater that twice their standard errors.

occupied housing, and, if the same relation holds for the housing contained in the current sample, we would expect to see a slight overestimate of the cost of housing a child, the magnitude of the overestimate depending on the proportion of renters in the given potential income group.

The families included in the following regressions were limited by five selection criteria: (1) head must be married with spouse present; (2) his race must be white; (3) his occupation and education must have been reported; (4) he must have been either an owner or a renter; and (5) his age must have been in the range 20 to 49. The last of these criteria was included because a family's adjustment to its actual housing needs often lags considerably behind those needs, and older couples often possess excess housing capacity after their children have left home. Inclusion of these couples in our regressions might lead to an underestimate of the actual housing requirements of children.[19]

Table 4–10 presents regression results for four potential income groups. Note that the regression equations omit a variable representing own/rent status, and this has pronounced effects on the family size coefficients, especially in the two upper income groups. With the home ownership variable omitted, the regression coefficients on family size reflect the differential incidence of home ownership among the four groups. In Groups 1 and 2 the incidence of home ownership is 74 and 69

Table 4–10. Determinants of Housing Size—Four Potential Income Groups

Dependent Variable: Number of Rooms in Dwelling

Independent Variable	Regression for Group Number			
	(highest) (1)	(2)	(3)	(lowest) (4)
No. children aged 0–5	.44[a]	.32[a]	.00	.24[a]
No. children aged 5–13	.36[a]	.35[a]	.18[a]	.17
No. children aged 13–18	.40[a]	.29[a]	.18[a]	.31[a]
No. adults (aged 18+)[b]	.74[a]	.43[a]	.42[a]	.39[a]
Date of survey				
1965	−0.29[a]	−0.14	−0.25[a]	−0.06
1970	—	—	—	—
Age of head	.05[a]	.04[a]	.03[a]	.04[a]
Intercept	1.99	2.46	2.97	2.72
R^2	.35	.30	.20	.15
N	695	569	636	160
Mean of dependent variable	5.96	5.50	5.25	5.50

Source: See Table 4–9.

[a]Absolute value of regression coefficient more than twice its estimated standard error.

[b]Excluding husband and wife.

percent respectively, while in the two lower groups percentage of families owning homes drops to 66 and 64 percent.[n] Thus the supply constraint implicit in the rental housing market may be operating differentially in each of the four income groups and may account for the differential impact of children as represented in the regression results.

In Table 4–10 the estimated coefficients for the dummy variable representing the 1965 survey are uniformly negative. Their size and the uniformity of sign appear to arise mainly from the omission of current income from the regression equation. With current disposable income included in the regression, the coefficient on the survey dummy becomes insignificant in all four cases. Thus the survey dummy acts as a partial surrogate for current income as a main determinant of differences in housing size between the two survey periods.

The coefficient for the variable "age of head" is also consistently positive in each of the four regressions. This is again due in part to the omission of disposable income as a predictor; however, the inclusion of disposable income merely reduces the size of the coefficient without

[n]Note that we have controlled for potential income in the analysis by dividing the sample into four potential income groups. Current income has consequently been omitted from the regressions; however, this omission results in only very minor increases in the family size coefficients, primarily because the "date of survey" dummy acts as a proxy for current income.

eliminating its significance. Thus there appears to be an effect, independent of income, operating through age of head to increase the consumption of housing as the head grows older. However, it may simply be the operation of the lag previously mentioned in the adjustment of housing size to needs.

Our interest centers around the impact of children on the quantity of housing consumed by the family. As these results conclusively show, the number of rooms occupied by the family increases with family size. In addition, a child's contribution to the consumption of housing is positively related to the potential income of the family. Note the differences in magnitude between the coefficients in the first two columns and those in the last two. This implies that children of high status families occupy more space than do the children of lower status couples, an impression that is further strengthened when mean housing cost per room is observed for the different groups. The last row of Table 4–9 presents mean annual cost per room for each of the four groups. Average cost per room is seen to be positively associated with potential income group, and it would appear that both quality and quantity are positively associated with economic status.

However, in Table 4–10 the progression from Group 1 to 4 is not entirely smooth. With respect to the impact of children, Group 3 appears to be rather dissimilar to the other three groups. The estimated impact of children aged 0–5 is nil, while it is positive but relatively low for children of other ages. Note also that on the average, Group 3 families occupy housing with the smallest number of rooms. With respect to the demographic features for which the groups can be compared, Group 3 is unexceptionable. The proportion of families renting, the age of head, and the mean number of children in the three age groups are all reasonably similar for the four groups. Nevertheless, even though mean annual disposable income is $1,000 higher for Group 3 families than for Group 4 families, mean size of dwelling is lower.

One possible explanation for this is that families in Group 3 are more heavily concentrated in central cities where supply constraints are operating. It is likely that the occupations found in Group 3 are more heavily concentrated in urban areas and that families in the group are not as likely to be able to afford suburban or spacious urban housing. The members of Group 3 are seen to be concentrated in jobs that may be considered to be urban in nature, while Group 4 contains farmers, farm managers, and ranchers, groups for which the housing supply constraint might not be as tight.[o]

---

[o]See Table 3–1. In the four-group classifications, the groups contain the following education-occupation subgroups (identified by rank on mean total expenditure in Table 3–1): 1(1,2,3,4,); 2(5,6,7,8); 3(9,10,11,12); 4(13,14,15,16).

Since consistent measures of location for the two sample surveys are not available, it is not possible to test this hypothesis; accordingly, I have proceeded with the assignment of cumulative housing cost for Group 3 by arbitrarily assuming that a child aged 0–5 requires the same amount of space as does a child of the same age in Group 4.[p] With this adjustment, cumulative housing expenditure on the average child in each potential income group ($CHE_j, j = 1, 4)$) can be calculated by summing over eighteen years the average annual cost of housing. That is:

$$CHE_j = 6 \ SIZ_{1j}P_j + 7 \ SIZ_{2j}P_j + 5 \ SIZ_{3j}P_j,$$

where P_j is mean expenditure per room in Group j, and SIZ_{ij} $(i = 1, 3)$ is the room requirement per child in each of the three different age groups for the four potential income groups. Cumulative housing cost for a child aged zero to eighteen is:

Group 1	Group 2	Group 3	Group 4
$2989	$2031	$1122	$997

These estimates are considerably smaller than those derived by Pennock.[20] Her estimates of the cumulative cost of housing children range from $5,500 to $6,900 in 1969 prices, while Group 1 expenditures do not even approach the low end of this range. The difference arises, I would suspect, due to the fact that Pennock allocates total annual expenditures on housing on a per capita basis, giving children the same share of total housing costs as their parents. But this would appear to overestimate the impact of children on housing costs. Couples living alone consume most of the housing (kitchen, bathroom, living room, garage, etc.) that is required by families with children. The cost of housing children is the cost of marginal additions to housing, and the per capita assignment of housing expenditures would appear to assign to children expenditures that would continue to be made in their absence. Thus the lower figures are probably closer to the true marginal cost of housing a child and to the parents' assessment of these costs.

The elasticity of cumulative housing expenditure per child is large; the double-log regression is:

$$E_{housing} = -9.53 + 1.46Y \quad R^2 = 0.74,$$
$$(0.43)$$

[p]Beverly Duncan suggests that the differences between Group 3 and Group 4 may arise because of a differential incidence of public housing in the two groups. She notes that in Census tract data, a primary way in which public housing is detected is through a decrease in room crowding. Unfortunately our data do not identify families living in public housing so we cannot explore her hypothesis.

suggesting that a 10 percent increase in cumulative income will lead roughly to a 15 percent increase in the cumulative cost of housing a child.

6. EDUCATION EXPENDITURES ON CHILDREN

The last of the major categories of expenditure on children may be, given present knowledge, the most difficult to assess. There are essentially two levels of education: (1) mandatory primary and secondary education, and (2) optional college, junior college, or technical education. Regarding the former, the question is not whether to send a child to school but rather where to send him. Post high school training offers considerably more choice both on the part of the parents and, possibly, the child. Note again that the ideal variables for our purposes would be direct measures of parents' perceptions of the educational requirements implied by child rearing. In the absence of these direct measures, we again resort to the assumption that young parents' expectations are essentially the product of a normative response to the behavior of older couples in the same potential income group. Since the sorts of educational commitments that high status parents make to their children are suspected to be considerably stronger than those of other parents, it would be particularly useful to have direct measures of a couple's status achievement motivation as well as its actual expectations regarding the cost of child rearing.

Preprimary, Primary, and Secondary Schooling

Since the quality of schooling that parents provide their children is open to choice, it might be suspected that couples making decisions about family size take into account the educational options open to them. Parents may perceive high or low substitutability among the different types and qualities of education available, and this will have a marked impact on their assessment of the cost of precollege schooling. Unfortunately we do not know the degree to which parents perceive different qualities of schooling to be substitutable, but given massive migrations of parents to suburbs and the vigor with which urban ethnics defend their "neighborhood" schools, it might be suspected that the quality of schooling matters very much to parents in all classes.

Even if data were available regarding parents' attitudes toward quality differentials, valuation of these different levels is no easy task. To obtain a given level of quality the couple has, theoretically at least, the option of sending a child to a private or parochial school or of moving to a district containing schools with the requisite features. There is a cost associated with this given quality level, but it may be very difficult to measure.

For example, if parents move to a suburb partly to obtain schools of a certain type, the cost of this choice may be reflected in higher property taxes, increased commuting costs for the husband, and so on. However, residential location is due to a host of factors only one of which may be desired school quality, and the problem of measuring the cost of achieving a certain type of schooling without direct access to parents' own perceptions appears to be virtually insurmountable.

Even given the difficulty of the task, there is a strong prima facie case to be made for the hypothesis that upper status parents do in fact spend more on their children's precollege education:

1. Among whites preschool attendance of children is strongly related to the education of the head of the household.[21] This relationship holds especially strongly for three- and four-year-olds, ages where public education is still rare. The relation also exists when school attendance is tabulated by job status [22] and by family income, although the latter relationship may be due in part to the contribution of working wives to family income.[23]
2. In addition, the composition of nursery school and kindergarten classes is heavily weighted toward upper income, white collar children, [24] an unsurprising finding in view of the fact that large proportions of upper income families send their children to private kindergartens and nursery schools.[25] The income and occupational composition of private primary and secondary schools also follows the pattern reported for nursery schools and kindergartens.
3. Moreover, private school attendance is closely associated with the metropolitan status of a community, with a higher proportion of total enrollment being found in private schools in central cities than elsewhere. This suggests that the private–public school dichotomy is representative of quality differentials in large cities.[26]
4. Finally, among Catholics the same sorts of considerations seem to apply, with upper status families more likely to send their children to parochial schools, especially when religiosity and other pertinent factors are controlled.[27]

These findings are suggestive, but the data are not available in enough detail to justify attempts to construct estimates of the precollege costs of educating children. The estimates of education costs to be reported below therefore omit precollege costs. This could bias our estimates of expected costs; however, this depends crucially upon the degree to which awareness of these precollege costs is actually incorporated into the fertility decision. As reference to Table 4–12 below will indicate, the quantitative impact of these costs appears to be very small and the spread between potential income groups similar to that for college expenditures. Consequently, possible measurement errors would not appear to be a serious problem.

Expenditures on College Education

The decision to educate children past the mandatory requirement necessitates two interdependent choices on the part of parents. The first is whether to send children to college at all and the second is where to send them. Parents of young children almost invariably expect their children to attend college. Lansing, Lorimer, and Moriguchi [28] found in 1960 that in families with children aged one to nine, 73 percent of the couples surveyed expected their children to attend college and 63 percent expected their children to graduate. This finding, confirmed in other surveys, is also illustrated by regression (1) in Table 4–11.

A subsample of white couples with children under age ten was selected from the Productive Americans Survey. They were asked the question, "Do you have any children who will go to college?" and their answer was scored "1" if yes and "0" if no. Eighty-seven percent of the couples replied that they expected at least one of their children to attend college. With a question such as this, the result may in fact tell us more about the form of the question than the intentions of the parents regarding their college plans for children. Nevertheless, it is interesting to note that even with a regression of such low explanatory power as regression (1) it is possible to detect a gross difference in the plans of high status couples and lower status couples. A place in one of the two highest potential income groups (husband) and some training past high school (wife) would seem to lead to a higher expectation of college attendance, a finding in accord with results to be presented below regarding actual college attendance.

Of course, many children never attend college; only 44 percent (49 percent male and 39 percent female) of all 1960 tenth-grade students had entered a degree credit granting college or university within one year after their scheduled graduation from high school.[29] Even allowances for the lower attendance rates of minority students would not result in a significantly higher attendance rate by white students. Two not necessarily conflicting conclusions can be drawn from these results: (1) parents of young children may be unwarrantedly optimistic about the chances of their children attending college; and (2) as the younger cohort approaches college age, the overall proportion of children attending college will rise significantly. Admittedly there has been a secular increase in the

Table 4–11. College Attendance (Actual or Planned) of Children of Parents from Different Potential Income Groups

Independent Variables	Regression 1[a]	Regression 2[b]
Education of wife		
0–5 grades	−0.34	−0.31[c]
6–8 grades	−0.17[c]	−0.10
9–11 grades	−0.04	−0.05
High school	—	—
High school +		
nonacademic training	0.09	0.15
College, 1–3 years	0.03	0.27[c]
College, college +		
graduate training	0.08	0.21[c]
Potential income group		
of husband		
(1) highest	0.14[c]	0.32[c]
(2)	0.14[c]	0.13
(3)	—	—
(4)	0.06	0.05
(5)	−0.01	−0.05
(6) lowest	0.04	−0.17[c]
Intercept	0.79	0.50
R^2	0.10	0.23
N	378	460
Mean of dependent variable	0.87	0.48

Source: Productive Americans Survey (1964).

[a]Couples selected for this regression are parents of children the oldest of whom is less than ten years old. The dependent variable was scored "1" if parents answered yes to the question, "Do you expect any of your children to attend college?" Otherwise it was scored zero.

[b]Couples selected for this regression were parents of at least one child eighteen years or older. The dependent variable was scored "1" if they answered yes to the question, "Are any of your children attending (or have they ever attended) college?" Otherwise it was scored zero.

[c]Absolute value of coefficient more than twice the estimated standard error.

proportion of eligible eighteen-year-olds who attend college,[q] but there is also evidence that the parents of young children are optimistic in their forecasts of college attendance.

Again our interest centers around the parents' perceptions of a college education as an input into the production function for children. If it could be measured directly, the ideal information would be information

[q]The proportion of the population having attended college has risen from about 7 percent (cohort of 1875–85, Lansing, Lorimer, and Moriguchi, *op. cit.,* p. 102) to almost 33 percent (cohort of 1941–45, U.S. Bureau of the Census, *Current Population Reports,* Series P-23, No. 37, "Social and Economic Characteristics of the Population in Metropolitan and Nonmetropolitan Areas: 1970 and 1960" Washington, D.C.: (U.S. Government Printing Office, 1971, Table 11, p. 53)). This trend might begin to flag if the rate of return to a college education falls relative to that attainable in occupations not requiring the degree.

on the parents' standards for their children, both in terms of college attendance or nonattendance and in terms of the perceived substitutability of different types and qualities of post high school education. An index of expected cost of college education could be developed from this measure that might be used as an indication of the seriousness with which future educational outlays are viewed.

Needless to say, the data necessary to generate these direct measures are not at hand and surrogate methods must be employed. The effort would appear to be worthwhile: a significant proportion of the white wives interviewed in the 1960 GAF survey gave as the primary reason for limiting their families to a given number the explanation that they "couldn't afford to educate more children."[30] It would appear, therefore, that a sizable proportion of couples are aware of the cost of educating children when they make their family size decisions.

To measure parents' expectations about future education costs, we will again assume that the parents of young children expect to spend about as much as older families in the same potential income group. For example, it is assumed that the young lawyer with preschool children plans to spend approximately as much on his children's educations as his older colleagues do on their children's. Even given this assumption, our estimates of educational expenditures remain crude. We can arrive at only very general estimates of expected quality (price) and the actual frequency of attendance is our only indication of the probability of future attendance.

Even so, there is some evidence indicating that the elasticity of educational expenditures with respect to potential income is high. Table 4–12 presents the results of six regressions calculated using data from

Table 4–12. Annual Education Expenditures on Children (1960–61 Dollars)

Dependent Variable: Total Annual Expenditure on Education in Dollars

Independent Variable	*Regression for Potential Income Group Number*					
	(1)	*(2)*	*(3)*	*(4)*	*(5)*	*(6)*
Number of Children						
0–17	12	8[a]	5[a]	3	5[a]	2
18+	281[a]	140[a]	58[a]	58[a]	59[a]	39
Intercept	59	32	15	22	14	10
R^2	.24	.16	.13	.10	.14	.09
N	1428	1474	1387	1383	1010	923

Source: Bureau of Labor Statistics, Survey of Consumer Expenditure Tape (1960–61).
[a]These coefficients are at least twice their standard errors.

the 1960–61 Survey of Consumer Expenditures. It shows that mean education expenditures per child (tuition, fees, books, supplies, etc.) rise precipitously from the lowest potential income group to the highest. In fact, the annual income elasticity of expenditure per child is 2.79, highest of any of the elasticities previously presented in this chapter. Note that mean annual expenditure even for the highest potential income group is low—the reason being, of course, that the coefficients represent mean annual expenditure per child whether in college or not. The sample includes many families who are not contributing anything toward the college education of those members eighteen or older.

To develop a measure of expected educational expenditures we (1) derive a prediction of expected annual cost for each potential income group, (2) predict the probability that a child in a given income group will actually attend college, and (3) define estimated educational expenditures as: 4 × (mean annual cost) × (probability of attending college) = expected educational costs.

Using this formula, the maximum expenditure possible for a child would be equivalent to a four-year education at a college of given quality.[r] The minimum possible expenditure would be zero years of college. Thus the expected cost of educating a child will be a function both of the predicted quality of the school and of the predicted probability of attendance.

Prediction of College Quality.   Attempts to relate the quality of a college attended by a son or daughter to the socioeconomic status of the parents are not plentiful. In 1966 the Census Bureau gathered information during a Current Population Survey that provides at least a partial understanding of the correlation between college quality and parents' status. Table 4–13 presents the reported results of this survey. The quality of the college is, in this case, represented by an index of freshman aptitude.[s] The table demonstrates that college quality and status are related, whichever measure of status is employed. The differences in attendance are most pronounced at the high and low quality institutions. In all instances children of higher status parents attend high quality schools with a much greater frequency (30–40 percent) than do children of the lowest status families (13–16 percent). The proportion attending low quality schools is reversed: between 6 and 16 percent of

[r]Postgraduate education is arbitrarily excluded from the calculations. If parents also consider these costs in formulating their fertility decisions, our cost estimates will be biased downwards.

[s]Rankings are based on aptitude scores derived in conjunction with "Project Talent." Annually, beginning in 1960, the test scores of high school students in the United States were combined in an index against which the aptitude scores of entering freshmen at various colleges were compared.

Table 4–13. Rank of College Attended by Dependent Family Members 14 to 34 Years Old Enrolled in College, by Education and Occupation of Family Head and Family Income, for the United States: October 1966

(Civilian noninstitutional population)

Subject	Total enrolled	Rank of College by Index of Freshman Aptitude			
		Low	Medium	High	Not Available
Percent Distribution					
Years of school completed by family head					
Total, dependent family members	100.0	17.0	43.3	21.5	18.2
3 years of high school or less	100.0	20.5	42.8	14.6	22.0
4 years of high school	100.0	19.5	45.8	17.3	17.5
1 to 3 years of college	100.0	16.7	43.7	20.8	18.9
4 years of college	100.0	10.6	38.0	37.3	14.3
5 or more years of college	100.0	6.9	41.2	39.9	12.5
Occupation of Family Head					
Total, dependent family members	100.0	17.0	43.3	21.5	18.2
Head in experienced civilian labor force	100.0	16.5	43.7	22.1	17.8
White collar workers	100.0	13.6	42.5	27.9	16.1
Professional, technical, & kindred workers	100.0	11.6	44.6	29.8	14.2
Other white collar workers	100.0	14.6	41.5	27.0	17.1
Blue-collar, service, and farm workers	100.0	20.8	45.4	13.5	20.3
Head not in experienced civilian labor force	100.0	22.9	39.4	16.0	22.1
Family income[a]					
Total, dependent family members	100.0	17.0	43.3	21.5	18.2
Under $3,000	100.0	24.5	25.8	14.5	35.8
$3,000 to $4,999	100.0	25.3	37.7	11.3	25.9
$5,000 to $7,499	100.0	20.5	47.6	13.3	18.7
$7,500 to $9,999	100.0	17.3	47.0	17.9	17.9
$10,000 to $14,999	100.0	15.9	45.7	22.6	16.0
$15,000 and over	100.0	9.5	38.9	39.9	11.9
Not reported	100.0	15.4	40.9	23.8	20.4

Source: U.S. Bureau of the Census, *Current Population Reports*, Series P20, No. 183, "Characteristics of Students and Their Colleges: October 1966," U.S. Government Printing Office, Washington, D.C., May 22, 1969, page 20.

[a]Income during preceeding 12 months.

high status children are attending low quality schools while 20 to 25 percent of the lower status children are attending low quality colleges.

The Census Bureau also reports that the educational level of the parents is associated with whether the children are enrolled in a two- or a four-year college.

> Among students enrolled in college, 21 percent of those whose family head had completed less than 4 years of college were attending 2-year college and 79 percent were attending a 4-year college. However, only 10 percent of those students whose family head had completed 4 or more years of college were enrolled in 2-year colleges and 90 percent were enrolled in 4-year colleges.[31]

Similar results were reported for differences by income and by occupation.

Table 4–14 suggests that family income and cost also are positively related. Thirty-four percent of the college students from families with an income of $15,000 or more attend high cost colleges, with the proportion declining to 8.9 percent for those families in the $3,000–$4,999 range. Also note from Table 4–14 that the proportion attending private colleges is positively correlated with income, a relation that holds even if those students attending church related schools are removed from consideration.

The findings of Lansing et al. contribute indirectly to the impression that higher status families pay more for the education of their children. These authors find a direct partial correlation between family income and contribution to a child's college expenses. In addition, the level of education of the husband or wife is positively correlated with the parents' contribution.[32]

The last source of evidence, which will be the basis of the estimations below, is a study by Roy Radner and L.S. Miller.[33] In this study Radner and Miller attempt to determine the probability that a student of given intelligence (as measured by a test score equivalent to that received on the Scholastic Aptitude Test) and family income will attend colleges of different types. They specify eleven different types of colleges spanning the range from a local publicly supported junior college to "superior" high cost private universities.

Data for the estimates come from two samples of 190 students each taken in California and Illinois. Using a generalized form of logit analysis, they arrive at a set of probabilities that exhaust the possibilities available to the high school senior: no school, or one of eleven different types of colleges. The predicting equation is designed so that the probabilities of attendance can be generated in any of a number of situations. For

Table 4-14. Family Income of Dependent Family Members 14 to 34 Years Old Enrolled in Four-Year Colleges, by Selected Characteristics of the College, for the United States: October 1966
(Civilian noninstitutional population)

Characteristics of the College	Total Enrolled	Under $3,000	Family Income[a]					
			$3,000 to $4,999	$5,000 to $7,499	$7,500 to $9,999	$10,000 to $14,999	$15,000 and Over	Not Reported
Percent Distribution								
Type of control								
Total	100.0	(B)	100.0	100.0	100.0	100.0	100.0	100.0
Public	57.6	(B)	69.3	59.7	65.5	55.7	46.4	55.5
Private	37.2	(B)	27.1	33.8	29.9	39.9	49.5	36.0
Private secular	18.5	(B)	10.0	15.6	13.2	20.1	28.2	19.8
Church related	18.6	(B)	17.1	18.2	16.7	19.8	21.3	16.3
Roman Catholic	8.8	(B)	2.1	6.5	7.6	9.9	11.8	11.9
Other	9.8	(B)	15.0	11.7	9.1	9.9	9.5	4.4
Not available	5.3	(B)	3.6	6.5	4.5	4.4	4.3	8.4
Tuition and Fees								
Total	100.0	(B)	100.0	100.0	100.0	100.0	100.0	100.0
Under $250	27.1	(B)	34.6	31.3	28.0	25.0	19.0	28.5
$250 to $499	31.3	(B)	37.1	29.5	38.3	31.1	27.2	28.5
$500 to $999	15.3	(B)	15.7	17.4	12.5	15.5	15.4	13.7
$1,000 and over	21.0	(B)	8.9	15.3	16.7	24.0	34.3	20.3
Not available	5.4	(B)	3.6	6.5	4.5	4.4	4.3	9.0

Source: U.S. Bureau of the Census, *Current Population Reports*, Series P-20, No. 183, "Characteristics of Students and Their Colleges: October 1966," Washington, D.C.: U.S. Government Printing Office, May 22, 1969, p. 13.

(B) Base less than 150,000.

[a]Family income preceding twelve months.

example, if there is no local junior college available to a student, the probabilities of attendance conditioned on that fact can be calculated.[t]

In Table 4–15 are calculated the probabilities that a student of average intelligence (SAT score of 550) will attend schools of different types given (1) that he must attend school (i.e., nonattendance is not an option), and (2) that he has all eleven types from which to choose. The assumption of average intelligence is admittedly arbitrary but not unreasonable when it is recognized that parents are making final decisions about fertility long before the success of their children in school has been established.

To compute the probabilities of attendance of each type of school it is necessary to compute P_{ik} the probability that person i attends school k from the expression:

$$P_{ik} = exp(aX_{ik} + bY_{ik})/ \sum_{j \in J_i} exp(aX_{ij} + bY_{ij})$$

where $X_{ij} = A_i S_j/1000$ and $Y_{ij} = C_{ij}/I_i$.

A_i is an ability score for student i, I_i is a measure of income for student i, S_j is a measure of the "selectivity" or "quality" of alternative j, and C_{ij} is the out-of-pocket dollar cost to i of going to j. J_i is the set of alternatives open to student i.[34]

As an example, suppose there exists a student of average ability ($A_i = 550$) and means (family income: $I_i = \$10,870$). The probability that he attends a local public state college ($C_{ik} = \$400$, $S_k = 519$)—given that all eleven types are available—is 0.22, the quantity shown in Table 4–15. The probability that the same student attends a superior high cost private university is only 0.04, while the probability that he attends a public local junior college is 0.13. Once we know the probability of attending each of the eleven types of institutions it is a simple matter to calculate the expected annual cost of college for a student of given intelligence and family income. For the student of our example, the expected annual cost is $1,012.

In Table 4–15 the expected annual expenditure on education is calculated for a typical student from each of the six potential income groups. The mean disposable income used for each group is the mean disposable income of all families in the group, provided that they have at least one child of college age. Younger families and childless couples are excluded because the Radner-Miller calculations are based on the current income of families with children of college age and inclusion of the

---

[t]The cost figures are unadjusted for scholarships, grants-in-aid or loans.

Table 4-15. Prediction of College Quality

Income of Family Ability of Student School Type	Cost	Selectivity	$20,002. 550.	$14,448. 550.	$11,720. 550.	$10,870. 550.	$9,316. 550.	$5,532. 550.
PUB-JC-LOCAL	290.	430.	0.090	0.109	0.124	0.131	0.144	0.199
PVT-JC-MEDIUM COST	2200.	430.	0.035	0.030	0.025	0.023	0.019	0.007
PVT-JC-HIGH COST	3200.	430.	0.022	0.015	0.011	0.010	0.007	0.001
PUB-ST-COL-LOCAL	400.	519.	0.160	0.190	0.213	0.222	0.242	0.308
PUB-ST-COLLEGE	1300.	519.	0.103	0.103	0.101	0.099	0.094	0.063
PVT-COL-MEDIUM COST	2200.	519.	0.067	0.056	0.048	0.044	0.037	0.013
PVT-COL-HIGH COST	3200.	519.	0.041	0.029	0.021	0.018	0.013	0.002
PUB-UNIV-LOCAL	540.	564.	0.206	0.238	0.261	0.270	0.287	0.331
PUB-UNIVERSITY	1440.	564.	0.133	0.129	0.123	0.120	0.112	0.068
PUB-UNIV-HIGH COST	3200.	564.	0.056	0.039	0.028	0.025	0.018	0.003
PVT-UNIV-SUPERIOR	3200.	625.	0.087	0.061	0.044	0.038	0.027	0.005
Expected mean annual cost			$1409.	$1207.	$1064.	$1012.	$907.	$618.
Potential income group number			(1)	(2)	(3)	(4)	(5)	(6)

younger couples and couples without children might result in distorted estimates of the group means.

Expected annual cost of educating a child is seen to be correlated with family income, rising from $618 for the lowest potential income group to $1,409 for the highest. Quality of schooling would therefore appear to be strongly related to the potential income group of the family.

Prediction of College Attendance.   As is evident from regression (1) of Table 4–11 virtually all parents of young children report high aspirations for their children; however, it is also evident from regression (2) that performance falls far short of intention. Our problem is to determine the degree to which aspirations and realities interact to influence the parents' perceptions of the future costs of educating their children.

Lansing, Lorimer, and Moriguchi demonstrate that many parents wait until their children are in high school before actually beginning the accumulation of the funds necessary to educate their children.[u] Nevertheless, the anticipation of these costs may be a very real element in the decision to limit family size. Regression (1) provides some support for the idea of differential aspirations among various status groups in the population, and regression (2) provides stronger evidence for differences in actual performance; however, neither of these measures is entirely adequate for our purposes.

Underlying a stated desire to send children to college is the commitment to send them, and it is this commitment that determines the seriousness with which parents view the impending costs. It is my suspicion that, on the average, the commitment to send children to college is positively related to the education and the socioeconomic status of the parents. Again, the lack of data truly germane to our needs seriously inhibits our ability to correctly assign expected educational expenditures, and we are forced to assume that actual performance in the potential income group is at least proportional to the commitment of the group as a whole.

Our analysis would gain considerably in explanatory power if we were to possess direct information concerning each couple's perception of the role of education in the rearing of its children. Use of the group's actual performance as a substitute is ultimately insufficient and implies that the aspirations represented by regression (1) carry no weight in the fertility decision. But in the absence of a plausible way in which to incorporate the parents' aspirations (as inadequately represented in the regression),

---

[u]Lansing, Lorimer, and Moriguchi, *op. cit.*, pp. 36–43. They indicate that only about half the families interviewed reported that they had money set aside that was available to finance their children's college education.

reliance upon the potential income group's actual behavior would appear to be the safer course to follow.

The last column of Table 4–16 presents the proportion of families in each potential income group with at least one child aged eighteen or more who has attended college. It is this column that we will use as our index of the commitment with which parents view the impending education of their children. The index itself is derived with no reference to whether the parents actually pay for college, or to whether the children actually complete the course of study. Furthermore, it must again be emphasized that the strength of the parents' commitment at the time of the fertility decision and their subsequent performance may for many reasons be quite dissimilar.

Note in Table 4–16 that with two exceptions college attendance is positively related to the family's potential income group and wife's education. The exceptions are the higher proportion of college attendance in Group 4 families than in Group 3 families and the apparently stronger impetus for attendance in families where the wife's education is "College, 1–3 years" as opposed to "College, college plus graduate training."

The reversal between Groups 3 and 4 may be due to sampling error, or it might represent an actual behavior difference. The latter possibility become credible if we note (Table 3–1) the education and occupation of members of the two groups. In Group 3 we find clerical and sales workers and craftsmen and foremen, both with an education of high school diploma or less. In Group 4, on the other hand, are self-employed businessmen, operatives and kindred workers, and laborers and service workers. Those included in the latter two groups possess education of nine or more grades while self-employed businessmen in Group 4 possess education up through a high school diploma. Group 4 thus contains the better educated members of two of the lower status occupation groups. Compared to the members of Group 3, families in Group 4 may well exhibit a higher degree of motivation to send their children to college. In calculating expected expenditure on education we will assume that the reversal of the two groups does in fact represent true behavior differences.

Both the regression and the cross-tabulation lead us to the conclusion that the potential income group of the father and the education of the mother have a strong positive impact on the college attendance of the children. Due to the small size of the sample it is not possible to account for both these effects; rather, as our index of commitment we will use the proportions displayed as the last column of Table 4–16. Thus the index for Group 1 families is 0.97 and that for Group 6 families is 0.24.

Using the formula presented earlier in this section we can calculate

Table 4–16. Proportions of Families with at Least One Child 18 Years and Older Who Has Attended or is Attending College

Husband's Potential Income Group	Wife's Education							
	0–5	6–8	9–11	HS	HS+	Col, 1–3	Col, Col+	Row Avg.
1. (highest)			(1)[a]	(.8)	(1)	(1)	1	.97
2.	(.12)	(.5)	(.6)	.53	.92	.92	(.75)	.74
3.	(1)	.45	.4	.58	(.67)	(.75)	(.5)	.47
4.		.4	.47	.68	.54	(.78)	(.67)	.56
5.	(.12)	.40	.30	.38	(.67)	(1)	(1)	.41
6. (lowest)	0.0	.21	.37	(.14)	(0.0)	(.6)	(1)	.24

Source: Productive Americans Survey, 1964.

[a]Cells containing ten cases or less are indicated by parentheses.

N = 460 cases.

Mean for entire sample = 0.48.

expected educational costs for a child from each of the six potential income groups:

Group 1	Group 2	Group3	Group 4	Group 5	Group 6
$5,467	$3,573	$2,000	$2,267	$1,487	$593

Calculated in this manner, expected educational costs run from 29 percent of the major cost of child rearing for Group 1 parents to 6 percent for Group 6 parents.[v]

Whether estimates such as these adequately represent the impact of expected educational costs on the parents' fertility decision is an open question. Two aspects of the estimates are open to query: do these estimates properly represent the order of magnitude of expected educational costs? Do they reflect the actual income elasticity of expenditure that prevails across the potential income groups?

With respect to the first question little can be said except to note again that the cost of educating children appears to be a major reason given for family limitation.[35] The impact thus represented would appear to be far more than the actual mean expenditure figures given in Table 4–12 above. With respect to the second question it is possible to compare the expenditure elasticities for (1) actual expenditures per child (Table 4–12) and (2) the predicted expenditures per child just developed. For actual expenditures we have:

$$E_{education} = -27.61 + 2.79Y \quad R^2 = 0.91$$
$$(0.44)$$

and for predicted expenditures the regression is:

$$E_{education} = -24.6 + 2.81Y \quad R^2 = 0.98.$$
$$(0.21)$$

The elasticity of predicted expenditure is 2.81 while the elasticity of actual expenditure is 2.79, which is remarkably close agreement considering the considerable differences in the methods by which the two expenditure figures are calculated. Therefore we can say with reasonable assurance that the elasticity of expenditure across potential income groups, whether actual or predicted, is quite high—a finding that may have particular importance for the fertility decision. Much of the difference in the perceived cost of child rearing between potential income groups may be due to the large impact of projected educational expenditures on the decisions of upper income parents.

[v]These percentages reflect the share of education in the undiscounted cumulative cost of child rearing. Discounted at a rate of 4 percent annually, the share of education costs in the present value of total money expenditures is 22 percent for Group 1 and 4.4 percent for Group 6.

7. SUMMARY

The goal of this chapter has been to approximate the perceived money cost of children to parents in each potential income group through the use of actual expenditure data. It was argued in Chapter Two that parents have to make final fertility decisions in the face of incomplete information about the future costs of children. In the absence of direct information about their expectations, we have proceeded on the assumption that couples in particular occupational-educational subgroups tend to look to older members of the same class in order to make their projections. Moreover, it was hypothesized that social and institutional factors dictate a rise in the perceived money cost of a child as potential income rises.

The data summarized in Table 4–17 provide striking evidence of the strong positive correlation of cumulative money expenditure per child with potential income of the parents. Intergroup income elasticities of expenditure are without exception positive, varying from 0.24 to 2.81, and the overall elasticity of expenditure per child is 0.99. Nevertheless,

Table 4–17. The Cumulative and Discounted Money Cost of a Child (in Dollars)

Potential Income Group	Food	Clothing	Rec- reation	Housing	Education	TOTAL
1960–61 prices						
1. (highest)	4444	2772	1070	a	a	
2.	4589	2474	937	a	a	
3.	4151	2428	834	a	a	
4.	3173	2172	664	a	a	
5.	3747	1813	446	a	a	
6. (lowest)	3865	1718	355	a	a	
1969 prices						
1. (highest)	5500	3439	1333	2989	5467	18,728
2.	5679	3070	1163	2031	3573	15,521
3.	5137	3013	1039	1122	2000	12,311
4.	3927	2695	827	1122	2267	10,838
5.	4637	2249	555	997	1487	9,925
6. (lowest)	4737	2132	442	997	593	8,947
1969 prices, discounted at 4 percent						
1. (highest)	3796	2242	876	2207	2536	11,657
2.	3900	2009	763	1493	1664	9,829
3.	3616	1959	674	841	932	8,022
4.	2780	1785	529	841	1056	6,991
5.	3273	1466	361	707	693	6,500
6. (lowest)	3457	1422	262	707	276	6,124

aCalculations made on the basis of 1969 prices.

although these findings suggest a strong positive correlation, they do not actually confirm that expectations of young couples do indeed correspond to the behavior of older couples in the same potential income group, nor that parents, by and large, take these expected expenditures as given rather than actively considering the quality-quantity tradeoffs proposed by Becker and his associates.

The actual role of expected costs of child rearing in the fertility decision cannot be understood from these data or from any other currently available; however, since the results provide strong support for the hypothesized positive correlation between expenditure per child and potential income, and since there is no empirical evidence favoring the quantity-quality tradeoff approach of Becker, we will, in the following chapters, proceed to test the structural model of Section 3, Chapter Two.

Although the money cost estimates of this chapter have been developed for use in an analytical model of fertility, it is useful to compare them with two recent statistical descriptions of the cost of raising a child. The first of these, developed by Reed and McIntosh for the U.S. Commission on Population Growth and the American Future, presented money cost estimates for low and moderate income families of $27,109 and $39,924 respectively (1969 prices).[36] Comparison with Table 4–17 shows that the Commission estimates are far higher than those developed here. Indeed, our estimate of a cumulative money cost of $18,728 for high status families is only 70 percent of the Commission estimate for low status families.

Clearly there are some major discrepancies between the two methods. However, the Commission estimates are based almost entirely on the cost estimates developed by the U.S. Department of Agriculture and Jean Pennock, which have been discussed earlier in the chapter. These estimates exhibit some severe methodological shortcomings that tend to inflate the cost of children considerably, and since the Commission estimates rely on them almost entirely, it can confidently be asserted that they too are likely to be considerably inflated.

The methodology employed in the recent monograph by Espenshade is to be preferred on all counts,[37] but especially because it displays a concern for analytical consistency not apparent in the USDA estimates. Espenshade applies a refined and extended version of a methodology first employed by Henderson to the urban sample drawn from the same Bureau of Labor Statistics Survey of Consumer Expenditures utilized in this chapter. He estimates the cumulative cost of rearing a child from birth to age eighteen for low, middle, and upper income families and finds that this cumulative expenditure per child in two-child families ranges from $27,971 to $35,822 in 1960–61 prices. Converting to 1969 prices[w] we find the cumulative per child cost for low, medium and high income families to be $34,493, $38,125, and $44,456 respectively. These estimates are again considerably higher than those developed in this chapter; indeed, Espenshade's estimate for middle income families is roughly the same as the Commission estimate reported above.

How might we account for the differences? First, it should be noted that the concerns that led Henderson to employ his methodology were quite different from those of the present chapter. Henderson was concerned with the impact of children upon the material welfare of parents; indeed, his definition of the cost of a child was ". . . that increase in the family income which will enable parents to spend as much on themselves as they did before they had a child."[38] Essentially, then, Henderson's purpose was to "compensate" parents for the presence of a child in the family, the amount of this compensation being equal to the actual reduction in resource expenditure on the parents necessary to support a child.

Ideally, every expenditure category should be reported separately for parents and their children so that actual expenditures per child might be ascertained. Unfortunately, the consumer expenditure data are rarely collected in a manner which makes this possible, and Henderson was forced to base his measure of adult well-being on the impact of children on the consumption of items for which it could safely be assumed that there is no demand from children. This led to his choice of expenditures on alcohol and tobacco as the instrument to measure differences in adult welfare between families of different sizes. However, as Espenshade correctly notes, expenditures on this category are frequently underreported and subject to strong taste variation.

To avoid this and other problems, Espenshade defines two families' standards of living to be equivalent if they spend the same proportion of their after-tax income on food. This represents a considerable departure from the original Henderson methodology and gives rise to two problems, one conceptual and the other empirical. Conceptually, when we measure the cost of children to parents we are attempting to measure the degree to which parents are required to spend money on their children that they would have spent on themselves in the absence of children— thus, Henderson's use of alcohol and tobacco expenditures. The key assumption in picking any expenditure category is that the requirement of children for the category is zero. Obviously, this does not hold for food expenditures. Who then is being compensated for the presence of children in Espenshade's analysis.?[x] Does this standard of living criter-

---

[w]Using the Gross National Product Deflator.

[x]Espenshade implies (*op. cit.*, p. 26) that he would have used expenditures on adult clothing had they been available on the version of the tape supplied to him.

ion accurately reflect the dollar loss of goods and services by parents as they have children?

Empirically there is another problem with the use of food as the standard of living measure. We observed in Section 2 of this chapter that total family expenditures on food declined with the addition of young children. It was hypothesized that this may be due to an abrupt change in the couple's life style as they become parents and begin eating more meals at home, while substituting home time for the market time embodied in convenience foods and restaurant meals. If so, how are we to assess the change in value of total food expenditures as a couple acquires children? Both the conceptual and empirical issues just noted raise some doubt about the use of food as the compensation criterion.

Moreover, due to a difference in data format on the tapes utilized by both Espenshade and me, we are able to compare estimates of expenditures made on clothing. Espenshade's tape did not provide a breakdown of family clothing expenditures for adults and for children separately, while the tape utilized in the present chapter does contain such a breakdown. Consequently, the cumulative expenditures on children's clothing reported in this chapter are as accurate as the underlying interview information will allow, and it is constructive to compare them with Espenshade's estimates.

It should be remembered that Espenshade is utilizing only the urban portion of the SCE sample and that he utilizes only three income categories; furthermore, the estimates in this chapter are confined to white couples only and family size is coded quite differently than the measure utilized by Espenshade. We will compare cumulative clothing expenditure estimates in my Potential Income Group 1 (the highest level) with Espenshade's upper income group.[y]

From Table 4–5 we can calculate cumulative clothing expenditures expressly for children in one- and two-child families. In a one-child family cumulative expenditure is estimated to be $3,002, which is less than half of the $6,167 calculated indirectly by Espenshade. Remember, the clothing expenditure data utilized in this chapter relate specifically to expenditures on children's clothing while Espenshade's estimates are derived from total family expenditure on clothing. In a two-child upper income family, Espenshade calculates that the average cost of clothing each child is $4,352, while the average cost calculated from Table 4–5 is $2,531.[z] Thus the Espenshade estimates are 72 percent higher than the

[y]Since the mean family income in Potential Income Group 1 is higher than the mean family income in Espenshade's upper income group, the comparisons made here will understate the true differences if Espenshade's clothing estimates are too high and will overstate the differences if they are too low.

[z]The exact figure depends on the timing and spacing of children. The mean figures reported in Table 4–6 are for one- and two-child families in a given age group.

actual money expenditures on clothing reported in the survey. Moreover, Espenshade's estimates imply a 29.4 percent fall in the average cost of clothing a child as family size increases from one to two children, while the decline implied in the direct expenditure data is only about 15.7 percent. Therefore, if the direct expenditure data are at all indicative, the sharp decline in expenditure per child on clothing noted by Espenshade may be in large part an artifact of the estimation method.

These rough comparisons imply, with respect to clothing expenditures at least, that Espenshade's estimates are rather considerably too high. Moreover, since he has demonstrated that the estimates are internally consistent, it must be asked whether or not there is a systematic upward bias in the total estimate. If for two-child families the upward bias is on the order of 72 percent mentioned above, the discrepancy between this chapter's money cost estimates and Espenshade's is largely resolved. However, the components of total cost derived in this chapter come from widely differing sources and a detailed comparison of them with Espenshade's estimates would likely reveal more about the differing assumptions made in analysis than the true money cost of children.

CHAPTER FOUR

1. See Thomas J. Espenshade, *The Cost of Children in Urban United States,* Berkeley, Calif.: Institute of International Studies Population Monograph Series No. 14, 1973, p. 42, for some comparable figures.

2. See, for example, S.J. Prais and H.S. Houthakker, *The Analysis of Family Budgets,* Cambridge, Eng.: Cambridge University Press, 1955; R.G.D. Allen and A.L. Bowley, *Family Expenditure: A Study of Its Variation,* London: Staples, 1935; J.R.N. Stone et al., *The Measurement of Consumers' Expenditure and Behavior in the United Kingdom, 1920–1938,* Vol. 1, Cambridge, Eng.: University Press, 1954; H.S. Houthakker and L.D. Taylor, *Consumer Demand in the United States* (2d. ed.), Cambridge, Mass.: Harvard University Press, 1970.

3. A.M. Henderson, "The Cost of Children," *Population Studies* 3 (1949): 130–150; 4 (1950): 267–298; See also W.F.F. Kemsley, "Estimates of Cost of Individuals from Family Data," *Applied Statistics* I (3) (November 1952): 192–198; and M.H. Quenouille, "An Application of Least Squares to Family Diet Surveys," *Econometrica* 18 (1) (January 1950): 27–44.

4. L.I. Dublin and A.J. Lotka, *The Money Value of a Man* (rev. ed.), New York: The Ronald Press, 1946, Chapter 4.

5. Espenshade, *op cit.;* Peter Lindert, "The Relative Cost of American Children," Madison, Wis.: University of Wisconsin Graduate Program in Economic History Discussion Paper No. 7318.

6. E.g., Bureau of Labor Statistics, *Three Standards of Urban Living for a Family of Four,* BLS Bulletin No. 1570–7.

7. See various issues of United States Department of Agriculture, Consumer and Food Economics Research Division, *Family Economics Review.*

8. R.A. Easterlin, "Relative Economic Status and the American Fertility Swing," Philadelphia, 1972 (mimeo.).

9. J.S. Duesenberry, "Comment," in Universities—National Bureau of Economic Research, *Demographic and Economic Change in Developed Countries,* Princeton: Princeton University press, 1960, p. 234.

10. See H.S. Houthakker, "An International Comparison of Household Expenditure Patterns, Commemorating the Centenary of Engel's Law," *Econometrica* 25 (October 1957): 532–551: Prais and Houthakker, *op. cit.,* pp. 93–98; and Houthakker and Taylor, *op. cit.,* p. 62.

11. Dublin and Lotka, *op. cit.,* pp. 49–50.

12. Jean L. Pennock, "Cost of Raising a Child," *Family Economics Review* (March 1970): 13–17.

13. See any issue of *Family Economics Review*—e.g., June 1970, pp. 11–13.

14. *Loc. cit.*

15. United Nations, *Determinants and Consequences of Population Trends,* Population Studies, No. 17, New York, 1953, Doc. No. ST/SOA/SER. A/17, p. 216. See also Cicely Watson, "Housing Policy and Population Problems in France," *Population Studies* VIII (1) (1953): 14–15.

16. See, for example, R.A. Haugen and A.J. Heins, "A Market Separation Theory of Rent Differentials in Metropolitan Areas," *Quarterly Journal of Economics* 83 (4) (November 1969): 660–672.

17. See Martin David, *Family Composition and Consumption,* Amsterdam: North-Holland Publishing Co., 1962, Chapter 5, for an example of this approach.

18. *Ibid.,* p. 79.

19. *Ibid.,* pp. 60–61, 70–71.

20. Pennock, *loc. cit.*

21. U.S. Bureau of the Census, *Current Population Reports,* Series P-20, No. 268, "Nursery School and Kindergarten Enrollment: October 1973," Washington, D.C.: U.S. Government Printing Office, 1974, Table 4.

22. *Ibid.,* Table 5.

23. *Ibid.,* Table 6.

24. *Ibid.,* Table 3.

25. U.S. Bureau of the Census, *Current Population Reports,* Series P-20, No. 222, "School Enrollment: October 1970," Washington, D.C.: U.S. Government Printing Office, 1971.

26. *Ibid.*

27. Andrew M. Greeley and Peter H. Rossi, "Correlates of Parochial School Attendance," *School Review* 72 (Spring 1964): 54–55. Dean E. Hinmon, "Why Some Parents Do/Do Not Enroll Their Children in Catholic Schools," *Catholic School Journal* (September 1966): 88 *et seq.*

28. John B. Lansing, Thomas Lorimer, and Chikashi Moriguchi, *How People Pay For College,* Ann Arbor: Survey Research Center, Institute for Social Research, September 1960, p. 100.

29. Paul Feldman and Stephen A. Hoenack, "Private Demand for Higher Education in the United States," in Joint Economic Committee of the Congress of the United States, *The Economics and Financing of Higher Education in the United States,* Washington, D.C.: U.S. Government Printing Office, 1969, p. 390.

30. P.K. Whelpton, A. Campbell, and J. Patterson, *Fertility and Family Planning in the United States,* Princeton: Princeton University Press, 1965, p. 68. Four to 9 percent of the wives (depending on age) gave this as the primary reason for not expecting more children.

31. U.S. Bureau of the Census, *Current Population Reports,* Series P-20, No. 183, "Characteristics of Students and Their Colleges: October, 1966," Washington, D.C.: U.S. Government Printing Office, 1969, p. 2.

32. Lansing, *op. cit.,* pp. 32–36.

33. R. Radner and L.S. Miller, "Demand and Supply in U.S. Higher Education: A Progress Report," *American Economic Review* LX (2) (May 1970): 326–334.

34. See Radner and Miller, *op. cit.,* p. 331. The coefficients *a* and *b* are derived using the sample of 190 California high school seniors.

35. Whelpton, et al., *loc. cit.*

36. Ritchie H. Reed and Susan McIntosh, "Costs of Children," in U.S. Commission on Population Growth and the American Future, *Economic Aspects of Population Change,* Elliott R. Morss and Ritchie H. Reed, ed., Vol. II of Commission research reports, Washington, D.C.: U.S. Government Printing Office, 1972, pp. 337–350.

37. Espenshade, *op. cit.*

38. Henderson (1950), *op. cit.,* p. 268.

Chapter Five

The Assignment of Income and Costs

1. INTRODUCTION

In this chapter the construction of the empirical measures of the theoretical variables defined in Chapter Two is described and discussed. The exact procedures utilized in the formation of empirical estimates of potential income, time costs, and money costs are set out in some detail; however, the reader who is more concerned with the substantive issues raised in this study may wish to proceed directly to the following chapter without taking the essentially technical detour that this chapter represents.

As has often been stressed in prevous chapters, the empirical validation of the socioeconomic theory of fertility presented in Chapters One and Two is made very difficult by the absence of many of the analytically relevant variables called for by the theory. In particular, information about the parents' projections of the opportunity cost of children (both time and money costs), and their estimates of long run income potential are lacking. We have proceeded on the assumption that these expectations can be approximated by utilizing the experience of older cohorts in the same occupational and educational groups. This is at best a crude assumption, which might introduce considerable error into our attempts to test the demand for children model empirically, but, given the data currently available, it is virtually unavoidable. Thus, the following sections of this chapter describe in some detail the manner in which the estimates of potential income and costs are constructed and applied to the sample families to be analyzed in Chapter Six.

2. DERIVATION OF EXPECTED WAGE STREAMS

The crucial element in the determination of the long range earning power of the husband and wife is the prediction of the wage rate expectations of each. The factors that determine the wage rate potential of the couple are numerous, and include ability, ambition, education, occupation, ethnic or religious identification, and so on. In the absence of direct information on the couple's wage rate expectations, wage streams will be assigned that depend exclusively upon the husband's education and occupation and the wife's education at the time of the survey. These expected wage streams will be utilized to generate the predicted component of the couple's potential income; this represents the mean lifetime earnings potential of a couple of given occupational and educational characteristics. The relative income component of potential income, described in Section 3, will be utilized to account for individual differences among couples that cause them to deviate from the expected group means. The relative income component will thus account to some degree for differences in ability, ambition, and tastes specific to given couples.

The Husband's Wages

Data used to predict the husband's wage stream come from the combined Productive Americans and Family Economics surveys. In these surveys, an hourly wage rate was computed for each husband based on total hours spent working and total income from work. Consequently, some of these wage rates represent composite remuneration from two or more jobs.[a] It should be reiterated that assignment of wages on the basis of current occupation may lead to measurement error because of the possibility of significant job mobility in the future.

The combined Productive Americans and Family Economics samples have been divided into four age groups in order to allow for temporal variation in the ranking of the occupation-education groups by wage rate and to allow for a closer approximation of actual wage changes over time. For each of the age groups a separate regression is performed with variables representing education, occupation, age, and survey included as predictors. The dummy variable representing survey is included to net out differences in wage rates resulting from the five years intervening between the two surveys. A metric variable representing age was in-

[a]For example, 22 percent of the employed family heads in the Family Economics survey held more than one job.

cluded in order to gain an idea of the annual rate of change in wages during each of the four age periods.

Table 5-1 presents estimates of male hourly wages at ages twenty, thirty, forty, and fifty by education and occupation. Use of these estimates and application of the annual rate of increase (also shown in the table) allows a wage stream for each of 56[b] occupation-education groups representing an hourly wage at each age from twenty to 59 years. Finally, each of these wage streams has been smoothed through an approximation with a polynomial regression of degree two. Samples of the resulting wage streams are graphed in Figure 5-1. These wage streams provide the basis on which the expected component of the husband's potential income is calculated.

The Wife's Wages

The value of a wife's time spent in market work is not only a component of the couple's potential income, it also represents the minimum value that a woman might put on the time she spends in activities outside the market. Therefore, knowledge of the woman's potential wage stream is important if the value of her time spent in child rearing is to be calculated.[c] Again, actual wage rates of women in the labor force are utilized to assign a price of time to each woman, working or nonworking, in the samples analyzed in Chapter Six. This procedure is rather more difficult to defend for wives than for their husbands. Married women exhibit a markedly higher incidence of interrupted labor force participation and occupational changes than do men or unmarried women. Moreover, many married women work part time, and this might be expected to affect their wage rates.

The procedure adopted here assigns to each woman the wage stream predicted for her on the basis of her education. Current occupation has not been utilized in the calculation since it is expected to be an especially poor predictor of future occupation for fecund married women whose career patterns are so fragmented. Use of education and the actual wage rate received by married women implies that each woman expects her earning power to be comparable to other women of the same

[b]Two of the education groups ("high school plus nonacademic training" and "college, one to three years") were combined when estimates were prepared for the Survey of Economic Opportunity tape because the metric variable representing education on that tape did not allow assignment of the husbands to one or the other of the two groups.

[c]In the absence of institutional constraints on her time allocation, the value of the time that a wife actually does spend in nonmarket pursuits will, except at the margin, be higher than her market wage rate. However, in the context of the fertility model presented in this study, utilization of the market wage in the valuation of the time cost of child rearing appears to be appropriate. See Chapter Two, Section 2.

Table 5-1. Male Hourly Wages, by Education and Occupation, Ages 20, 30, 40, and 50: 1969

Occupation	Education						
	0–5	6–8	9–11	HS	HS+	COL 1–3	COL, C+
Age 20[a]							
Professional, technical	2.45	2.48	2.77	2.82	2.77	3.07	3.65
Managers, officials	2.37	2.41	2.70	2.75	2.70	2.99	3.57
Self-employed businessmen	1.33	1.36	1.65	1.70	1.65	1.95	2.53
Clerical, sales	1.86	1.89	2.19	2.23	2.18	2.48	3.06
Craftsmen, foremen	2.18	2.21	2.50	2.55	2.50	2.79	3.37
Operatives & kindred	1.89	1.92	2.21	2.26	2.21	2.50	3.08
Laborers & service workers	1.58	1.61	1.90	1.95	1.90	2.19	2.77
Farmers, farm managers	0.51	0.55	0.84	0.89	0.84	1.13	1.71
Annual wage increase in dollars = 0.153							
Age 30							
Professional, technical	2.33	2.51	2.89	3.32	3.60	4.01	5.07
Managers, officials	3.07	3.26	3.64	4.07	4.34	4.75	5.82
Self-employed businessmen	2.63	2.82	3.19	3.63	3.90	4.31	5.38
Clerical, sales	2.24	2.43	2.80	3.23	3.51	3.92	4.98
Craftsmen, foremen	2.83	3.01	3.39	3.82	4.10	4.51	5.57
Operatives & kindred	2.51	2.70	3.07	3.50	3.78	4.19	5.25
Laborers & service workers	1.72	1.90	2.28	2.71	2.99	3.40	4.46
Farmers, farm managers	0.97	1.15	1.53	1.96	2.24	2.65	3.71
Annual wage increase in dollars = 0.136							
Age 40[a]							
Professional, technical	4.48	4.53	4.89	5.04	5.22	5.53	7.32
Managers, officials	4.61	4.66	5.02	5.16	5.35	5.66	7.45
Self-employed businessmen	3.94	3.99	4.36	4.50	4.68	4.99	6.79
Clerical, sales	3.95	4.00	4.36	4.50	4.69	5.00	6.79
Craftsmen, foremen	4.23	4.28	4.64	4.78	4.97	5.28	7.07
Operatives & kindred	3.43	3.48	3.85	3.99	4.17	4.48	6.27
Laborers & service workers	2.34	2.39	2.76	2.90	3.08	3.39	5.19
Farmers, farm managers	1.77	1.82	2.18	2.33	2.51	2.82	4.61
Annual wage increase in dollars = 0.035							

Age 50

Professional, technical	3.56	3.92	4.48	4.67	4.69	4.74	6.97
Managers, officials	4.31	4.67	5.23	5.42	5.44	5.49	7.72
Self-employed businessmen	2.81	3.16	3.72	3.91	3.93	3.98	6.22
Clerical, sales	3.06	3.41	3.97	4.16	4.18	4.23	6.47
Craftsmen, foremen	3.41	3.76	4.32	4.51	4.53	4.58	6.82
Operatives & kindred	2.90	3.25	3.82	4.01	4.02	4.08	6.31
Laborers & service workers	1.96	2.31	2.88	3.07	3.08	3.13	5.37
Farmers, farm managers	1.91	2.26	2.83	3.02	3.03	3.09	5.32

Annual wage increase in dollars = 0.008

[a]In these two age groups the tabular values for the 0–5 grades education group have been altered since the underlying regression coefficients exhibited considerable instability due to small sample size.

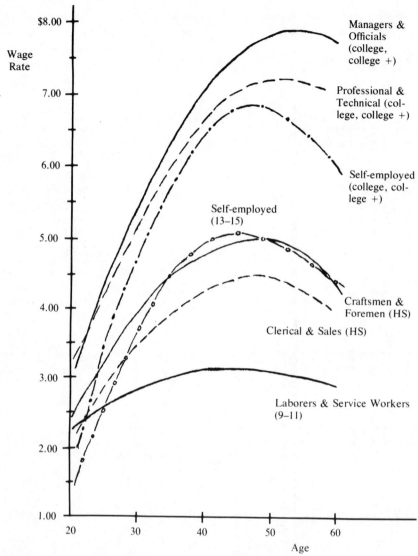

Figure 5–1. Selected Male Wage Streams

educational qualifications. However, recent studies are providing new evidence that married women's wages vary considerably due to the so-called "job interruption effect,"[1] and many women might be aware of this effect as they plan their fertility.

As a result, the potential wage stream of the wife may well be endogenous to the fertility model, with the wife's wage expectations being determined jointly with her expected family size. This implies (1) that wives project ahead their labor force participation over the child rearing cycle, and (2) that they can associate wage effects with the periods during which they are out of the labor force. To the degree that wives can do this, the measures of their potential wages generated in this chapter will, to a greater or lesser extent, be inaccurate. Note, however, the mere existence of the job interruption effect is not sufficient to require that wage expectations be made endogenous in the fertility model; what is required is that couples perceive the effect and consider it relevant to their fertility deliberations. This is an empirical question for which the data of the present study are insufficient to provide an answer. The new data sets being developed by the author and others will shed new light on the issue and will determine whether the method adopted in the present study is appropriate to the analysis of fertility.

The wage streams calculated for women (Fig. 5–2) are again generated from the Productive Americans and the Family Economics surveys. Women were chosen for analysis if they were (1) Caucasian, (2) currently employed with defined occupation and education, (3) between the ages of 20 and 59, and (4) either the head or the wife of the head of a

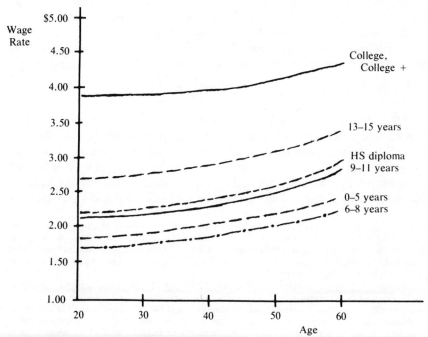

Figure 5–2. Female Wage Streams

household. Division of the sample into age groups did not produce the changes in rank orderings expected, and since the rate of change in wages was not very pronounced, women's wage streams were calculated by the use of only one regression with explanatory variables representing age, age squared, education, and survey date. The wage streams illustrated in Figure 5-2 are utilized to calculate the wife's contribution to expected potential income and to value her time inputs into child rearing.[d]

3. CALCULATION OF POTENTIAL INCOME

The Main Components of Family Income

In a given year a couple can obtain money income through the sale of the husband's and wife's labor on the market or through the receipt of income from capital assets or transfers. For older couples in particular, capital income may derive from savings and investments generated as the result of past work effort but not consumed as received; however, a significant portion might come from gifts and inheritances, which involve no market work on the part of the couple. Indeed, these latter sources may be significant elements of a couple's potential income and it would be highly desirable to obtain measures of them.

It will be remembered from Chapter Two that our empirical measure of potential income contains three elements which are represented as:

$$I = I_p + I_r + V,$$

where I_p is the predicted potential wage income for a couple based on that couple's occupational and educational characteristics, I_r is the "relative" income component that accounts for the deviation of a particular couple's wage and salary potential from the predicted values due to such unmeasured factors as ability and ambition, and V is the present value of income arising from nonlabor sources such as gifts and inheritances.[e]

[d]Note that the predicted wage rate for women with 0 to 5 grades of education is slightly higher than that for women with 6 to 8 grades. This anomalous result is likely to be due to the fact that the regression coefficient upon which the estimates are based was computed from only nineteen cases out of the 1,752 cases in the sample (estimated coefficient is –0.404 while its standard error is 0.524).

[e]Another important source of income derives from public and private transfers such as unemployment compensation, social security, noncontributory public welfare, private pension benefits, and other transfers such as alimony/child support payments. These sources of income do not appear to be very important for the present study. Recipients of public transfers are disproportionately nonwhite, members of families headed by women, over age sixty-five, and poorly educated. Private transfers generally arrive late in life (pensions)

Our estimate of potential income will include measures of I_p and I_r but not of V. That portion of V that comes from nonlabor sources simply cannot be estimated from the sample data utilized in the following chapter, and this might mean the introduction of significant measurement error into our construct I. A couple's family size decision may depend disproportionately on the expectation of a future inheritance, which might, for example, be entirely committed to finance the children's education. Therefore, knowledge simply of the couple's wage income potential is not sufficient to account for the differences in fertility behavior that might ensue from the expectation of future gifts and inheritances.

Fortunately, many inheritances are not large. The median inheritance for those families reporting in the 1960 Michigan study just cited was in the range of $950 to $4,949, and 82 percent of those families receiving inheritances received a sum less than $9,950.[2] That is, for the great proportion of families, income from inheritances totals less than $600 annually (at a yield of 6 percent), and the quantitative impact of this discounted stream would not appear to be very large. However, if parents treat these expected inheritances as special use funds, even a modest inheritance of a few thousand dollars may play an inordinate role in the fertility decision, and measurement error from this source may remain a problem.

Predicted Potential Income (I_p)

The predicted wage streams for husband and wife derived in Section 2 can be utilized to compute the couple's predicted potential income on the basis of assumptions made about the maximum amount of work effort each is able to supply to the market.[f] We proceed on the assumption that institutional and biological constraints limit the maximum amount of market work performed per year by the husband and wife to 3,000 and 2,000 hours respectively. In recognition of their primary responsibility for the management of the home, wives are arbitrarily limited to a maximum of one full time job, while husbands are assumed capable of sustaining a full time job as well as a secondary job of approximately twenty hours per week. Utilization of these figures pro-

---

and are correlated with wage income, or are unexpected by the couple planning a family (alimony or child support payments); consequently both forms of transfers will be disregarded in the construction of the potential income estimates. See James N. Morgan, Martin David, Wilbur Cohen, and Harvey Brazer, *Income and Welfare in the United States* (New York: McGraw-Hill, 1962) for a discussion of the sources of family income.

[f]Note that since it will be assumed that all couples can supply potentially the same maximum amount of time to the market, the choice of maximum hours per year for both the husband and wife is somewhat arbitrary; however, this has no effect on the analytical results of the following chapter.

vides a realistic, if somewhat arbitrary, picture of the family's maximum long range earning power.[g] Thus, predicted potential income is calculated according to the formula:

$$I_p = I_p{}^w + I_p{}^h$$

$$= 2000\left[\sum_{t=t_k}^{t_k+30} \frac{w_t{}^e}{(1+r)^{t-t_k}}\right] + 3000\left[\sum_{t=t_j}^{t_j+30} \frac{w_t{}^g}{(1+r)^{t-t_j}}\right],$$

where $I_p{}^w$ and $I_p{}^h$ are the potential wage incomes of the wife and husband respectively, t_k and t_j are the respective ages of wife and husband at the birth of their first child, $w_t{}^e$ is the wife's wage at age t (given an education of type e), $w_t{}^g$ is the husband's wage at age t (given an occupation and education of type g), and r is the couple's subjective rate of time discount. Since other studies have demonstrated that higher status couples tend to have children later than lower status couples, we have attempted to capture the resulting cost and resource differentials by basing both the potential income and the time cost calculations on the age of birth of the first child. The choice of a discount rate for these calculations is discussed in Section 5 below.

Relative Potential Income (I_r)

As Figure 2–1 illustrated, a couple may, for a variety of reasons, expect either more or less income than other couples of similar occupational and educational characteristics. If the actual wage expectations of the husband and wife were available as data, the potential income variable, I, would represent exactly their long range projections. Our empirical analog must, however, decompose potential income into the predicted component and the relative component, the latter being assigned on the basis of additional information about the given couple. Thus, the relative income component serves as a correction to the main component of potential income, I_p, just derived.

Each of the two surveys utilized to test the fertility model in Chapter Six provides an opportunity to assign a relative income measure to each couple in the samples. The 1960 Growth of American Families (GAF) study actually contains the wife's assessment of the family's income position in relation to friends and other relatives, and thus presents no problem; however, the 1967 Survey of Economic Opportunity (SEO)

[g]Two and three thousand hours were chosen in order to put the quantitative impact of children on the total resources of the parents into sharper focus; the total cost of children can thus be easily compared with the maximum money income available to parents from wage and salary sources.

contains no information on expected income, thus it is necessary to build a relative income measure utilizing data about the family's current income. This is accomplished by assessing a family's total income in relation to families whose heads exhibit similar age, occupation, and education characteristics.[h]

Controlling for age and potential income group, we can identify those families that exhibit an income considerably above or below the average of all couples in the group. The control on husband's age is instituted to eliminate income differentials arising from the families' different positions in the life cycle; thus, a member of Potential Income Group 1 who reports an income of $18,000 would not be considered atypical if his age is 40 or above, but if the head is below age 40 an income of this magnitude puts the family in the upper quartile in that potential income–age group. Upper and lower bounds are computed for each age–potential income group, and couples in the extreme upper and lower income quartiles are identified. Construction of the relative income variable in this manner is admittedly crude, but it does provide a way in which to sharpen our estimates of potential income.[i]

4. ASSIGNMENT OF TIME COST AND MONEY COST

In Chapter Two it was noted that our measure of the price of a child for each couple would rely on ex post expenditure data, which would prohibit analysis of the impact of a change in the price of an input into child rearing on P, the price of a child, except in the unlikely occurrence of fixed factors in the "production" of children. Thus, we approximate the theoretical price P as follows:

$$P = C^s(p, w)$$

$$\approx \sum_i (\text{market expenditure per child})_i{}^g$$

$$+ (\text{value of wife's time per child}),^e$$

[h]Two other variables in the SEO data set that were of great potential use in the assessment of potential income were "net worth of family" and "husband's hourly wage rate." However, the first variable was left uncorrected, even for known omissions, and the resulting measure represents a shifting collection of reported and unreported assets and liabilities. The second variable was subject to a nonresponse rate of 36 percent in that portion of the sample chosen for analysis. Hourly remuneration of the head would have been extremely useful in the identification of those husbands whose special qualities had led to wage rates significantly different from those of men of comparable occupation and education.

[i]See the discussion in Chapter Six for a description of how the relative income variables are included in the analysis.

where total expenditure per child is divided into a money cost component and a time component, with g representing the husband's potential income group and e the wife's education group.

Time Cost

Although there is reason to suspect that child care behavior varies with religion and potential income group, the available data were not sufficient to develop a differential set of estimates for time spent on child care. Instead, each mother is assumed to devote the same amount of time to her children during their eighteen years in the family, regardless of religion or potential income groups. To assign a time cost to a child in a given family, the valuation of the mother's time depends on (1) her predicted wage rate and (2) the age at which she begins her family. Derivation of the mother's predicted wage stream is described above in Section 2, and is assumed to depend solely upon her attained education.

The period in the life cycle that a couple chooses to bear and raise its children also affects the opportunity cost of a child. Women who wait until their late twenties or early thirties to start their families will in general be using higher priced time for child rearing than if they had borne their children early. We attempt to account for cost differences arising from variations in timing by applying the wage rates predicted for a woman during the eighteen years after her first birth. For example, if one woman with a college education starts her family at age 22, the time she spends in child rearing over the eighteen years is valued at the wage rates predicted annually for the span from 22 to 40. For another woman of equal education who begins her childbearing at age 28, the time spent in child rearing is valued with the set of wage rates beginning at age 28 and continuing to age 46. In this rather crude manner we hope to acknowledge the cost differentials that arise because of delayed childbearing.

Finally it should be noted that we have not attempted to account for differentials in spacing or in completed family size, although Chapter Three has presented some evidence that these do exist. The data have not allowed a precise enough breakdown to make the effort worthwhile, and for couples expecting larger families any assignment would be excessively arbitrary. Consequently, the approximate time cost per child of a family with two and a half children has been used so as to reflect the mean family size of couples in the original samples.

Likewise, although spacing differences were shown to result in variations in the cumulative time cost of child rearing, no attempt was made to account for them in the assignment of opportunity costs. Cost differentials implied by spacing variations did not appear to be large enough to warrant the considerable effort necessary to include them. Therefore, in assigning a measure of time cost per child, we base the calculation solely on the wife's education and upon her age at the first birth. The measure is thus sensitive to delays in the initiation of a family but not to differentials arising from variations in spacing.

Money Cost

As explained earlier, data problems have forced us to derive money expenditure estimates for only six potential income groups (see Table 4–17). Therefore, each couple in the samples is assigned a money expenditure figure solely on the basis of the husband's education and current occupation at the time of the survey. Again, the money cost estimates are based on the expenditure per child in a two child family— although it was noted in Chapter Four that there is some evidence of declining marginal expenditure as family size increases. Presumably data will eventually be collected that will allow a considerably more precise estimation of expected money expenditures on children.

5. CHOICE OF A SUBJECTIVE DISCOUNT RATE

Because they begin and complete their fertility while they are relatively young, parents must commit resources to child rearing many years into the future. For many parents this future commitment may be an important element of the family size decision; however, current costs and benefits associated with allocative decisions are usually presumed to play a larger role in current decisions than are future costs and benefits. That is, a dollar spent paying the obstetrician's fee is presumed to play a larger role in the fertility decision than is a dollar spent for college tuition twenty years hence.

To represent the temporal weighting that decision makers are presumed to apply to future costs and benefits, economists often assign subjective rates of discount to these future values. These discount rates are not market rates; they are numerical reflections of the internal time orientations of the husband and wife and they may be expected to vary with psychological makeup, social and cultural background, and so on.

Since couples must make family expenditure commitments long before the payments are actually due, these future payments must be discounted to take account of the decreased importance of future expenditures on current decisions. Ideally, a measure of the time orientations of each husband and wife included in the analysis would be available such that discount rates might be applied to each couple individually. Unfortunately, as so often been the case in this study, data on time orientation are not available for the couples to be analyzed. Indeed, I am aware of no previous attempts to measure subjective discount rates for individuals in a sample survey context.[j]

Consequently, we have proceeded on the assumption that each couple displays identical time orientation characteristics. This assumption might be a source of considerable error if couples from different potential income groups display systematically different subjective discount rates. Moreover, couples may discount different items of expenditure at different rates, being, for example, particularly concerned about the future costs of college education for their children while ignoring, say, clothing and recreation costs of teenagers. In the absence of concrete evidence the assumption of uniformity seems least damaging.

A discount rate of 4 percent has been chosen for these calculations mainly because it represents a commonly available rate of return for virtually all families in 1969.[k] The rate is admittedly arbitrary and is rather lower than that chosen by other students of fertility doing related work.[3] However, in the absence of direct information on the time orientation of couples we have little firm theory on which to base our choice of discount rates. This is a problem of possibly major importance in the empirical analysis of fertility models, and the new data sets designed to test them must obtain reliable measures of time orientation in order to adjust future cost and resource estimates properly.

Given the discount rate, present values of the costs of children and the potential income of parents can be calculated. Samples of the potential income and opportunity cost calculations are presented in Table 5-2 for couples of varying occupational and educational characteristics. Since the cost and potential income calculations are dependent upon the age of the parents as they begin their child rearing, two sets of calculations are presented for couples beginning their families at ages 23 and 30. Note that these two ages represent only two of approximately 400 age, income, and occupation combinations; however, the total cost and potential income calculations are representative of many of the couples in the survey.

The last column of the table presents the opportunity cost of a child as a percent of the couple's potential income. Note that these costs are not related to the couple's actual income but to the maximum income that could be earned if the husband and wife devoted full effort to market work for 30 years. The family's potential income totals and the opportunity cost per child figures of Table 5-2 are examples of the values that will be assigned to each couple for the analysis of the

---

[j]I am presently engaged in some sample survey research that seeks to achieve accurate measures of individual subjective rates of time preference that, hopefully, will allow this sort of information to be gathered routinely as a part of future fertility surveys.

[k]This was the maximum interest rate available on conventional savings accounts in 1969.

Table 5-2. Potential Income and the Cost of Raising a Child[a]

Wife's Education	Husband's Education Occupation, and Potential Income Group	Wife's Potential Income	Husband's Potential Income	Family's Potential Income	Time Cost per Child	Money Cost per Child	Opportunity Cost per Child	Opportunity Cost as a Percent of Potential Income
Wife and husband age 23:								
College, college +	college, college/ manager-official (1)	143,254	330,447	473,701	19,315	11,657	30,972	6.5
High school	clerical/sales (3)	84,514	204,814	289,328	11,223	8,022	19,245	6.6
6–8 grades	operative/kindred (5)	65,985	171,611	237,596	8,670	6,500	15,170	6.4
Wife and Husband age 30:								
College, college +	College, college +/ manager official (1)	147,204	378,297	525,501	19,730	11,657	31,387	6.0
High School	clerical/sales (3)	88,465	226,581	315,046	11,638	8,022	19,660	6.2
6–8 grades	operative/kindred worker (5)	69,936	184,697	254,633	9,086	6,500	15,586	6.1

[a]Discount Rate = 4 percent, measured from age at which first child is born.

socioeconomic model of fertility reported in Chapter Six, to which we now turn.

CHAPTER FIVE

1. Jacob Mincer and Solomon Polachek, "Family Investments in Human Capital: Earnings of Women," *JPE Supplement, 1974,* pp. S76–S108; see also, George E. Johnson and Frank P. Stafford, "The Earnings and Promotion of Women Faculty," *American Economic Review* LXIV (6) (December 1974): 888–903.

2. Morgan, et al., *op. cit.,* pp. 86–94.

3. See Peter Lindert, "The Relative Cost of American Children," Madison, Wisconsin: University of Wisconsin Graduate Program in Economic History Discussion Paper No. 7318, pp. 16–17.

The Demand for Children

1. INTRODUCTION

The construction of our proxies for income and the costs of child rearing completed, we are now able to estimate the demand for children. However, before the empirical results are presented it will be useful to summarize briefly the underlying themes of this study.

The fundamental postulate of this work is that for many American couples, procreation is a decision problem necessitating choices about the long range allocation of the family's resources. Consequently it is argued at some length (in Chapters One and Two) that the economic theory of the consumer, suitably modified, is an appropriate vehicle for the analysis of fertility differentials.

This study represents a particular adaptation of consumer theory to the study of fertility, an adaptation which places particular emphasis on the role of social and psychological factors in shaping family size decisions. Great pains have been taken to emphasize that the consumer theory approach is not incompatible with the analyses of fertility based in other disciplines; indeed, the various approaches are complementary and each remains incomplete without the others. Economists have traditionally paid insufficient attention to differential social, institutional and psychological influences on the couple, while other social scientists have undervalued the advantages of a well articulated theory of choice.[1]

Figure 1–1 has been offered as a prototype of a modified decision model suitable for the study of fertility. In this model a number of factors, economic and noneconomic, are illustrated as having an effect on the fertility decision. Background social and demographic characteristics as well as basic personality traits are shown to have impacts not only on the couple's relative preferences for children versus other activities, but on the couple's ability to generate income and wealth and on the underlying standards by which the children are raised. A wealth of information exists on the relation of sociodemographic variables to fertility, but hardly ever before have these variables been included in an explicit fertility decision model. Moreover, the direct association of sociodemographic variables with completed or expected fertility has proven relatively unfruitful in adding to our understanding of fertility as a social process. The consumer theory approach outlined in Chapters One and Two provides new avenues for sociodemographic factors to influence fertility through their impact on preferences, resource expectations, and the price of children—the latter being the factors of immediate relevance in any allocation decision.

However, there is a major problem associated with the implementation of the behavioral model of Chapter One—the lack of suitable data. Couples make family size decisions on the basis of their preferences for children versus other activities, their perceptions of the resource impact of children, and their expectations of the time and money resources available to them over the life cycle. None of the national fertility studies undertaken to this date has contained the sort of information needed to test adequately a decision theory model of fertility, and this has required a major effort to synthesize proxies for the needed data. Chapters Three, Four, and Five of this study represent efforts to produce the sort of economic variables necessary, but heretofore never gathered, to the estimation of a socioeconomic model of differential fertility.

The behavioral model of Figure 1–1 makes an explicit attempt to illustrate the manner in which sociodemographic factors influence both parental "tastes" for children and the underlying standards that couples bring to the child rearing process. Since only meager data on preferences are in fact available, the estimation model actually adopted[a] represents a significant truncation of the fully articulated model of Chapter One. In particular, we are again forced to rely on social and demographic variables as proxies for different dimensions of the preference structure. In selecting these variables we have, of course, been immeasurably aided by the insights of the numerous scholars cited in Section 2 of Chapter One; however, it will ultimately be necessary to go beyond these insights to measure directly those elements of couples' preferences relevant to the fertility decision.

Sociodemographic factors have also been utilized to construct new

[a]See Chapter Two, Section 3 and, especially, Figure 2–1.

estimates of the price of children and the potential income of couples. Again, direct information regarding parental perceptions of the resource requirements of child rearing would have been preferable to the estimates constructed in Chapters Three through Five. However, these estimates demonstrate conclusively that the opportunity cost of child rearing is strongly connected to the potential income of parents.[b]

This does not confirm the hypothesis advanced in Chapter Two that parents choose a family size on the basis of preconceived notions of the cost of children, but it does indicate that simple correlations between income and family size are inadequate to illustrate the connection between income and fertility. Awareness of the role of the price of a child is important not only for purposes of statistical estimation but for consideration of various economic policies which might be designed to alter aggregate fertility. By various means, governmental policy might be used to alter equilibrium family size.[c] However, in order to assess numerically the comparative static impact on family size of a change in the price of a child it is necessary to remove the effects of differential preference structures. As the analysis of Section 5 will demonstrate, this is a particularly difficult task given the data sets utilized in the present chapter.

This chapter draws together, therefore, the sociodemographic insights reviewed in Chapter One and the price and income variables constructed in Chapters Three through Five for the estimation of the socioeconomic model of the demand for children presented in Chapter Two. The demand equations to be estimated in Sections 3, 4, and 5 represent the final objects of attention and synthesize the social and economic approaches to the study of fertility. Section 3 utilizes data from the Survey of Economic Opportunity (1967). This survey, while not intended primarily as a fertility survey, contains information sufficient to estimate the demand equation proposed for analysis. Section 4 presents the results of a similar analysis of data from the 1960 Growth of American Families (GAF) study.[2] Section 5 analyzes both samples for the presence of interaction effects which might serve to distort our interpretation of the price and income elasticities estimated from the entire sample. Preliminary to the discussion of the empirical results, however, Section 2 discusses methodological issues relating to the statistical estimation of the model.

---

[b]See Tables 4–17 and 5–2.

[c]Because parents consider the opportunity cost of a child to be a datum in the fertility decision model of Chapter Two, we will in this chapter use the terms "price" and "opportunity cost" interchangeably.

2. MEASURING THE DEMAND FOR CHILDREN

An Empirical Measure of Quantity Demanded

Throughout this study we have proceeded as if an empirical analog for the demand for children is readily available. Economists have assigned a precise meaning to the term "demand" that is at variance with the commonly used synonyms such as wants, needs, requirements, desires, and so forth. To the economist, the demand for something is "the desire for it constrained by the resources at the consumer's disposal." One measure of the demand for children might be completed fertility, but obviously this variable is available only for couples from older cohorts. If we are to utilize data from a sample of all married couples at a point in time, we must have a measure of the demand for children that includes those children yet to be born.

The national surveys of fertility begun in 1955 and continued every five years since then have attempted to devise measures of prospective fertility. The object of these attempts was to derive short run predictions of aggregate fertility, and a number of competing measures were developed. Women were asked how many children they expected to have, intended to have, and desired to have. Moreover, they were asked about the ideal number of children for the average American family. The latter variable is almost entirely unacceptable for our purposes since, conceptually at least, it bears little relation to the couple's own demand for children.

However, the other variables (number of children, expected, intended, and desired) would appear to be closely analogous to the economist's conception of demand. Ryder and Westoff have undertaken a careful comparison of the conceptual and numerical differences between these measures using data from the 1965 National Fertility Study (NFS).[3] From their discussion it is apparent that measures of family size intentions represent the closest analogs to the demand for children. A measure is wanted that reflects the parents' actual choice constrained by their own social and economic position and by their expectations of the future.

When parents are asked how many children they want or desire to have they are perhaps more likely to respond according to their unconstrained preferences. This would appear to be the case for the NFS data since the mean number of children desired is invariably higher than the mean number intended, even if religion or education is controlled.[4] This suggests that measures of the number of children intended represent the preferred indicators of the demand for children.

Unfortunately, the sample surveys utilized in this chapter do not contain measures of family size intentions; rather, they contain variables representing expected parity: women in both samples are asked how many children they ultimately expect to have. This question also appears on the NFS questionnaire and Ryder and Westoff are able to compare measures of expected and intended family size. They find no statistically significant differences between the two measures even though conceptually they are rather different. In fact, mean expected parity invariably exceeds mean intended parity for the aggregate sample and for subgroups classified by education and religion.[5] However, the differences are not large and, after an extended analysis, Ryder and Westoff conclude that ". . . the number expected and the number intended are very much alike on both an individual and an aggregate basis."[6] From this, we may conclude that a measure of prospective fertility that is conceptually quite close to the demand for children is available for our analysis.

There are, however, other problems with the expected family size variable that should be mentioned. First, family size expectations vary over the couple's life cycle, making it very difficult to pinpoint the stage in which they stabilize. Independent studies have demonstrated that the various measures of prospective fertility do show a high degree of aggregate stability but that this result is a consequence of many compensating changes.[7] Furthermore, Ryder and Westoff,[8] in analyzing the data from the NFS, have found that there appears to be a systematic tendency for the fertility expectations of a cohort to increase with age; moreover, this rise does not appear to be uniform.

Second, although the fertility expectations of women at parity two have proved to be very accurate predictors of actual aggregate fertility over a long period there appear to be numerous compensating differences.[9] These differences are rather closely related to the parents' success at family planning and thence to various measures of their socioeconomic status. This is unfortunate, since if the compensating errors were distributed independently of the various status variables, use of the expectation variable in place of actual completed fertility would result in unbiased estimates of the parameters in a demand equation for children. As it is, our confidence in this measure is weakened.

Finally, we must face the possibility that neither measures of prospective fertility nor completed fertility itself are accurate indicators of the demand for children. As Freedman, Coombs, and Bumpass argue:

> . . . it seems reasonable that any specific response about the number of children wanted or expected is usually the center of a personal range or distribution of values. If the answer is "three," often what this really

means is that three is the number valued most (perhaps much more than any other) but that two or four are not completely out of the question. They may, in fact, be close alternatives.[10]

If response "errors" of this type are randomly and independently distributed, they need not cause us problems of interpretation; however, if they are correlated with the explanatory variables of the demand equation they present another souce of bias. More satisfactory would be a measure of expected parity which accounted for the probability of alternative parities, perhaps utilizing the methodology described by Lolagene Coombs in a recent paper.[11]

Even data on completed family size may provide poor measures of the demand for children. It is difficult to identify completely those couples whose fertility was in fact entirely intended or those couples whose subfecundity prevented their attainment of the intended number. It is obvious, therefore, that none of the measures available for service as a proxy for the demand for children is completely above suspicion. Nevertheless, certain steps, to be described in the next subsection, can be taken to improve the expected parity variable so that it more closely approximates the demand for children.

Exclusion of Ineffective Planners and the Subfecund

In Chapter One the significant incidence of unwanted pregnancy was discussed and it was argued that either the statistical model explaining completed fertility should also be designed to explain fertility regulating behavior or that ineffective family planners should be excluded from the analysis. In the absence of the data necessary to test a decision model of fertility regulating behavior, the latter course has been chosen. Presumably the couples retained for analysis are those whose fertility expectations correspond well with their intentions.

The GAF sample presents no problem in identifying effective family planners, since the survey's investigators developed specific measures of contraceptive efficacy. Moreover, the GAF sample contains relatively precise measures of subfecundity and we are therefore able to exclude ineffective family planners and the subfecund on the basis of directly gathered information. The SEO, however, presents rather more severe problems in that no measures of family planning success or fecundity are available and we must base our selection on alternative criteria. To insure that the most severe cases of sterility and subfecundity are excluded, only couples with at least one child ever born are included for analysis. As noted in Chapter One, family size expectations begin to stabilize after the birth of the second child. The regressions reported in

Section 3 were also computed using only those couples with two or more children; there were very few differences among the regressions and consequently the results reported below are for couples with at least one child ever born.

Exclusion of unsuccessful family planners presents a more difficult problem. The GAF studies and the National Fertility studies have demonstrated that unsuccessful family planners are concentrated disproportionately among the less educated and low income couples in the population. To exclude poor family planners in the SEO sample, all couples in which either the wife possessed an eighth grade education or less or the husband was a member of Potential Income Group 6 were dropped from the analysis. We risk losing a group that displays singular preferences about family size with such a procedure; however, since we cannot explain statistically the incidence of contraceptive failure in the decision framework, it seems best to eliminate poor family planners from the outset.[d]

Model Structure and Method of Estimation

In Chapter Two it is argued that parents choose a family size on the basis of expectations regarding future resources and the future requirements of child rearing. The production function for children is regarded as predetermined and related to the socioeconomic status of the parents. There is, therefore, for any given set of wages, prices, tastes and nonlabor wealth a minimum cost mode of production for any number of children. Parents are presumed to choose a family size subject to the constraint posed by the perceived production function, the form of which is determined by physiological considerations as well as by individual preferences and social norms.

The deterministic model of Chapter Two, Section 3 is, therefore, recursive as represented in Figure 2–1. In this chapter we will proceed as if the stochastic model is also recursive although, given the diversity of the data sources that make up the model, it is not possible to insure that the conditions defining a recursive model are fully met.[e] Thus the demand for children is a function of two predetermined (but endogenous)

---

[d]The lower end of the status distribution was not excluded from the GAF regressions, and less educated women would indeed appear to possess distinct preferences for children. See Section 4 below.

[e]The model: $By + Cx + e = 0$ (where y is a vector of endogenous variables, x is a vector of exogenous variables and e is a vector of errors) ". . . is said to be recursive if there exists an ordering of the endogenous variables such that the matrix B is triangular and if the covariance matrix of e is diagonal." E. Malinvaud, *Statistical Methods of Econometrics* (Chicago: Rand McNally & Co., 1966, p. 512.) We cannot demonstrate that the condition on e is satisfied.

variables, price and income, and of a number of exogenous variables representing preferences and various sociodemographic factors. Ordinary Least Squares (OLS) regression will be utilized to estimate the equations.

3. SEO SAMPLE RESULTS

The first two columns of Table 6–1 present the results of a regression calculated on sample drawn from the SEO data. Before the findings are discussed in detail a brief description of the sample is in order. The Survey of Economic Opportunity was conducted by the Bureau of the Census in February–March 1967. The sample was spread over 357 clusters comprising 701 counties and independent cities.[f] Each of the 50 states and the District of Columbia were included. Approximately 29,000 occupied households were eligible for interview. The SEO sample was selected so that blacks and other races were overrepresented, and a weighting scheme was used to account for this. Since our attention is restricted to white families, only the original, self-weighting portion of the sample was utilized. Nonwhites, and families in the armed forces are excluded as are currently married wives who have had previous marriages. Thus the sample represents white couples from all but the lowest income strata who are, hopefully, effective family planners.

Note that cluster samples are less efficient than simple random samples and the correct estimates of sampling variance are larger than those that would be derived from formulas designed for random samples. While corrected estimates of the variance of sample means are easy enough to calculate, the same cannot be said for estimates of standard errors of regression coefficients, F-statistics for analyses of covariance, etc. Since the loss of efficiency is directly related to the degree of homogeneity within each of the sample clusters, calculation of corrected statistics is sample specific and commonly available regression programs do not incorporate options to account for the effects of clustering. Consequently the statistical results of this chapter almost certainly understate variances and overstate levels of significance to some degree. This should be kept in mind when interpreting the sample results as the discussion will proceed as if the underlying data come from simple random samples.

Age of Wife

In societies where fertility is well controlled we expect that the fertility rates of different cohorts will vary in response to changes in

---

[f] Independent cities are those cities whose governmental status is equivalent to and independent of county government (e.g., Baltimore, St. Louis, and numerous cities in Virginia).

Table 6–1. Regression Results

Dependent Variable: Total number of children expected

Independent Variable	SEO		GAF	
	Coefficient	Standard Error	Coefficient	Standard Error
Size of wife's family of orientation	—	—	.076	.020
Age of wife				
≤(32 SEO), (25 GAF)	.044	.017	−.040	.029
≥(47 SEO), (39 GAF)	.118	.018	−.16	.036
Farm background[a]				
Both some	.060	.050	−.008	.033
Both none	.074	.027	−.059	.028
Wife's work experience since marriage				
Has worked; doesn't like it	—	—	−.12	.026
Has worked; likes it	—	—	−.092	.033
Religion				
Both Catholic	—	—	.15	.046
Neither Catholic	—	—	−.12	.041
Extrafamilial activity: Wife[c]	—	—	.087	.024
Couple's ability to plan ahead				
Can plan	—	—	−.037	.028
Cannot plan	—	—	−.032	.042
Wife's age at first marriage				
<19	.084	.017	.047	.028
≥23	−.084	.018	−.091	.032
Husband and wife disagree	—	—	−.041	.023
Cost of child rearing	−.001	.106	.40	.15
Potential income of family[b]	−.136	.073	−.20	.071
Wife's education				
≤8	—	—	.16	.049
>	.074	.024	.011	.044
Wife's work in 1966				
No work	.034	.018	—	—
Full time	−.107	.021	—	—
Current relative income				
Bottom Quartile	−.020	.020	—	—
Top Quartile	.047	.018	—	—
R^2	0.075		0.14	
Number of cases	4,184		1,221	

[a]In SEO sample "farm background" refers to residence at age sixteen. In GAF sample it refers to any farm experience before marriage.

[b]The variable for potential income in the GAF sample has been adjusted for current relative income; in the SEO sample this variable represents expected potential income only.

[c]If the wife attends at least one meeting of a nonchild-oriented club per month the dummy variable representing extrafamilial activity is scored one.

social and economic conditions. That completed fertility for different cohorts has shown considerable variation in the United States is well illustrated in Figure 1–2. Dummy variables representing the wife's age have been introduced into the demand equation specifically to account for intergenerational differences in tastes and socioeconomic conditions that would otherwise have been uncaptured.

In the SEO sample two variables representing women aged twenty to 32 and 47 or older have been introduced. Given the sharp drop in completed fertility experienced by these older cohorts of women it is unsurprising to find that the expected family size of women aged 47 and older was considerably less than that for younger women. These women were, of course, bearing children before, during and immediately after the Depression, when aggregate fertility had reached its lowest level of the century until the early 1970s. The expectations of younger women in the survey (born in 1935 or later) appear to have remained high in 1967; the coefficient of 0.044[g] is somewhat higher than the fertility of the cohorts represented by the excluded dummy variable. The latter cohorts (1934–1920) experienced the highest fertility in the twentieth century. In any case, it obviously is necessary to account for generational differences in preferences. The possible indirect effects of age will be explored below in Section 5.

Farm Background

The work of David Goldberg and others [12] leads us to include dummy variables representing farm experience in the backgrounds of the husband and wife. The variables available in the SEO and GAF studies are not comparable since the SEO sample refers to each spouse's residence at age sixteen while the GAF study refers to any farm experience before marriage. Furthermore, once education and occupation are controlled, it is not clear that the net impact of farm experience will be very large. Since size of family of orientation is not available in the SEO sample, farm background variables may act as proxies for the former. In any case our weak prior opinion is that lack of a farm background will tend to reduce expected family size and presence of a farm background will tend to increase it somewhat. The sample results agree in sign with our expectation and imply roughly a difference of 0.31 in expected family size due to differences in farm background. Again, possible interaction effects are explored in Section 5.

---

[g]Remember that the dependent variable in this regression is the natural logarithm of expected family size; the coefficients reflect, therefore, the impact of the independent variable on the log of family size, not on the actual value. For example, a coefficient of −0.12 represents (given the mean expected family size for the sample of 2.44) a reduction of 0.28 children from the number expected by the 33 to 46 age group.

Age at First Marriage

The age at which a woman marries may affect completed family size in a number of ways. First, the younger she is at marriage the longer she is regularly exposed to the risk of conception. Second, early marriage might, as Bumpass suggests, be indicative of a higher level of fecundity resulting in premarital pregnancy and subsequent marriage. Third, early marriage might signify stronger tastes for marriage and children among these women as opposed to those who marry later. Finally, early marriage might be a manifestation of poor ability to engage in contraception.

On the other hand, later than average marriage might represent the opposite of some of these factors. Women who marry late may exhibit a significantly stronger commitment to nonfamilal activities. Also they may be less fecund or be able to utilize contraception more effectively. The possibility that age at marriage is acting as a proxy for fecundity and family planning differentials is especially strong with respect to the SEO sample. Our measures of fecundity and family planning skill are extremely crude and it is likely that the age at marriage variable is representing some of these differentials that have not been filtered out in the initial sample selection process. Thus the age at marriage variables are included as proxies for preferences for children versus other activities, and possibly as proxies for fecundity status and family planning efficacy.

A reviewer has complained that age at marriage is an endogenous variable and that its inclusion in the regression may lead to bias. I agree that the decision to marry and the arrival of the *first* child may, in some sense, be simultaneous events; however, we are dealing with effective family planners whose ultimate family size decisions are, in general, made long after marriage. There does not, therefore, seem to be a particularly strong case for treating age at marriage and ultimate fertility as simultaneously determined.

The sample coefficients tend to support our prior expectations about the impact of age at first marriage. Early marriage leads to increased fertility expectations while late marriage leads to reduced fertility expectations. The influence of the well known age at marriage interaction is explored in Section 5.

Education of Wife

Prior sociodemographic research [13] has led to a strong expectation that fertility and the wife's education should, for a variety of reasons, be negatively related. Education is included here as an additional proxy for the wife's preferences for children versus other activities. We expect that education past high school should be negatively associated with expected family size; however, the SEO data do not support this interpretation. Indeed, the sample suggests rather strongly that the effect is positive, not negative. We might conclude from this that any negative impact exerted by the wife's education upon fertility is exerted indirectly through the opportunity cost variable. This result is at considerable variance with previous findings, however, and caution in accepting it too easily is advised. When new and more appropriate data are collected, special attention should be paid to the separate paths by which education affects fertility.

Wife's Work Status in 1966

It was noted in Chapter Two that a wife's work experience since marriage is strongly correlated with expected family size; however, the causal implications of this relationship are far from clear. Previous sociodemographic studies often implicitly have assumed that the line of causation runs from work to family size choices. That is, differential work experience after marriage somehow leads to differential preferences regarding children. Women who work, it is argued, are manifesting their preferences for smaller family sizes. Certainly work and child rearing compete for a mother's time, especially when there are preschool children in the family; however, the question of whether the wife's market work is a cause or result of differential family size expectations remains unanswered. The static analysis employed here (and implicitly in the other studies analyzing the market work–fertility relationship) is ultimately unsuitable. What is needed is an expressly dynamic model and a data set markedly superior to any presently available.

In a life cycle model of resource allocation of the type suggested by Robert Willis, the wife's previous market work would be simultaneously determined with the fertility decision, and inclusion in an OLS regression would be inappropriate. However, since we reject the notion that marriage, fertility and work-leisure decisions are made simultaneously at the outset of marriage, we regard the wife's previous market work as predetermined on the date of the survey. This is not to say that the wife's time allocation would not be endogenous in the full dynamic model suggested above; however, our data are simply not able to support the full dynamic model.

Consequently, a variable representing the wife's market work relationship is included in regressions estimated for both samples. In the SEO sample the dummy variable categories are (1) no market work in 1966, (2) full time work in 1966, and (3) part time work in 1966.[h] Again these dummies may actually be representing several underlying factors. They may partially represent differential tastes for children and market

---

[h]"Full time" means more than 40 weeks worked while "part time" means more than zero but less than 41 weeks worked. The latter dummy is the excluded variable in the regression.

work as is occasionally presumed. Or, given the poor quality of our controls upon fecundity, they may represent fecundity differentials to some degree.

Our expectations that full time market work will be associated with smaller expected family size are confirmed by the sample. The coefficient on the dummy variable "full time market work" is -0.107 with a standard error of 0.021. The coefficient on the dummy variable "no market work" is 0.034 with a standard error of 0.018. The difference in expected family size between women who work full time and those who work not at all is roughly 0.32 children.

Predicted Potential Income and the Price of Children

Both Appendix A and Chapter One have presented arguments that suggest that, contrary to much of the sociodemographic literature, potential income of the couple should be a major determinant of family size. The failure of various income measures to perform well in previous cross-sectional studies has been ascribed to model misspecification, in which the perceived price (or opportunity cost) of child rearing has been incorrectly omitted from statistical analysis. Given the strong positive covariation between price and potential income,[i] the omission of price as an explanatory variable in cross-section regressions has resulted in downward bias in the income coefficients that has obscured the true role of income in the fertility decision.

However, inclusion of the price variable in the SEO regression does not lead to stronger estimates of the price and potential income elasticities. The price elasticity coefficient (-0.001), while of the proper sign, is exceedingly small and is accompanied by a large standard error. Likewise, the predicted potential income elasticity (-0.136) is accompanied by a standard error (0.073) that would not allow the rejection of the null hypothesis at, say, the 0.95 level. A clue to the reasons for the poor performance of these variables is contained in Figure 6–1: the joint confidence region is thin and slanted toward the northeast quadrant of the parameter space, the region where we might expect the "true" elasticities to lie. From this we might conclude that multicollinearity is obscuring the true price elasticities.

Given the strong covariation between the price and expected potential income variables, it would not be surprising to find our coefficient estimates being disturbed by multicollinearity manifested in a number of ways—standard errors on certain coefficients are large, signs on

---

[i]The zero order correlation between the two variables in the GAF and SEO samples is on the order of 0.84.

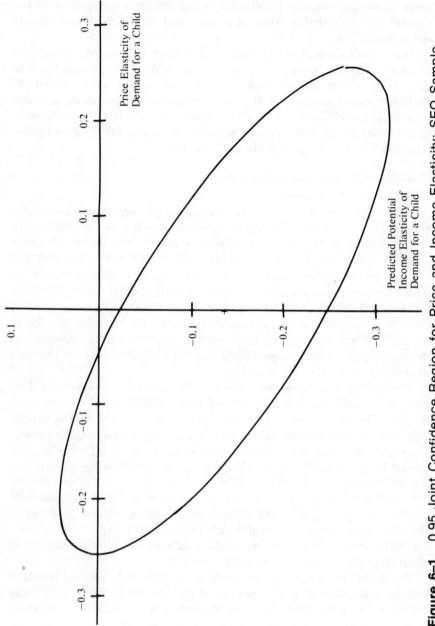

Figure 6-1. 0.95 Joint Confidence Region for Price and Income Elasticity: SEO Sample

coefficients are "wrong," and confidence regions may overlap unlikely areas of the parameter space. Moreover, parameter estimates are extremely sensitive to differences in specification and are unstable in repeated sampling:

> . . . what multicollinearity means is that the data are unable to provide independent information about the parameter values. Instead, the data provide weak suggestions of appropriate values together with trade-offs between individual coefficients which do not conflict with the sample evidence.[14]

Clearly, then, multicollinearity may present major problems in interpreting these two coefficients.

One way to mitigate the effects of multicollinearity is to incorporate additional information about the elasticities by utilizing that information to modify the sample results. In my dissertation [15] I attempted to do this by adopting a Bayesian framework, within which prior opinions as to the true values of the regression coefficients are modified through a systematic application of the sample likelihood function. However, the size of the sample was large enough so that the sample results overpowered the priors for any reasonable degree of prior precision.

Another factor that might complicate the situation still further is the problem of measurement error. We have gone to some extremes to create proxies for the underlying variables required by the theory, but there is no way in which the accuracy of our proxies may be assured. Moreover, since the price and income variables are so highly correlated, measurement error in only one of the variables might be producing bias in both parameter estimates.

Finally, to make matters even worse, there may be important interaction effects obscuring the true values of the underlying elasticities. In the theoretical discussion in Appendix A it was assumed that preference structures across couples are homogeneous. If so, then a positive income elasticity of demand for children within each family should also be manifested across families. However, if preferences for children vary systematically by social status or by potential income group, or by age at marriage, then the overall income elasticity as measured by the regression of Table 1–1 may well be negative while the within-group income elasticities would be positive. The impact of these possible interaction effects will be explored more fully in Section 5.

The Relative Income Component

As developed in the analytical model of Chapter Two, potential income should measure the couple's *expectations* of the present value of the maximum income stream attainable over the life cycle. In the absence of direct information on these expectations an empirical proxy for potential income has been constructed that includes a predicted component and a relative component designed to provide information about how the couple expects to do relative to couples of similar occupation and education.

Current family income was utilized as the indicator of relative income in the SEO sample.[16] Couples with current family income markedly higher or lower than others in their peer group are represented by dummy variables in the regression. The regression coefficients tend to indicate the couples in the top quartiles of their respective status groups expect more children than do couples of average or less income. The coefficient is not large (0.047) but it is significant, and it does provide independent confirmation of Deborah Freedman's 1963 findings.[j]

The coefficient for the bottom quartile is also positive; however, it is small in magnitude and accompanied by a large standard error. The existence of the positive income effect for the relative income component of potential income casts further doubt on the income elasticity estimated for the predicted potential income component, and suggests that improved measurement both of potential income and of the price of a child will be necessary if the theory is to receive an adequate statistical test.

4. GAF SAMPLE RESULTS

Table 6-1 also presents results for a regression calculated from data collected in the 1960 Growth of American Families survey. Since this survey contains additional valuable information, it is possible to estimate a more elaborate demand equation for children. Direct comparisons between the SEO and GAF results may be made for only a few of the explanatory variables since definitions of these variables often differ between the two samples.

Wife's Family of Orientation

In Chapter One it was noted that previous fertility research has detected a relationship between the size of the families of orientation of the husband and wife and the couple's own expected family size. Net of other factors such as previous farm residence and educational differences it is not unreasonable to consider this variable as a taste variable. Our hypothesis is that, in general, parents who were brought up in large families tend to prefer large families of their own. Reference to Table 6-1 illustrates this hypothesis with the GAF data. The natural

---

[j]Deborah Freedman, *op. cit.* See also the discussion of her work in Chapter Two.

logarithm of the size of the wife's family of orientation enters with a coefficient of 0.076 and a standard error of 0.02. It would appear, therefore, that there is a significant direct effect operating on the demand for children through this variable.

Age of Wife

In the GAF sample the intergenerational difference in completed family size again is manifested for older couples with those families over age 39 exhibiting a coefficient of -0.16 and a standard error of 0.036. The cohorts included in each of the three age groups are approximately the same as in the SEO sample even though the chronological ages have been altered to account for the seven years between surveys. Younger couples, on the other hand, appear to expect slightly fewer children than does the middle group of parents; however, coefficients for the younger couples in both surveys are accompanied by relatively large standard errors and the degree to which younger couples differ from the middle aged group remains unclear.

Farm Background

These dummy variables have a different meaning than do those in the SEO sample. In the GAF sample "farm experience" includes any farm experience of the husband or wife from birth to marriage. It is, therefore, a much more inclusive classification than the SEO grouping by residence at age sixteen. Nevertheless, lack of a farm background on the part of either spouse continues to exert a negative effect upon fertility. The effect of farm background is, in this survey, measured net of the possibly related effect of the size of the wife's family of orientation and would therefore appear to be a somewhat closer approximation of an independent farm experience effect. (The two coefficients on farm background do not exhibit high pairwise correlations with size of wife's family of orientation.) From both samples it would appear that any effect on family size exerted through farm background is present if only one spouse has experienced it. In neither regression do couples in which both spouses have farm experience expect a significantly different number of children from those in which only one of the spouses has a farm background.

Wife's Work Experience
Since Marriage

The GAF sample contains data on the wife's total market work experience according to whether the wife has worked and "likes it" or "doesn't like it." We would expect this classification to reflect preferences for nonfamilial activity more accurately than a simple work history. More specifically, a wife who works and likes to work might be thought to value nonfamilial activity more highly than a wife who has not worked or who has worked but not enjoyed it. The data do not provide evidence that differential tastes toward market work affect fertility. Women who have worked for any reason expect fewer children than those women who have not worked since marriage. Wives who have not liked working actually expect slightly more children than do wives who have liked working but the difference is not large. It would seem, therefore, that the work experience, not necessarily the attitude towards it, is the main factor related to fertility.

Religion

The two included dummy variables representing religious association are expected to reflect strongly differences in preferences and in-stitutional pressures that surround members of the different denomina-tions. The coefficient estimates in Table 6–1 conform well to our prior opinions, with couples in which neither spouse is Catholic expecting the fewest children and with couples in which both are Catholic expecting the most. Mixed marriages represent an intermediate position between the two extremes, perhaps signaling compromise between the husband and wife in choosing a completed family size.

The mean expected family size for couples in the GAF samples is 2.95 children and the spread of 0.27 between Catholic and non-Catholic families represents a difference in expected family size of 0.91 children. The direct effect of religion upon family size expectations would, there-fore, appear to be sizable, even net of the separate effect of the wife's age at first marriage. In the following section we test to determine if religious differences interact with the other socioeconomic determinants of family size.

Wife's Extrafamilial Activity

If the wife attends at least one meeting of a nonchild oriented club per month the dummy variable representing extrafamilial activity is scored one. Again, we expect this variable to reflect differential preferences regarding activities competing with child rearing. A wife who is active in nonchild centered activities would be expected to desire fewer children than other wives, according to the sociopsychological literature reported in Chapter Two. However, such is not the case with wives included in the GAF sample. Wives active in outside organizations appear to expect more children than do inactive wives. The coefficient estimate is 0.087 with a standard error of 0.024. This variable appears to be tapping some dimension of the preference structure, but it is not the dimension that we had supposed. Again, the lack of direct information on preferences is seen to inhibit our understanding of differential fertility.

Ability to Plan Ahead

Each wife in the GAF study was asked to assess her own ability to foresee future events and to plan ahead. Answers were grouped according to three types of response: (1) the wife feels confident of her ability to plan ahead; (2) she feels unable to plan ahead effectively; (3) she has some doubts about her ability to plan ahead effectively. We would expect that those wives who are confident of their ability to plan ahead will expect fewer children than the other wives and, although the sample confirms this, we cannot assert with any reasonable degree of confidence that a wife's assessment of her planning ability has any bearing on expected family size. Both those wives who felt they could plan and those who felt that they could not plan expected fewer children than the wives who were unsure; however, standard errors are large enough on both coefficients to prohibit rejection of a null hypothesis at any reasonable level of significance.

Age at First Marriage

The GAF regression results agree in sign though not in relative magnitude with the SEO results. Later marriage appears to lead to expectation of smaller families and early marriage seems to imply slightly larger families. The relative impact of late marriage is large (-0.091) compared to that of early marriage (0.047) in the GAF sample, while the impacts are similar in the SEO regression. Since the controls on fecundity and family planning ability are somewhat superior for the GAF data, these dummies might represent family orientations more accurately than do the same variables in the SEO regression.

Education of Wife

Since wife's education is not used as a control variable in the GAF sample, women with education only through the eighth grade are included for analysis. Women with eight or less years of education would appear to expect larger families, the coefficient on the appropriate dummy variable being 0.16 with a standard error of 0.049. College educated women do not appear to exhibit significantly different tastes for children from women with eight through twelve years of schooling. Indeed, the expected negative impact of a college education on the demand for children is not found in either of the samples analyzed in this study, and this suggests that the education variable may represent a set of underlying influences, the elements of which should be studied separately.

For women with very few years of schooling, education might have an independent effect upon family size in addition to its effect on the wife's opportunity wage; however, this variable may in fact be a proxy for differential success at birth control. Even though we have eliminated women who had demonstrated excess fertility by the date of interview, we have not eliminated those women who might have gone on to exceed their desired family size. Since these women tend to be concentrated at the lower educational levels, the significant coefficient on the dummy variable may be reflecting these women's expectations regarding possible future contraceptive failures. Given the basic difficulties inherent in the use of expected family size as a proxy for number of children demanded, we should not take it for granted that differences in education lead to differential tastes for children.

Potential Income and the Cost of Children

The GAF study asked each wife to assess the couple's relative economic position in relation to friends and relatives. We are thus able to incorporate another measure of relative income in the GAF sample that closely relates to the couple's own perceptions of their status. The information on relative income has been incorporated into the analysis in two ways. First, we have adjusted our measure of potential income by a factor of 0.25 in either direction to account for a response indicating either high or low relative income. (The results of a regression using this formulation are reported in Table 6–1.) Second, a regression using predicted potential income and two dummy variables representing relative potential income was computed. The results for the latter regression are generally similar to the SEO results and will not be discussed except to note that the dummy variables denoting relative income performed less well than the analogous dummies utilized in the SEO sample.[k]

Use of the adjusted potential income variable was intended to produce a more accurate proxy for the couple's perceived potential income. The estimated coefficients are, however, even more solidly placed in the southeast quadrant of the parameter space (Fig. 6–2). The estimated income elasticity is −0.20 with a standard error of 0.071 and the estimated price elasticity is 0.40 with a standard error of 0.15. Contrary to expectation, the adjustment factor seems to have accomplished nothing more than a slight reduction of the collinearity between the potential income and price variables. It would appear that the comments in Section 3 that relate to the potential income and price variables also apply here. Multicollinearity is not as serious as in the SEO regression; how-

---

[k]Estimated coefficients for the second regression are (standard errors in parentheses): Potential Income = −0.57 (0.11); Price = 0.86 (0.19); High Relative Income = 0.021 (0.027); Low Relative Income = −0.016 (0.048). Another regression was also computed. It contained the disaggregated components of potential income and opportunity cost. Signs on the estimated price and income elasticities are the same as for the aggregated version reported in the text.

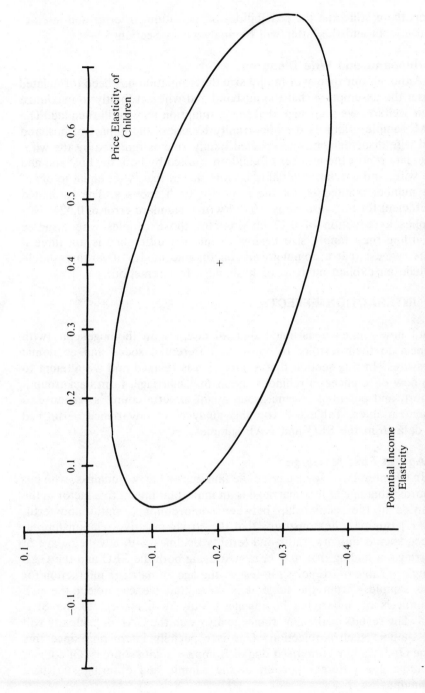

Figure 6–2. 0.95 Joint Confidence Region for Price and Income Elasticity: GAF Sample

ever, there still exist the possibilities of measurement error and interaction effects and the latter will be analyzed in Section 5.

Husband and Wife Disagree

Although our theory of family size determination has been formulated under the assumption that the husband and wife act jointly to maximize their welfare, we recognize that the assumption may be ill founded. The GAF sample offers us the opportunity to assess the impact of husband and wife disagreement on expected family size as reported by the wife. The data report the number of children wanted by both the husband and the wife, and a dummy variable is constructed that is set equal to one if the number wanted is not the same for both spouses. The estimated coefficient for this variable is -0.041 with a standard error of 0.023. This implies a reduction of 0.12 children for those couples who disagree regarding their family size desires. While the difference is not large it does suggest that a complete microeconomic model of fertility should include an explicit analysis of husband-wife interaction.

5. INTERACTION EFFECTS

Until now we have assumed that all couples are homogeneous with respect to their fertility response to differential social and economic pressures. In this section that assumption is relaxed and we attempt to see how differences in religion, age at first marriage, farm background, cohort, and potential income group might affect a couple's response to other variables. Table 6–2 contains analyses of covariance performed on data from the SEO and GAF samples.

Age at First Marriage

In Chapter Two we discussed the findings of Larry Bumpass, who has reported that age at first marriage is an important interactive factor in the analysis of the relationship between socioeconomic status and fertility.[17] Bumpass demonstrates that the strong negative relationship between socioeconomic status and fertility declines with advancing age at marriage, a finding that may be tested using both the SEO and the GAF samples. Table 6–2 reports the test of the age at marriage interaction for both samples—from the table it is clear that we can reject the null hypothesis of underlying homogeneity only with respect to the SEO data. The results of the covariance analysis on the GAF data clearly will not support such a rejection. This is especially interesting since this same GAF sample comprised one of Bumpass's data sources. Of course, he utilized a different portion of the sample and differing statistical techniques.

Table 6-2. Analyses of Covariance: GAF and SEO

Source	Residual Sum of Squares	df	Mean Square
SEO: Expected Family Size by Age at First Marriage			
Entire Sample	8.32×10^2	4191	.199
Separate Equations	8.26×10^2	4171	.198
Incremental SS	9.53	20	.476
F-value[a]	2.40		
SEO: Expected Family Size by Farm Background			
Separate Equations	8.29×10^2	4171	.199
Incremental SS	5.83	20	.292
F-value[a]	1.47		
SEO: Expected Family Size by Age of Wife			
Separate Equations	8.26×10^2	4171	.198
Incremental SS	8.79	20	.439
F-value[a]	2.22		
SEO: Expected Family Size by Potential Income Group			
Entire Sample[c]	8.32×10^2	4171	.199
Separate Equations	8.26×10^2	4145	.199
Incremental SS	6.14	26	.236
F-value[d]	1.19		
GAF: Expected Family Size by Age at First Marriage			
Entire Sample	1.87×10^2	1202	.155
Separate Equations	1.82×10^2	1170	.156
Incremental SS	4.71	32	.147
F-value[b]	0.94		
GAF: Expected Family Size by Farm Background			
Separate Equations	1.79×10^2	1170	.153
Incremental SS	7.70	32	.241
F-value[b]	1.58		
GAF: Expected Family Size by Religion			
Separate Equations	1.78×10^2	1170	.152
Incremental SS	9.13	32	.285
F-value[b]	1.88		
GAF: Expected Family Size by Potential Income Group			
Entire Sample[c]	1.74×10^2	1152	.151
Separate Equations	1.61×10^2	1114	.145
Incremental SS	1.23×10	38	.325
F-value[e]	2.24		

[a]F needed to reject is 1.57 at the 0.95 level.

[b]F needed to reject is 1.45 at the 0.95 level.

[c]These two analyses of covariance were performed after tape deterioration had caused the destruction of a small number of cases in the two samples (20 cases in the SEO sample and 18 cases in the GAF sample).

[d]F needed to reject is 1.50 at the 0.95 level.

[e]F needed to reject is 1.40 at the 0.95 level.

Of special interest are the variables representing different aspects of socioeconomic status in the regression equation estimated for each marital group shown in Table 6–3. As age at first marriage increases, the strong negative coefficient on potential income becomes positive while the positive coefficient on the price variable becomes negative. This would appear to confirm our suspicions that our potential income variable is acting in the equations more as an indicator of overall status without a well measured price variable to represent the correlated expenditures per child adequately. Under this interpretation, the coefficients on the potential income variable behave as Bumpass would lead us to expect, with the relationship between status and fertility changing from negative to positive as age at marriage increases. Needless to say, if the price variable was an accurate measure we would expect its coefficient to be negative for each of the three regressions.

Also of interest is the behavior of the coefficients on the current relative income dummies. The low income coefficients change from positive to negative while the high income coefficients become more strongly positive. We cannot attribute this to multicollinearity since the two coefficients are not strongly related either with each other or with other coefficients. These sign changes further confirm that an increasing age at marriage tends to strengthen the positive relation between income and fertility.

Education, entering as a taste variable, also has its positive effect upon fertility strengthened as age at marriage increases, although the standard errors of the estimated coefficients are too large for us to place much weight on them. In any case, these results tend to confirm the existence of an age at marriage interaction that must be satisfactorily treated if misleading inferences are to be avoided.

Religion
Numerous studies have found that Catholics and non-Catholics behave differently with respect to the impact of socioeconomic variables

Table 6–3.   Status Coefficients: Age at First Marriage

	Age at First Marriage		
Variable	Under 19	19 to 22	23 and over
Potential Income	−0.27[a]	−0.25[a]	0.13
Price	0.005	0.071	−0.14
Current Relative Income			
Low	0.07[a]	0.007[a]	−0.04
High	0.006	0.04	0.09[a]
Wife's Education			
>High School	0.05	0.07	0.09

[a]These coefficients at least twice their standard errors.

on fertility.[18] We are able to test for the religion interaction in the context of our demand equation utilizing data from the GAF sample. From Table 6–2 we see that it is possible to reject the homogeneity hypothesis. The sample is divided into three groups: (1) husband and wife are both Catholic, (2) only one spouse is Catholic, and (3) neither spouse is Catholic. Again, the status variables tend to vary systematically with membership in one of the three groups.

The price elasticity coefficient rises from 0.18 for non-Catholic couples to 1.24 for the Catholic couples while the adjusted income elasticity shows no apparent progression. It should be noted that the adjusted potential income variable may not now correspond nearly as closely to the overall status of the couple as does the price variable because of the addition of the relative income component.[1] Again, the behavior of the price elasticity coefficient would suggest the need to account for the religious interaction in future research with new data.

Farm Background
Although tests of this interaction on both samples turned up one significant interaction, examination of the separate regressions computed for the GAF sample produced only one interesting discovery. In couples where both spouses had farm experience before marriage the coefficient on the price variable was −0.37, while for couples with no farm experience the price elasticity was 0.62. In couples where one spouse had farm experience the price coefficient was 0.37 and there would appear to be a systematic progression from negative to positive.

Age of Wife
This interaction is tested because it is very important to know if a couple's response to social and economic variables is a function of the ages of the husband and wife. We observed in Sections 3 and 4 that generational differences do make a difference with respect to total expected family size, but the question remains as to whether older couples respond differently to social and economic factors than do younger couples.

The test of interaction performed here can only be suggestive of intergenerational differences since many of the explanatory variables represent underlying theoretical concepts only imperfectly. For example, a wife's work experience in 1966 is irrelevant to the fertility expectations of older wives who have passed the fecund period. Likewise, some of the explanatory variables represent influences which

---

[1]In addition, sample sizes in two of three groups are 252 and 107; this, combined with the effect of the adjustments to the potential income variable, might be enough to weaken the relationship between status and the adjusted variable.

become increasingly irrelevant with the passage of time. Farm background, for example, appears to play a stronger role in the fertility of older women, which is to be expected since relatively few of the younger women have had farm experience.

The potential income and price elasticities estimated for each of the three age groups also vary considerably although in none of the regressions is either of the coefficients accompanied by a standard error less than half its absolute value. Here the fundamental inadequacy of our proxy variables becomes most apparent. How can we expect these variables to reflect the vast differences in personal and cultural experience represented by these couples of such widely differing ages? More than ever the need for individual data becomes apparent if we are to understand the quantitative nature of the influences affecting completed fertility.

Potential Income

None of the interaction variables thus far examined represents long range economic and social status; however, it is reasonable to suspect that preference structures may well be status related. In the absence of direct measures of status, the potential income group of a couple has been selected in order to determine whether or not income and status interactions are affecting the coefficient estimates obtained for the entire SEO and GAF samples. In both cases the samples have been divided into three potential income groups (Table 6-4), although the groups are not identical because of sample size differences. Because we are concerned mainly with the possible impact of statistical interaction upon the price and income elasticity estimates, other coefficient estimates have been omitted from the table.

Price and income elasticity estimates in the SEO sample remain unimpressive; for example, none is significantly different from zero at the 0.95 level. Moreover, the analysis of covariance reported in Table 6-2 will not allow us to reject the hypothesis of homogeneity among couples in different potential income groups. However, this hypothesis may be rejected for the GAF sample. Potential income elasticities are consistently negative and significant and there are considerable differences between the three interaction groups. However, only in the first interaction group (Potential Income Groups 1 and 2) is the estimated price elasticity both positive and significant as in the total GAF sample. In the other two groups the estimated price elasticities are negative and are accompanied by large standard errors; thus we are unable to rule out interaction effects as contributing factors to the problem of estimating the price and income elasticities of the model.

In the absence of more suitable data on the expectations of parents

Table 6–4. Potential Income and Price Coefficients for Potential Income Interaction Groups

Interaction Group Potential Income Group	*SEO*			*GAF*		
	I *(1)*	*II* *(2&3)*	*III* *(4&5)*	*I* *(1&2)*	*II* *(3&4)*	*III* *(5&6)*
Potential Income	−0.112	−0.276	−0.416	−0.478[a]	−1.14[a]	−0.617[a]
Elasticity (Std Error)	(0.091)	(0.162)	(0.328)	(0.168)	(0.324)	(0.263)
Price Elasticity	−0.071	−0.341	−0.072	0.840[a]	−0.217	−0.109
(Std Error)	(0.15)	(0.299)	(0.737)	(0.204)	(0.338)	(0.410)
Sample Size	2298	1652	234	557	475	139

[a]These coefficients at least twice their standard errors.

regarding the cost of a child and of their expectations regarding their income potential, it will be difficult to demonstrate that the theoretical model has been afforded an adequate empirical test. Multicollinearity, measurement error, and interaction effects all remain as potential barriers to the estimation of the price and income elasticities suggested by the theory.

6. CONCLUSIONS

In this chapter various versions of the demand equation suggested by the microeconomic theory of Chapter Two have been estimated and analyzed. Of special concern has been the performance of the newly constructed proxies for the opportunity cost (price) of a child and the couple's potential income. Specific price effects ordinarily have not been considered in the sociodemographic analyses of differential fertility that have predominated in the fertility literature, and the analysis of Chapter Two leads us to suspect that the omission is serious.

The performance of the price and income proxies has not been impressive. The expected positive income elasticity and negative price elasticity failed to emerge in the analysis of the total sample; however, the presence of statistical interaction effects has served to complicate the issue. Tests confirmed the continuing presence of a number of previously identified interaction effects that serve especially to cloud the interpretation of the price and income elasticities estimated from the two samples. In some cases the presence of the interaction effects was shown to have a nonnegligible effect on the magnitude and sign of the two coefficients. This is an important finding because it suggests that the coefficients estimated in the total cross-section may not be analytically equivalent to the theoretically derived price and income effects of Chapter Two.

In order to understand the comparative static response of couples to changes in the opportunity cost of a child or to changes in potential income, it is necessary to insure that the underlying differences in couples' preferences structures are adequately accounted for; otherwise, the interactions of the noneconomic and the economic factors will produce biased estimates of the comparative static effects predicted by the theory.

In addition, the empirical analysis of the price and income variables is complicated by two more factors that hinder the interpretation of the coefficients. The first is multicollinearity, which is manifestly present in the set of predictors. Without the application of extraneous information, the harmful effects of high intercorrelation among the explanatory variables cannot be reduced. Given the high correlation between the constructed income and price proxies, the poor performance of these two variables is unsurprising, although the strength of the coefficient estimates in the GAF regression is certainly unexpected.

Unfortunately, no data exist that would allow us to incorporate extraneous information into our analysis of the price and income coefficients. Indeed, given the considerable efforts needed to construct even these crude proxies for the price of a child and potential income, it is not likely that new insights will be forthcoming until researchers have actually started from the beginning and collected directly the data required by the microeconomic theory. Then, of course, the need to refine the estimates of the opportunity cost of a child produced in Chapters Three and Four will disappear since the appropriate data will be at hand.

The second problem, closely related to the first, is that the crudity of the measures of price and potential income virtually guarantees that measurement error is obscuring the true value of the underlying price and income coefficients. Since the estimates of Chapters Three and Four cannot be compared with other estimates of the total opportunity cost of a child, there is no way that the accuracy of the proxies can be assured. Consequently, multicollinearity, measurement error, and statistical interaction may all be working to obscure the interpretation of the true impact of price and potential income on the demand for children. Chapter Seven will discuss some of the new data on price and income that should be collected in order to eliminate the empirical problems encountered in this chapter.

Additional suggestive findings have emerged from this chapter. Perhaps the most intriguing is the impact of a wife's education net of the opportunity cost component on the demand for children. Contrary to commonly accepted findings, the education of a woman past high school may have positive, rather than negative, effects on family size expectations. If this is indeed a valid finding, it suggests that the traditionally accepted sociological explanations of the impact of education on family size will have to be modified.

The SEO data provide independent support for the existence of a relative income effect of the type described by Deborah Freedman. If it were possible to measure potential income properly, the significance of the relative income effect for the comparative static impact of income on fertility could be analyzed directly. In any case the findings of this chapter suggest that couples who are doing better economically than their peers expect to have more children, and this may indicate that there is indeed a positive income effect operating at some level relative to the demand for children.

Other factors, such as size of family of orientation, religion, farm background, and age at first marriage were shown to exhibit effects on fertility predicted by previous research. However, the presence of husband-wife disagreement over family size might also have an effect upon fertility, and the findings of this chapter suggest that it may not be enough to analyze only the outcomes of the fertility decision process. Rather, the process itself may also be an appropriate object of study, if the fertility decision is to be fully understood.

CHAPTER SIX

1. See Judith Blake, "Are Babies Consumer Durables?" *Population Studies* XXII (1) (March 1968): 5–25.

2. A detailed discussion of the sample drawn for this study can be found in Pascal K. Whelpton, Arthur A. Campbell, and John E. Patterson, *Fertility and Family Planning in the United States,* Princeton: Princeton University Press, 1966, Appendix A.

3. Norman B. Ryder and Charles F. Westoff, *op. cit.,* Chapter II.

4. *Ibid.,* p. 28.

5. *Ibid.,* p. 22.

6. *Ibid.,* p. 25.

7. See Ronald Freedman, Lolagene C. Coombs, and Larry Bumpass, "Stability and Change in Expectations About Family Size: A Longitudinal Study," *Demography* 2 (1965): 250–275; and Larry L. Bumpass and Charles F. Westoff, *The Later Years of Childbearing,* Princeton: Princeton University Press, 1970.

8. *Op. cit.,* Chapter III.

9. Bumpass and Westoff, *op. cit.,* Chapter IV.

10. Freedman, Coombs, and Bumpass, *op. cit.,* p. 259.

11. Lolagene C. Coombs, "The Measurement of Family Size Preferences and Subsequent Fertility," *Demography* 11 (4) (November 1974): 587–612.

12. See Chapter One.

13. See the references in Chapter One.

14. Edward E. Leamer, "Inference with Non-Experimental Data: A Bayesian View," unpublished PhD dissertation, University of Michigan, 1970, p. 38.

15. Boone A. Turchi, "The Demand for Children: An Economic Analysis of Fertility in the United States," unpublished PhD dissertaion, University of Michigan, 1973, pp. 275–291.

16. See Chapter Five, Section 3.

17. Larry L. Bumpass, "Age at Marriage as a Variable in Socioeconomic Differentials in Fertility," *Demography* VI (1) (February 1969): 45–54.

18. See Charles F. Westoff, Robert Potter, and Phillip E. Sagi, *The Third Child,* Princeton: Princeton University Press, 1963; Ronald Freedman, David Goldberg, and Larry Bumpass, "Current Fertility Expectations of Married Couples in the United States: 1963," *Population Index* 31 (1) (January-March 1965: 3–20; and Paschal K. Whelpton, Arthur A. Campbell and John E. Patterson, *Fertility and Family Planning in the United States,* Princeton: Princeton University Press, 1966.

Chapter Seven

Summary and Conclusions

1. CONTRIBUTIONS OF THE STUDY

Although interest in the microeconomic analysis of fertility decisions has increased markedly in recent years, the substantive impact of the consumer theory approach has remained relatively minor. A major goal of this study has been to increase the acceptance of the micro theory approach to fertility by placing it firmly in the general social and psychological context within which family size decisions are made. The second major goal of the study has been to develop an integrated socioeconomic model of completed family size that takes account of the noneconomic factors affecting allocative decisions. The third major goal has been the statistical estimation of this integrated socioeconomic theory.

These primary objectives have led to some secondary objectives of independent interest and importance. The theoretical model developed in Chapter Two calls for the measurement of a couple's perceived opportunity cost of children, and, in the absence of any preexisting attempts to measure this magnitude directly, it has been necessary to generate a proxy for this variable through the use of actual data on parental expenditures of time and money on their children. Consequently, in the course of the estimation of the economic model of fertility, new estimates of the opportunity cost of children by social class have been developed. These estimates provide a new slant on class differentials in expenditures on children, and conflict rather significantly with other published estimates in the field.

The fundamental justification for introduction of the microeconomic theory of consumer behavior into fertility research is the recognition that, once the ability of couples to control fertility is well established, the number of children born becomes largely a matter of choice. This choice is tempered by the obviously large resource requirements of children and the limitations of resources available to the couple. American couples clearly are making these choices. Family size intentions have been modest ever since family level data began to be collected in the mid 1950s. Indeed, for many couples, the ability to avoid excess fertility has become absolute as a result of the Supreme Court's decision legalizing abortion. Consequently, completed family size is now largely a matter for choice, and consumer theory is expressly designed to deal with just this sort of decision.

However, as has been repeatedly stressed, fertility cannot be regarded as simply another consumer purchase problem. Parenthood is a social and religious institution of profound dimensions, and noneconomic factors can be expected to play an important role in this allocative decision. Chapter One discussed in some detail the many ways in which social and psychological factors may influence the fertility decision. Some of these influences may operate directly, altering the relative preferences of couples for children versus other activities or affecting their time orientation in a way that produces differences in fertility.

Most important, perhaps, is the influence of noneconomic factors on the couple's perceptions of the cost of child rearing. A husband and wife may enter into the family size decision with preconceived notions about the resource cost of children that are largely determined by the social class within which they reside, and differences in the perceived price of a child may well account for many of the observed differences in fertility exhibited by American couples.

The microeconomic model of fertility presented in Chapter Two is an explicit attempt to create a rigorous theory of the family size decision that pays more than lip service to the noneconomic factors that influence fertility. It emphasizes the noneconomic factors that may influence the perceived opportunity cost of a child and assumes that couples enter into fertility decisions constrained by preconceived notions of the cost of children. This formulation allows the theoretical exploration of the impact of price and income changes on the couple's optimum family size. The comparative static implications of the model lead further to suggestions as to how government expenditure and revenue policy might be utilized to alter aggregate fertility.

However, policies designed to change fertility rates need not be economic, and the fertility model of Chapter Two allows the comparison of various policy approaches, both economic and noneconomic in nature. The advantage of a decision model in the analysis of fertility is that, for most American couples, family size is the outcome of explicit decisions to engage in or not to engage in overt fertility regulating behavior. From a scientific point of view it is essential to understand the factors—economic and noneconomic alike—that influence those decisions. Likewise, in the absence of directly coercive measures to control fertility, government policy makers must also understand the same factors if an effective and politically acceptable population policy is to be achieved. Hence the need for an integrated decision model for fertility analysis.

The development of this decision model has led directly to the identification of two economic variables of prime importance: (1) the opportunity cost (or price) of a child, and (2) the couple's potential income. The analysis suggests that because parents must make long range commitments to their children, and because these commitments must be made long before the resource expenditures occur, each couple makes its ultimate fertility decision based upon projections of future income and time available and of the expected resource costs of a child.

Ideally, for purposes of fertility analysis it would be desirable to have young couples' direct answers to questions designed to elicit this information. Unfortunately this information has not yet been gathered and in this study we have been forced to develop alternative estimates of the time and money cost of children. To do this, it was assumed that younger couples base their judgments upon their perceptions of the actual behavior of older couples of comparable social and economic status. Consequently, the estimates that have been developed in this study are estimates derived from actual behavior and thus represent new and independent estimates of the cost of children that can be contrasted with others that have recently been developed.

Chapter Three documents the sizable commitment of time that the average white American wife makes to her children. From the time a child is born until he/she leaves home at age eighteen a mother will perform approximately 6,300 hours of housework for each child that she has. In a two-child family of moderate spacing this means that for the approximately 7,300 days that she has a child at home, a mother will perform 1.77 hours of housework per day for her children. An only child appears to receive even more attention than a child in larger families, receiving, on the average, 9,274 hours of a mother's housework time in an eighteen-year period, or 1.4 hours per day. An only child appears to receive 43 percent more time from his mother than does a child in a two-child family and 51 percent more time than a child in a three-child family.

Clearly, the time cost of a child is enormous in terms of the market commodities foregone due to child care commitments. In 1969 the cumulative cost of a child in a two- or three-child family was $24,600 for a college educated woman, $14,300 for a woman with a high school diploma, and $13,600 for a woman with at least some high school education.

Moreover, child rearing involves another cost in addition to the direct time expenditures on child rearing. Children appear to be responsible for an additional loss of approximately 2,440 hours of market work during the time that they reside in the family. This loss of market work appears to come about because of rigidities in the labor market and the lack of alternative child care options. Although it is improper to argue that the market value of these 2,400 hours represents an additional cost of child rearing (see the discussion in Chapter Three), this loss of market work serves to increase the opportunity value of time utilized directly in child rearing activities.

Another aspect of the time cost of children documented in the present study is the declining time inputs required by them as they age. As long as at least one child in the family is of preschool age, the average mother commits approximately 2.6 hours per day to child rearing. Once all the children are in school the mother's time expenditure drops 40 percent to about 1.6 hours per day. The entrance of the last child into high school signifies a drop to approximately 45 minutes of housework per day, only 28 percent of the requirement for preschoolers. Therefore, the entry of a mother's last child into grade school represents a major decline in her time commitment and probably accounts for the sharp decline in the incidence of childbirth for couples whose youngest child has reached school age.

Children also claim significant outlays of parental income. By classifying parents as members of long range potential income groups, it has been possible to develop estimates of the cumulative money cost of children by social and economic status. The breakdown into six different potential income groups represents, as far as I am aware, the most detailed breakdown of money expenditures by income group currently available. The results of Chapter Four demonstrate the substantial economic impact of children at all income levels. The cumulative money cost of a child (in 1969 prices) ranges from $18,728 for high status parents to $8,947 for the lowest potential income group surveyed.[a] This represents an overall income elasticity of expenditure per child equal to 1, suggesting that the respective standards of living of parents and their children are highly interdependent.

[a]It will be remembered that money income expenditures on only five expenditure items were generated: food, clothing, housing, recreation, and education. This accounts for approximately 80 percent of total money expenditures on children and including the missing expenditure components might raise the money cost per child range to $11,200–$23,410. It should be noted that these expenditure totals continue to be far below those widely cited from U.S. Commission on Population Growth and the American Future sources.

Within expenditure categories, however, there is considerable variation in the income elasticity of expenditure. Food and clothing expenditures are income inelastic (0.25 and 0.67 respectively), while expenditures on housing, recreation, and education are elastic.[b] In particular, the sizable elasticity associated with expenditures on post high school education suggests that a primary difference in the fertility decisions made by lower and upper status parents is the prime importance the latter accord to the future education of their children. This feature of the opportunity cost of children may indeed be a major factor in the explanation of fertility differentials across income groups.

When the money costs and the time costs of child rearing are combined, the economic consequences of parenthood are demonstrated to be formidable indeed. A high status couple in 1969 could expect each child in a two- or three-child family to represent upwards of $43,000 in opportunity cost, while for the more typical couple the cumulative opportunity cost of a child would be approximately $27,000. That parents are routinely making the decision to have children in spite of the magnitude of this commitment suggests the strength of the social and psychic returns that couples receive from parenthood.

As informative as these estimates of the time and money cost of children may be, their suitability for use in the estimation of the demand for children remains in doubt. The theoretical model requires each individual couple's perceptions of future resources and the opportunity cost of children. We suspect that these individual expectations are highly influenced by the couple's social and economic position; however, to substitute group means for individual expectations, as has been done in this study, is to apply a crude solution to a difficult problem.

The performance of the income and price variables in the demand equations for children suggests that the empirical proxies generated here are not of sufficient accuracy to allow successful estimation of the model. And since this study represents one of the most extensive attempts yet to utilize existing cross-section data sources to test an economic model of fertility, it becomes apparent that successful empirical tests of economic models of fertility may have to await the creation of data sets appropriate to that purpose.

Estimation of the current demand model has been hampered by three factors acting together: (1) measurement error, which has arisen naturally as part of the attempt to approximate individually perceived prices and incomes with empirically derived group means; (2) statistical interaction effects, which are present because the absence of individual social and psychological data has forced the use—indeed the overuse—of social and demographic variables as proxies for tastes and prefer-

[b]The elasticities are: education, 2.81; recreation, 1.56; and housing, 1.46.

ences; (3) multicollinearity, which has arisen because social and demographic variables have been forced to do double duty, acting both as proxies for psychological variables and as determinants of the constructed measures of time cost, money cost, and potential income.

Simply stated, the data collected in the five national fertility surveys and in numerous other sociodemographically oriented fertility surveys remain ultimately unsuited for the testing of a microeconomic decision model of family size. If models of this type are to have an opportunity to demonstrate their full potential for explanation and policy purposes, they must be tested with appropriate data. The following section suggests some steps that should come next.

2. THE PATH AHEAD

Since marital fertility is associated with decisions made both jointly and independently by the husband and wife, analysis of those decisions requires data at that level. Consequently, sample surveys continue to represent the preferred way to gather appropriate data for the analysis of the fertility decision. Moreover, these surveys should be longitudinal in design so that the decision models of fertility can be formulated and tested as fully dynamic models. Static models may be appropriate for the analysis of completed family size, but other important topics—e.g., spacing and timing decisions, and fertility regulating behavior—require a dynamic decision framework. Given the longitudinal design, the following are areas that will require major new measurement efforts in order to produce data appropriate to test the microeconomic models of fertility.

The Preference Structure

In this study we have been forced to rely on social and demographic variables in place of a number of dimensions of individual preferences. New attempts need to be made to measure directly the husband's and wife's relative preferences for parenthood versus other activities, including market work, that provide psychic rewards. The direct measurement of preferences is a difficult undertaking, but recent developments in the theory of measurement and nonmetric multidimensional scaling provide a framework within which to direct this effort.

Another element of the psychological makeup of parents that requires measurement is the time orientation of the husband and wife. The manner in which couples weight present versus future rewards and costs may play an important role in the outcome of fertility decisions and also may help to explain variations in contraceptive effectiveness.

The final element of the couple's preference structures that must be measured in detail is the set of standards parents bring to child rearing.

It is a fundamental hypothesis of this study that couples enter into parenthood with at least a rough conception of the resource requirements of their children. In order to know how parents will respond to changes in the prices of inputs into child rearing and to changes in their own expected wages and incomes, it is essential to understand the underlying structure of the parents' perceived production function for children. Questions that need to be answered include:

1. What inputs and what quantities are perceived to be the minimum necessary to raise a child?
2. How much substitutability among inputs do parents perceive in the production of their children?
3. To what degree to differential social and institutional pressures limit the flexibility of couples to vary the inputs used in child rearing?
4. Do parents perceive economies or diseconomies of scale in child rearing?

Income and Cost Expectations

Given the sociopsychological framework within which they operate, couples must make fertility decisions based upon their projections of future resources and the expected costs of children. The difficulties of interpretation encountered in Chapter Six suggest that these projections must be measured directly, especially since changes in these projections over time will form the basis for the dynamic analysis of fertility changes.

Fertility Regulating Behavior

Since fertility intentions do not necessarily correspond to fertility outcomes, the analysis of the demand for children requires that attention be paid to fertility regulating behavior. In Chapter One it was argued that the initiation and cessation of contraception are decision problems and should be analyzed as such. This will require data somewhat different from those usually collected in the national fertility surveys. In particular, the data collected should relate specifically to the factors affecting the adoption of one method over another. Some of these factors are: (1) the perceived effectiveness of each method; (2) the use qualities and side effects of each method; (3) the cost of each method. Once a better understanding of the regulating decision is achieved, our understanding of fertility outcomes will also improve.

The Dependent Variables

In order to make better predictions of both completed fertility and spacing and timing events, more complete measures of the dependent variables are necessary. For example, it is not sufficient simply to ask a respondent the number of children that he or she intends to have. What is needed is a more complete assessment of fertility intentions, including not only the most likely number of children but also the respondent's relative feelings about alternative family sizes. In this way family size expectations will be measured as preference weighted averages rather than as single response quantities.

Husband-Wife Interaction

Finally, more attention must be paid to husband-wife interaction with respect to fertility. The device of treating the fertility decision as a joint utility maximization problem has advantages in terms of mathematical simplification, but husbands and wives often disagree and their disagreements may distort the outcomes of the fertility decision process. Unless the nature of husband-wife conflict is studied, its impact on the predictions of the microeconomic model of fertility will remain unknown.

3. CONCLUSIONS

Aggregate fertility in the United States is now potentially more volatile than at any previous time in the nation's history. In 1974 the total fertility rate fell to 1.86, lowest in United States history, and yet only seventeen years before, aggregate U.S. fertility was at a peak. Levels of fertility and fluctuations in those levels are coming to have important ramifications for virtually every sector in the economy. Rapid population growth generates excess demands for services such as education while rapid declines in the rate of growth result in excess capacity, displacement of factors of production, and the potential for long term economic stagnation.

A better understanding of the determinants of aggregate fertility and of fertility differentials is essential if effective policy to stabilize and direct fertility rates is to be made possible. The microeconomic theory offers the promise of facilitating the understanding of fertility trends and of providing policy alternatives. What is needed now are data sets capable of exploiting the theory's potential for providing a new and enlightening view of fertility decisions.

Appendixes

Appendix A

Are Children "Inferior Goods"?

In his original article on fertility, Gary Becker argues that "Since children do not appear to be inferior members of any broader class, it is likely that a rise in long run income would increase the amount spent on children."[1] In essence, he is making the traditional consumer theory argument that child rearing is a "normal" consumption activity, where normality implies that in the absence of changes in other determining factors, a rise in income will raise the optimal number of children desired by the representative couple.[a] In light of the well known negative correlations between income and family size, it is useful to present a theoretical argument underlying this proposition.

To do this we can utilize some of the insights into consumer theory that have evolved out of the "new theory of demand" presented formally by Kelvin Lancaster.[2] Lancaster argues that it is not consumption activities but the characteristics of consumption activities that provide utility to the consumer. The consumer is thus pictured as maximizing utility with respect to characteristics rather than activities.[b] The advantage of this extension from a conceptual point of view is that it enables demand theory to provide some insight as to why various bundles of consumption activities are chosen over others. For our purposes, adoption of the characteristics framework allows us to examine the conditions under which child rearing might be considered to be a normal activity.

[a]Assume for the purposes of this discussion that all preference structures are homogeneous so that the behavior of a homogeneous group of parents may be discussed.
[b]The relation between consumption activities and characteristics is "objective" (Lancaster, *op. cit.*, p. 134)—that is, the transformation of activities into characteristics is governed by forces intrinsic to the activities and not by individual preferences.

A major assumption of this study is that children possess characteristics that, on balance, make child rearing a desirable activity, and indeed there is considerable evidence that children are sources of pleasure to their parents. A survey of mental health conducted in 1957 produced data identifying children and economic well-being as the two most frequently mentioned (29 percent of the sample for each) sources of individual happiness. Conversely, children were mentioned as sources of unhappiness by only seven percent of the sample.[3] Indeed, these studies seem to have found greater ambiguity surrounding the husband-wife relationship than around the parent-child relationship.

The characteristics of children that make them of value to parents are not easy to measure or even to list completely. However, the recent interest exhibited by psychologists in this area suggests that new measures of the psychic role of children will soon be available. A spur to this activity was the seminal article by Hoffman and Hoffman, which attempted to catalog the various characteristics of children that fulfill psychic needs of parents.[4] In their list it was suggested that children possess characteristics that meet the following psychic needs:

1. Adult status and social identity (women's major role).
2. Expansion of the self, tie to a larger entity, "immortality."
3. Morality: religion; altruism, good of the group; norms regarding sexuality, impulsivity, virtue.
4. Primary group ties, affection.
5. Stimulation, novelty, fun.
6. Creativity, accomplishment, competence.
7. Power, influence, effectance.
8. Social comparison, competition.

From this list and from others that might be developed we can state the obvious and note that children play a major social and psychic role in the United States; moreover, it is not clear that any activity that might compete with children for parents' time and money would be as efficient in satisfying these needs as are children.

Assume that inferior characteristics do not exist and that parents exist in a two-characteristic, multiactivity world in which child rearing is a relatively efficient supplier of characteristic C_1 and a relatively inefficient supplier (relative to a composite "alternative consumption activity") of characteristic C_2. Two cases are of interest: (1) all characteristics are nonsatiable, and (2) the collection of characteristics (C_1) for which child rearing is a relatively efficient supplier is subject to satiation. Then, by observing the preference map of the parents we can determine the conditions under which child rearing is not an inferior activity.

Case 1

First, we assume that neither of the two characteristics is satiable and that child rearing has a comparative advantage in the production of characteristic C_1. On the axes in Figure A–1a differing quantities of each of the two characteristics are shown. The straight lines from the origin represent different consumption activities. Since child rearing has a comparative advantage in the production of C_1 the activity ray labeled "child rearing" has a flatter slope than the other activity rays.

If we are initially given a couple's income and all the prices of inputs into the two activities we can locate two points, E and F, denoting the maximum amount of each of the activities that can be purchased, given prices and incomes. A straight line between these two points is the locus of the possible combinations of the two activities attainable, given prices and income; EF is the couple's initial budget constraint. Point A represents the activity bundle actually selected by the couple, given the budget constraint EF and the indifference curves (not shown). Consumption of children is at level OH.

Now, suppose we increase the income available to the couple. Under what conditions is it possible for child rearing to be an inferior good (i.e., for the consumption of the activity to decline as income rises)? As the budget line shifts out from the origin (parallel to EF), the geometric condition for inferiority is that the new equilibrium point is somewhere in the triangle ADG. Only then will consumption of the child rearing activity have declined as income rises. In the triangle AJG consumption of child rearing will have risen. If the new equilibrium actually is in AGD, this implies that the income elasticity of demand for characteristic C_1 is low relative to that for C_2.

Note, however, that if the Other Consumption Activity provides none of characteristic C_1 (i.e., ray OE coincides with the vertical axis), then the triangle AGD collapses to the line segment AD and the income elasticity of demand for C_1 is zero. In this case child rearing cannot become an inferior activity since, at the least, consumption remains constant as income rises. The larger the angle between the child rearing ray and its closest substitute the lower the chance that child rearing is an inferior activity.

Case 2

Figure A–1b demonstrates the situation in which characteristic C_1 is satiable, and consumption past C_1^* confers negative utility on the couple. Again we start from an initial equilibrium position A and determine how consumption of the two activities changes as income is increased. As income increases, continued increases in the consumption of C_1 will eventually lead to declining utility. Therefore we expect that the

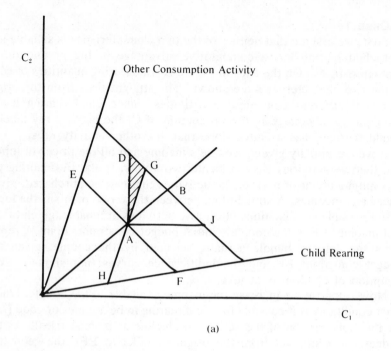

(a)

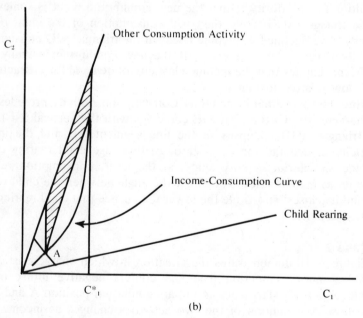

(b)

Figure A–1. Child Rearing as an Inferior Activity

income consumption curve will eventually bend upwards and force the consumption of child rearing to decline as it enters the shaded area. Note again, however, that if the Other Consumption Activity does not provide the characteristic C_1 then child rearing can never become an inferior activity, even if the characteristic is satiable at some finite level of consumption.

These two cases provide a general idea of the circumstances under which child rearing may be an inferior activity. If there are substitute activities that are reasonably efficient in providing the characteristics for which child rearing is the most efficient, then an increase in income may induce a decline in the level of child rearing if these characteristics are subject to satiation or to a low income elasticity of demand.

However, the list of parental needs satisfied by children—and, more importantly, the discussion by Hoffman and Hoffman of these needs— suggests that while there are many alternative activities that also supply attractive characteristics to the couple, few of them provide for these needs as efficiently and comprehensively as child rearing. That is, child rearing appears to provide a large and important collection of characteristics to a couple for which other activities are poor substitutes. This reduces the likelihood that child rearing is an inferior member of a broader class of consumption activities. Moreover, we have no evidence to suggest that the income elasticity of demand for the characteristics specific to child rearing is low or subject to satiation.

While the foregoing is certainly not a proof of the assertion that child rearing is a normal activity, it provides a reasonable basis for the assumption. It should be remembered however, that this is an argument about an individual utility structure and it is silent as to whether preference structures might systematically vary across social and economic groups, an occurrence that might severely distort attempts to determine the "true" income elasticity of demand for children.

APPENDIX A

1. Becker (1960), *op. cit.,* p. 211.

2. Kelvin J. Lancaster, "A New Approach to Consumer Theory," *Journal of Political Economy* LXXIV (2) (April 1966): 132–175.

3. Lois W. Hoffman and Martin L. Hoffman, "The Value of Children to Parents," in *Psychological Perspectives on Population,* James T. Fawcett (ed.), New York: Basic Books, 1973, p. 23.

4. *Ibid.*

The Estimation of Expenditures on Food and Recreation

The estimation of food and recreation expenditures on children in Chapter Four is complicated by the availability only of total family expenditure on these two items. Total family expenditure on food and recreation must, therefore, be allocated among parents and children of different ages. The procedure adopted in Chapter Four is the simplest and most direct; total family expenditures on food and recreation are merely allocated on the basis of potential income and family type, with children of a given age and age distribution being assigned the mean expenditure of families of a given type and potential income classification. However, this method may lead to underestimates of the requirements for actual expenditures on children, as may be easily demonstrated.

From the economic theory of the consumer it is known that in the absence of variations in prices, the expenditure of a family on any particular commodity or commodity group depends on the family's income after taxes:

$$e_i = f_i(y),\tag{1}$$

where e_i is total family expenditure on commodity i and y is income after taxes. Equation (1) is, of course, the famous Engel curve, which relates total family expenditures on a commodity to family income.

If our interest is in the impact of different family members on expenditures for commodity i the Engel curve may be written in per capita terms as:

$$e_i/N = f_i(y/N),\tag{2}$$

where N is the total number of persons in the family. However, we are expressly concerned with the differential requirements of specific family members on total family consumption and can modify equation (2) so that it reflects this concern:

$$\frac{e_i}{\Sigma k_{ij} n_j} = f_i\left(\frac{y}{\Sigma k_{oj} n_j}\right). \tag{3}$$

In equation (3) N, the total number of family members, has been replaced with $\Sigma k_{ij} n_j$, the number of "equivalent adult consumers" of commodity i in the family and $\Sigma k_{oj} n_j$ is the number of "equivalent adult consumers" for total family expenditure in general.

The number of equivalent consumers for any given commodity may or may not be equal to the number of equivalent consumers for total consumption, even though the latter is nothing more than a weighted average of the equivalent adult scales for each separate commodity. Note that n_j is the number of persons in the jth category—for example, n_1 may be the number of preschool children, n_2 the number of grade school children, and so on. The index k_{ij} represents the specific relative requirement of a person in the jth category for commodity i. If the index for adults is always normalized to equal one, then the requirement in dollars of expenditure for commodity i for a person of type g is:

$$k_{ig}\left(\frac{e_i}{\Sigma k_{ij} n_j}\right).$$

Statistically, then, the problem is to measure the specific scales for children and adults. Note that these scales depend on the biological and social constraints on child rearing discussed in Chapter Two. Estimation of the specific scales is complicated by the dependence of overall family consumption upon the income available to the family. That is, the addition of a new member to the family has two effects: first, the new member brings his own requirements for the commodity in question; second, the consumption of that item by other family members may alter as the new member is added. For example, to illustrate the impact on consumption of commodity i on the addition of a person of type g, the partial derivative of (3) with respect to n_g can be computed, remembering that the income elasticity of demand for the commodity is given by:

$$\epsilon_i = \frac{y}{e_i} \frac{\partial e_i}{\partial y} = \frac{y}{e_i} \frac{\Sigma k_{ij} n_j}{\Sigma k_{oj} n_j} f'_i.$$

The impact of the addition of a person of type g is, therefore:

$$\frac{\partial e_i}{\partial n_g} = k_{ig}\left(\frac{e_i}{\Sigma k_{ij} n_j}\right) - \epsilon_i e_i\left(\frac{k_{og}}{\Sigma k_{oj} n_j}\right), \tag{4}$$

which is composed of two separate effects, the specific effect (first term right-hand side) of adding the individual, and the redistribution effect upon the consumption of the other members of the family. Thus, unless the commodity or commodity class exhibits an income elasticity of zero, the addition of a type *g* person will result in an increase in consumption somewhat less than the specific requirement of that person, the difference being made up by the reduced consumption of other family members.

The method utilized in Chapter Four to estimate the specific food and recreation requirements of children produces estimates of the *net* impact of children, which includes both the specific impact as well as the redistribution effect. Its originators, Kemsley and Quenouille,[1] focused on expenditure items of low income elasticity such as particular food items, and for these items the downward bias is not very important. However, recreation expenditures are highly income elastic and it is to be expected that the estimates of Chapter Four underestimate the requirements of children for expenditures of this type.

APPENDIX B

1. W.F.F. Kemsley, "Estimates of Cost of Individuals from Family Data," *Applied Statistics,* I (November 1952): 192–98; M.H. Quenouille, "An Application of Least Squares to Family Diet Surveys," *Econometrica* 18 (1) (January 1950): 27–44.

Bibliography

Allen, R.G.D. *Mathematical Economics*. 2nd ed. London: Macmillan & Co. Ltd., 1964.

―――― and Bowley, A.L. *Family Expenditure: A Study of Its Variation*. London: Staples, 1935.

Becker, Gary S. *Human Capital*. New York: National Bureau of Economic Research, 1964.

――――. "A Theory of the Allocation of Time." *Economic Journal* LXXV (September 1965): 493–517.

――――. "An Economic Analysis of Fertility." *Demographic and Economic Change in Developed Countries*. Universities—National Bureau of Economic Research. Princeton: Princeton University Press, 1960.

―――― and Lewis, H. Gregg. "On the Interaction Between the Quantity and Quality of Children." *JPE Supplement, 1973*, S279–S288.

Ben-Porath, Yoram. "Economic Analysis of Fertility in Israel: Point and Counterpoint." *JPE Supplement, 1973*, S202–S233.

Berelson, Bernard. "Beyond Family Planning." *Science* 163 (February 7, 1969): 533–543.

Blake, Judith. "Are Babies Consumer Durables?" *Population Studies* XXII (March 1968): 5–25.

――――. "Income and Reproductive Motivation." *Population Studies* XXI (November 1967): 185–206.

――――. "Population Policy for Americans: Is the Government Being Mislead?" *The American Population Debate*. Edited by Daniel Callahan. Garden City, N.Y.: Doubleday and Co., 1971.

Bumpass, Larry L. "Age at Marriage as a Variable in Socio-Economic Differentials in Fertility." *Demography* VI (February 1969): 45–54.

―――― and Westoff, Charles F. *The Later Years of Childbearing*. Princeton: Princeton University Press, 1970.

Cain, Glen G. and Weininger, Adriana. "Economic Determinants of Fertility: Results from Cross-Sectional Aggregate Data." *Demography* 10 (May 1973): 205–223.

227

Callahan, Daniel, ed. *The American Population Debate.* Garden City, N.Y.: Doubleday and Co., 1971.

Cho, Lee-Jay, Grabill, Wilson H., and Bogue, Donald J. *Differential Current Fertility in the United States.* Chicago: University of Chicago Community and Family Study Center, 1970.

Coombs, Lolagene C. "The Measurement of Family Size Preferences and Subsequent Fertility." *Demography* 11 (November 1974): 587–612.

Cyert, Richard M. and March, James G. *A Behavioral Theory of the Firm.* Englewood Cliffs, N.J.: Prentice-Hall, 1963.

David, Martin. *Family Composition and Consumption.* Amsterdam: North-Holland Publishing Co., 1962.

Deardorff, Alan and Stafford, Frank. "Labor Supply in Labor-Leisure and Household Production Models." Unpublished. Ann Arbor, Michigan: University of Michigan Department of Economics, October 1973.

Demeny, Paul. "The Economics of Population Control." *Rapid Population Growth.* Prepared by the National Academy of Sciences. Baltimore: The Johns Hopkins Press, 1971.

De Tray, Dennis N. "Child Quality and the Demand for Children." *JPE Supplement, 1973,* S70–S95.

Dublin, L.I. and Lotka, A.J. *The Money Value of a Man.* Rev. ed. New York: The Ronald Press, 1946.

Duesenberry, J.S. "Comment." *Demographic and Economic Change in Developed Countries.* Universities—National Bureau of Economic Research. Princeton: Princeton University Press, 1960.

Duncan, Otis Dudley. "Farm Background and Differential Fertility." *Demography* II (1965): 241–249.

———, Freedman, Ronald, Coble, J. Michael, and Slesinger, Doris. "Marital Fertility and Size of Family of Orientation." *Demography* II (1965): 508–515.

Dyck, Arthur J. "Population Policies and Ethical Acceptability." *The American Population Debate.* Edited by Daniel J. Callahan. Garden City, N.Y.: Doubleday and Co., 1971.

Easterlin, Richard A. "Towards a Socioeconomic Theory of Fertility." *Fertility and Family Planning.* Edited by S.J. Behrman, Leslie Corsa, Jr., and Ronald Freedman. Ann Arbor, Michigan: University of Michigan Press, 1969.

———. *Population, Labor Force, and Long Swings in Economic Growth: The American Experience.* New York: Columbia University Press, 1968.

———. "Relative Economic Status and the American Fertility Swing." Philadelphia: University of Pennsylvania, Department of Economics, 1972.

———. "The Economics and Sociology of Fertility: A Synthesis." Philadelphia: University of Pennsylvania, Department of Ecnomics, July 1973.

Espenshade, Thomas J. "Adapting Consumer Theory to the Fertility Decision." Tallahassee, Florida: Florida State University Department of Economics, 1973.

———. *The Cost of Children in Urban United States.* Berkeley, Calif.: Institute of International Studies Population Monograph Series No. 14, 1973.

Feldman, Paul and Hoenack, Stephen A. "Private Demand for Higher Education in the United States." *The Economics and Financing of Higher Education in the United States.* The Joint Economic Committee of the Congress of the United States. Washington, D.C.: U.S. Government Printing Office, 1969.

Fisher, Franklin M. "Tests of Equality Between Sets of Coefficients in Two Linear Regressions: An Expository Note." *Econometrica* XXXVIII (March 1970): 361–366.

Fortney, Judith A. "Achievement as an Alternative Source of the Emotional Gratification to Childbearing." Paper presented at the Annual Meetings of the Population Association of America, April 1972.

Freedman, Deborah. "The Relation of Economic Status to Fertility." *American Economic Review* LIII (June 1963): 414–426.

Freedman, Ronald, and Coombs, Lolagene. "Economic Considerations in Family Growth Decisions." *Population Studies* 20 (November 1966): 197–222.

———. "Childspacing and Family Economic Position." *American Sociological Review* 31 (October 1966): 631–648.

———, Coombs, Lolagene C., and Bumpass, Larry. "Stability and Change in Expectations About Family Size: A Longitudinal Study." *Demography* II (1965): 250–275.

———, Goldberg, David; and Bumpass, Larry. "Current Fertility Expectations of Married Couples in the United States: 1963." *Population Index* XXXI (January–March 1965): 3–20.

———, Whelpton, Pascal K., and Campbell, Arthur A. *Family Planning, Sterility, and Population Growth.* New York: McGraw-Hill Book Company, 1959.

———. *The Sociology of Human Fertility: An Annotated Bibliography.* New York: Appleton-Century-Crofts, 1974.

Friedman, David. *Laissez-Faire in Population: The Least Bad Solution.* New York: The Population Council, 1972.

Galbraith, V.L. and Thomas, D.S. "Birth Rates and the Interwar Business Cycles." *Journal of the American Statistical Association* XXXVI (1941): 465–476.

Gershenkron, Alexander. "Review of *Demographic and Economic Change in Developed Countries.*" *Journal of the American Statistical Association* 56 (December 1961): 1006–1008.

Ghez, Gilbert R. and Becker, Gary. "The Allocation of Time and Goods Over the Life Cycle." Report No. 7217. Chicago: Center for Mathematical Studies in Business and Economics. University of Chicago, April 1972.

Gibbs, J.P. "Norms: The Problem of Definition and Classification." *The American Journal of Sociology* 70 (March 1965): 586–594.

Goldberg, David. "The Fertility of Two-Generation Urbanites." *Population Studies* XII (March 1959): 214–222.

———. "Another Look at the Indianapolis Fertility Data." *The Milbank Memorial Fund Quarterly* XXXVIII (January 1960): 23–36.

Gramm, Wendy Lee. "The Demand for the Wife's Non-Market Time." *Southern Economic Journal* 41 (July 1974): 124–133.

Greeley, Andrew M. and Rossi, Peter H. "Correlates of Parochial School Attendance." *School Review* LXXII (Spring 1964): 52–73.

Gronau, Reuben. "The Effect of Children on the Housewife's Value of Time." *JPE Supplement, 1973,* S168–S201.

Haitovsky,Yoel. "Multicollinearity in Regression Analysis: Comment." *Review of Economics and Statistics* LI (November 1969): 486–488.

Haugen, R.A. and Heins, A.J. "A Market Separation Theory of Rent Differentials in Metropolitan Areas." *Quarterly Journal of Economics* LXXXIII (November 1969): 660–672.

Hauser, Phillip M. "Comments." *Milbank Memorial Fund Quarterly* XLVIII (Part 2) (April 1970): 235–239.

Hawthorn, Geoffrey. *The Sociology of Fertility.* London: Collier-MacMillan, 1970.

Heckman, James J. "Effects of Child-Care Programs on Women's Work Effort." *JPE Supplement, 1974,* S136–S163.

Hendler, Reuven. "Lancaster's New Approach to Consumer Demand and Its Limitations." *American Economic Review* LXV (March 1975): 194–199.

Henderson, A.M. "The Cost of Children (Part I)." *Population Studies* III (1949): 130–150.

——. "The Cost of Children (Part II)." *Population Studies* IV (1950): 267–298.

Henderson, James M. and Quandt, Richard E. *Microeconomic Theory.* New York: McGraw-Hill Book Company, 1971.

Hicks, John R. *Capital and Growth.* New York: Oxford University Press, 1965.

Hill, C. Russell and Stafford, Frank P. "Allocation of Time to Preschool Children and Educational Opportunity." *Journal of Human Resources* 9 (Summer 1974): 323–341.

Hinmon, Dean E. "Why Some Parents Do/Do Not Enroll Their Children in Catholic Schools." *Catholic School Journal* (September 1966): 88–96.

Hoffman, Lois W. and Hoffman, Martin L. "The Value of Children to Parents." *Psychological Perspectives on Population.* Edited by James T. Fawcett. New York: Basic Books, 1973.

Houthakker, H.S. "An International Comparison of Household Expenditure Patterns, Commemorating the Centenary of Engel's Law." *Econometrica* XXV (October 1957): 532–551.

—— and Taylor, L.D. *Consumer Demand in the United States* (2nd ed.). Cambridge, Mass.: Harvard University Press, 1970.

Johnson, George E. and Stafford, Frank P. "The Earnings and Promotion of Women Faculty." *American Economic Review* LXIV (December 1974): 888–903.

Johnston, John. *Econometric Methods* (2nd ed.). New York: McGraw-Hill Book Company, 1972.

Jones, Ronald W. "The Structure of Simple General Equilibrium Models." *Journal of Political Economy* LXXXIII (December 1965): 557–572.

JPE Supplement, 1973. Journal of Political Economy 81 (March/April 1973, Part II).

JPE Supplement, 1974. Journal of Political Economy 82 (March/April 1974, Part II).

Kemsley, W.F.F. "Estimates of Cost of Individuals from Family Data." *Applied Statistics* I (November 1952): 192–198.

Kirk, Dudley. "The Influence of Business Cycles on Marriage and Birth Rates." *Demographic and Economic Change in Developed Countries.* Universities—National Bureau of Economic Research. Princeton: Princeton University Press, 1960.

Kiser, Clyde V. and Whelpton, Pascal K. "Resumé of the Indianapolis Study of Social and Psychological Factors Affecting Fertility." *Population Studies* VII (November 1953): 95–110.

Kish, Leslie. "Confidence Intervals for Clustered Samples." *American Sociological Review* XXII (April 1957): 154–165.

———. *Survey Sampling.* New York: John Wiley & Sons, 1965.

Lancaster, Kelvin J. "A New Approach to Consumer Theory." *Journal of Political Economy* LXXIV (April 1966): 132–175.

Lansing, John B., Lorimer, Thomas, and Moriguchi, Chikashi. *How People Pay for College.* Ann Arbor: Survey Research Center, 1960.

Leamer, Edward E. "Inference with Non-Experimental Data: A Bayesian View." Unpublished PhD dissertation, University of Michigan, 1970.

Leibenstein, Harvey. "An Interpretation of the Economic Theory of Fertility: Promising Path or Blind Alley?" *Journal of Economic Literature* XII (June 1974): 457–479.

———. *Economic Backwardness and Economic Growth.* New York: John Wiley & Sons, 1957.

Leibowitz, Arleen. "Women's Allocation of Time to Market and Non-Market Activities: Differences by Education." Unpublished PhD dissertation, Columbia University, 1972.

Lindert, Peter H. "Remodelling the Household for Fertility Analysis." Madison, Wis.: Center for Demography and Ecology Working Paper 73–14, May 1973.

———. "The Relative Cost of American Children." Madison, Wis.: University of Wisconsin Graduate Program in Economic History Discussion Paper No. 7318, March 1973.

Lindley, D.V. *Introduction to Probability and Statistics: Part 2, Inference.* Cambridge, Eng.: Cambridge University Press, 1965.

Malinvaud, E. *Statistical Methods of Econometrics.* Chicago: Rand McNally, 1966.

Michael, Robert T. "Education and the Derived Demand for Children." *JPE Supplement, 1973,* S128–S164.

——— and Willis, Robert J. "Contraception and Fertility: Household Production Under Uncertainty." New York: National Bureau of Economic Research, Working Paper No. 21, December 1973.

Mincer, Jacob. "Market Prices, Opportunity Costs, and Income Effects." *Measurement in Economics: Studies in Mathematical Economics and Econometrics in Memory of Yehuda Grundfeld.* Edited by Carl Christ. Stanford, Calif.: Stanford University Press, 1963.

——— and Polachek, Solomon. "Family Investments in Human Capital: Earnings of Women," *JPE Supplement, 1974,* S76–S108.

Morgan, James N. "Housing: The Relation of Quantity to Quality (cost to number of rooms) and the Relation of Housing Consumption (costs) to Income." Ann Arbor, Mich.: Survey Research Center, February 1971.

―――, David, Martin, Cohen, Wilbur, and Brazer, Harvey. *Income and Welfare in the United States.* New York: McGraw-Hill Book Co., 1962.

―――, Sirageldin I.A., and Baerwaldt, N. *Productive Americans.* Ann Arbor, Mich.: Institute for Social Research, 1966.

Namboodiri, N. Krishnan. "Some Observations on the Economic Framework for Fertility Analysis." *Population Studies* XXVI (July 1972): 185–206.

Nash, A.E. Kier. "Going Beyond John Locke? Influencing American Population Growth." *Milbank Memorial Fund Quarterly* XLIX (January 1971): 7–31.

Okun, Bernard. *Trends in Birth Rates in the United States Since 1870.* Baltimore: Johns Hopkins Press, 1958.

Pennock, Jean L. "Cost of Raising a Child." *Family Economics Review* (March 1970): 13–17.

Phillips, Llad, Votey, Harold, and Maxwell, Darold E. "A Synthesis of the Economic and Demographic Models of Fertility, An Econometric Test." *Review of Economics and Statistics* LI (August 1969): 298–308.

Pollak, Robert A. and Wachter, Michael L. "The Relevance of the Household Production Function and its Implications for the Allocation of Time." *Journal of Political Economy* LXXXIII (April 1975): 255–77.

Prais, S.J. and Houthakker, H.S. *The Analysis of Family Budgets.* Cambridge, Eng.: Cambridge University Press, 1955.

Pratt, Lois and Whelpton, Pascal K. "Extra-Familial Participation of Wives in Relation to Interest and Liking for Children, Fertility, Planning, and Actual and Desired Family Size." *Social and Psychological Factors Affecting Fertility.* Edited by Clyde Kizer and P.K. Whelpton. Vol. 5. New York: Milbank Memorial Fund, 1958.

Quenouille, M.H. "An Application of Least Squares to Family Diet Surveys." *Econometrica* XVIII (January 1950): 27–44.

Radner, Roy and Miller, L.S. "Demand and Supply in U.S. Higher Education: A Progress Report." *American Economic Review* LX (May 1970): 326–334.

Reed, Ritchie H. and McIntosh, Susan. "Costs of Children." U.S. Commission on Population Growth and the American Future, *Economic Aspects of Population Change.* Elliott R. Morss and Ritchie H. Reed, Editors. Vol. II of Commission Research Reports. Washington, D.C.: U.S. Government Printing Office, 1972, pp. 337–350.

Reid, Margaret. *Housing and Income.* Chicago: University of Chicago Press, 1962.

Ritchey, P. Neal and Stokes, C. Shannon. "Residence, Background, Migration and Fertility." *Demography* IX (May 1972): 217–230.

Robinson, Warren C. and Horlacher, David E. "Population Growth and Economic Welfare." *Reports on Population/Family Planning,* No. 6 New York: The Population Council, February 1971.

Rubin, Zick. "Do American Women Marry Up?" *American Sociological Review* XXXIII (1968): 750–760.

Ryder, Norman B. and Westoff, Charles F. *Reproduction in the United States: 1965.* Princeton: Princeton University Press, 1971.

————. "Wanted and Unwanted Fertility in the United States: 1965 and 1970." U.S. Commission on Population Growth and the American Future, *Demographic and Social Aspects of Population Growth.* Charles F. Westoff and Robert Parke, Jr., Editors. Vol. I of Commission Research Reports. Washington, D.C.: U.S. Government Printing Office, 1972, pp. 467–487.

Schumpeter, Joseph A. *The Theory of Economic Development.* Cambridge, Mass.: Harvard University Press, 1949.

Silver, Morris. "Births, Marriages and Business Cycles in the United States." *Journal of Political Economy* LXXIII (June 1965): 237–255.

Simon, Julian L. *The Effects of Income on Fertility.* Chapel Hill, N.C.: Carolina Population Center, 1974.

Simon, Herbert A. "The Theories of Decision Making in Economics and Behavioral Science." *American Economic Review* 49 (June 1959): 253–283.

Sobel, Marion G. "Correlates of Present and Expected Future Work Status of Married Women." Unpublished PhD dissertation, University of Michigan, 1960.

Stafford, Frank P. "Student Family Size in Relation to Current and Expected Income." *Journal of Political Economy* LXXVII Part 1 (July/August 1969): 471–477.

Stone, J.R.N., Rowe, D.A., Corlett, W.J., Hurstfield, R., and Potter, M. *The Measurement of Consumers' Expenditure and Behaviour in the United Kingdom, 1920–1938.* Vol. I. Cambridge, Eng.: Cambridge University Press, 1954.

Sweet, James A. "Family Composition and the Labor Force Activity of American Wives." *Demography* VII (May 1970): 195–210.

Terhune, Kenneth W. and Kaufman, Sol. "The Family Size Utility Function." *Demography* 10 (November 1973): 599–618.

Theil, Henri. "Specification Errors and the Estimation of Economic Relationships." *Review of the International Statistical Institute* XXV (1957): 41–51.

Turchi, Boone A. "The Demand for Children: An Economic Analysis of Fertility in the United States." Unpublished PhD dissertation, University of Michigan, 1973.

Udry, J. Richard. *The Social Context of Marriage.* Philadelphia: J.B. Lippincott, 1966.

United Nations. *Determinants and Consequences of Population Trends.* Population Studies No. 17, Document No. ST/SOA/SER. A/17. New York, 1953.

U.S. Bureau of the Census. *The Methods and Materials of Demography.* Henry S. Shryock, Jacob S. Siegel, and Associates. Washington, D.C.: U.S. Government Printing Office, 1971.

U.S. Bureau of the Census. *Current Population Reports,* Series P-20, No. 183. "Characteristics of Students and Their Colleges: October, 1966." Washington, D.C.: U.S. Government Printing Office, 1969.

U.S. Bureau of the Census. *Current Population Reports,* Series P-20, No. 222. "School Enrollment: October 1970." Washington, D.C.: U.S. Government Printing Office, 1971.

U.S. Bureau of the Census. *Current Population Reports.* Series P-20, No.

263. "Fertility Histories and Birth Expectations of American Women: June 1971." Washington, D.C.: U.S. Government Printing Office, 1974.

U.S. Bureau of the Census. *Current Population Reports.* Series P-20, No. 268. "Nursery School and Kindergarten Enrollment: October 1973." Washington, D.C.: U.S. Government Printing Office, 1974.

U.S. Bureau of the Census. *Current Population Reports,* Series P-20, No. 269. "Prospects for American Fertility: June 1974." Washington, D.C.: U.S. Government Printing Office, September 1974.

U.S. Bureau of the Census. *Current Population Reports.* Series P-20, No. 271. "Marital Status and Living Arrangements: March 1974." Washington, D.C.: U.S. Government Printing Office, 1974.

U.S. Bureau of the Census. *Current Population Reports,* Series P-23, No. 37. "Social and Economic Characteristics of the Population in Metropolitan and Nonmetropolitan Areas: 1970 and 1960." Washington, D.C.: U.S. Government Printing Office, 1971.

U.S. Bureau of the Census. *Current Population Reports.* Series P-25, No. 521. "Estimates of the Population of the United States and Components of Change: 1973 (with Annual Data from 1930)." Washington, D.C.: U.S. Government Printing Office, 1974.

U.S. Department of Labor. Bureau of Labor Statistics. *Three Standards of Urban Living for a Family of Four.* BLS Bulletin No. 1570-7.

U.S. Department of Labor. Bureau of Labor Statistics Staff Paper No. 4. *A Micro Model of Labor Supply.* M.S. Cohen, S. Rea, and R. I. Lerman. Washington, D.C.: U.S. Government Printing Office, 1970.

Warren, Bruce. "A Multiple Variable Approach to the Assortative Mating Phenomenon." *Eugenics Quarterly* XIII (1966): 285–290.

Watson, Cicely. "Housing Policy and Population Problems in France." *Population Studies* VIII (1953): 14–45.

Westoff, Charles F., Potter, Robert G., Jr., Sagi, Philip C., and Mishler, Elliot G. *Family Growth in Metropolitan America.* Princeton: Princeton University Press, 1961.

———. *The Third Child.* Princeton: Princeton University Press, 1963.

Whelpton, Pascal K., Campbell, Arthur A., and Patterson, John E. *Fertility and Family Planning in the United States.* Princeton: Princeton University Press, 1966.

Wilkinson, Maurice. "An Econometric Analysis of Fertility in Sweden, 1870–1965." *Econometrica* 41 (July 1973): 633–642.

Willis, Robert J. "A New Approach to the Economic Theory of Fertility Behavior." *JPE Supplement, 1973*, S14–S64.

Winter, Sidney G. "Concepts of Rationality in Behavioral Theory." Ann Arbor, Mich.: Institute of Public Policy Studies Discussion Paper No. 7, August 1969.

Index

About the Author

Boone A. Turchi was born in Portland, Oregon in 1941. He completed his undergraduate work at Harvard College in 1963 with an honors degree in economics and spent most of the ensuing three years in Europe as a lieutenant in the United States Army. Following his discharge, Mr. Turchi studied at Boston University and at the University of Michigan where he received the doctorate in economics. Currently he is Assistant Professor of Economics at the University of North Carolina, Chapel Hill.